Library Services to Latinos

Also by Salvador Güereña

Latino Librarianship: A Handbook for Professionals
(McFarland, 1990)

Latino Periodicals: A Selection Guide
(with Vivian M. Pisano; McFarland, 1998)

Library Services to Latinos

An Anthology

edited by
SALVADOR GÜEREÑA

McFarland & Company, Inc., Publishers
Jefferson, North Carolina, and London

Publisher's note: All of the essays in this collection are original to this volume

Library of Congress Cataloguing-in-Publication Data

Library services to Latinos : an anthology / edited by Salvador
Güereña.
    p. cm.
    Includes bibliographical references and index.
    ISBN 0-7864-0911-8 (softcover : 50# alkaline paper) ∞
    1. Hispanic Americans and libraries.   I. Güereña, Salvador.
Z711.8.L53 2000
027.6'3—dc21   00-26849

British Library cataloguing data are available

Cover image ©2000 Photodisc

Manufactured in the United States of America

*McFarland & Company, Inc., Publishers
  Box 611, Jefferson, North Carolina 28640
   www.mcfarlandpub.com*

To my wife
Linda M. Güereña

Acknowledgments

First, I wish to thank all the contributors to this work. Their dedication to their profession is inspiring and is a lamp to illuminate the way for Latino librarians who are eager to learn how to better serve their communities. It is a fact that Latinos make up barely 1.8 percent of the librarian work force. Very few of these have the time to write for publication, and of those who do, fewer yet can count on receiving any support to be able to so. Thus I fully realize and appreciate the personal commitment made by each of the contributors to this book. I wish to thank my wife Linda to whom this book is dedicated, as well as the rest of my family for their patience and moral support while I was compiling and editing this work. I also wish to thank Lupita García who assisted me with final manuscript preparation, and Ixchel Vargas-Mendoza for helping to index the book.

A word of thanks also is due the university libraries of the University of California, Santa Barbara, my home institution, whose support of my work has made this, and many other projects, a reality, in the interest of service to the Latino community.

Contents

ELECTRONIC RESOURCES

Introduction

This anthology has been some time in the making. Essentially, it is an answer to the prodding of colleagues who had been urging me to compile another anthology of professional readings. I was reminded that a decade had gone by and another volume was needed to complement my earlier compilation of *Latino Librarianship: A Handbook for Professionals* (1990) that also was published by McFarland & Company. The purpose of *Library Services to Latinos* is to contribute something useful to a very limited body of literature, a paucity that especially prevails in the form of monographic works in the field of Latino librarianship. The present volume was conceived as a means to share some effective strategies in service, to inform through the use of selected case studies that demonstrate client-centered innovations, whether they involve the organization of Spanish-language collections, to meet the needs of children, or to examine developments in electronic resources. This book's intent also is to stimulate some discussion about some of the pressing professional issues of relevance to Latino librarians such as leadership development, recruitment and mentorship.

Edward Erazo begins this book with a discussion of leadership from a Latino perspective. He defines the characteristics of leaders, explores cultural variables that set apart Latino leaders from others, and gives his personal insights from recent leadership roles that he has held. Also addressing professional issues, Tami Echavarria writes on recruitment strategies to bring Latinos into the library profession. She examines the slow progress in this area and discusses measures, such as developing mentorship programs, that librarians and educators can take to reverse this pattern, to move towards the goal of institutionalizing diversity. Rhonda Rios Kravitz completes the section by sharing her findings from a research study she conducted to determine if Latino librarians and librarians of color encounter barriers to advancement in the workplace. In her article she gives the implications of her findings and provides some strategies for action.

In the section on language issues, Sonia Ramírez Wohlmuth argues for the need for librarians to be properly equipped in language and cultural competence to serve Spanish-speaking Latinos. According to Ramírez Wohlmuth second language instruction should be incorporated into library education and continuing education programs for librarians. Danelle Crowley has studied, lived and worked in Latin American countries. As a Spanish language cataloger for the San Antonio Public Library, Crowley gives practical ideas to libraries on how to expand their Spanish and bilingual collections, and on how to improve the library's abilities to meet its objectives of access and education. She describes ways to improve existing services and explains various options for providing better access to collections including the development of bilingual on-line catalogs, cataloging and marking, signage, printed and on-line instructions, and importantly, by providing language competent staff members. Graciela Berlanga-Cortéz follows a different take on the language issues debate by examining it from the aspects of cross-cultural communication. In her discussion she identifies the major cultural and linguistic barriers between information providers and information seekers who are Spanish-speaking. She also recommends in her article ways that libraries can eliminate such barriers across different cultures, through improved training, adaptations in the physical environment, and culturally sensitive materials and services.

Jon Sundell discusses in his in-depth case study how his library serves the growing and largely Mexican immigrant population of Forsyth County, North Carolina. While he describes many aspects of library service to the Spanish-speaking community, especially noteworthy is the major thrust of their strategy in networking with many organizations serving the same population. Carnesí and Fiol, writing from Queens Borough, New York, discuss their work in the New Americans Program of the Queens Borough Public Library that serves the most ethnically diverse borough in the City of New York. A winning and innovative outreach program, the New Americans Program's charge is exclusively to meet the needs of immigrants, many of whom are monolingual Spanish-speakers who experience adjustment difficulties that are ameliorated through this important program.

Working in another area of the country, Ben Ocón writes about efforts to reach the Latino community, but gives a paradigm for successful outreach touching upon his experiences in Salt Lake City, Utah. He underscores the importance of doing outreach, outlining proven techniques and provides a model for any public library setting. Ghada Kanafani Elturk, like Ocón, has been doing outreach but in Colorado. In her article, a case study of the Boulder Public Library, she stresses how important it is for libraries to exercise a leadership role in the communities that they serve. Elturk states it most eloquently that a leader is "one who is able to balance his or her own vision with people's needs and aspirations."

Academic libraries are represented by Susana Hinojosa who writes about an innovative curriculum in a university setting that gives new and transfer Chicano/Latino students to her campus an introduction to university life and to the library. A collective piece by junior college librarians coordinated by John Ayala talk about methods that can work in reaching out to Latino students in junior colleges.

This book offers two articles that cover the field of children's services. Latino children are the fastest growing segment of the population and it makes sense for libraries to devote attention to addressing their needs. Oralia Garza de Cortés is a well-known expert and advocate for library services to children. She brings much wisdom to bear on how libraries can do a better job of building reliable Spanish-language collections for children. In her article she delivers practical and cogent advice on developing a collection development policy, on establishing and maintaining content and culturally balanced collections. She reviews pertinent selection tools and strategies and even states the implications for library school educators who help produce future children's librarians. Hector Marino's article completes this section by focusing on the concerns of school libraries and examining how well prepared they are to serve limited-English-proficient school children. Marino gives his recommendations and strategies to more effectively develop well-planned school library and media centers. According to Marino, it will take no less than "long-term commitment, sensitivity, and hard work" so that the school library may succeed in playing its own important role in educating our Spanish-speaking children.

The final part of this book is devoted to a review of the expanding availability of information resources for Latinos that are found on the World Wide Web. In Susan Vega García's article she looks at the kinds of information that are available, who produces it, and to which Latino group(s) they pertain. Her coverage encompasses seven Latino groups—Chicanos (Mexican Americans), Puerto Ricans, Cuban Americans, Salvadoreans, Dominicans, Colombians, and Guatemalans residing in the U.S. Vega García reviewed the information she found, organized it by type of resource, and evaluated it, providing an excellent listing of recommended web sites. Romelia Salinas is a rising star whose in-depth work as the project manager for the Chicano/LatinoNet for its first five years give her a unique perspective to write about its inception and development as a leading agent in the rapid growth in Internet-based information for the Latino community.

As I pointed out to readers in my last compilation, this book must not be construed as an authoritative guide to Latino librarianship. What it does is to build on the work of others who have published in the field and helps to close some gaps. It was part of my original plan for this book to include topics such as library planning methods, perspectives of top Latino administrators, and on how to promote Latino library advocacy through "friends of the library" groups and trustees. Fortunately, at least several of these topics are addressed in a recent book I highly recommend, *Serving Latino Communities: A How-to-Do-It Manual for Librarians* by Camila Alire and Orlando Archibeque (Neal-Schuman, 1998).

PROFESSIONAL ISSUES

Learning to Lead a Library Association: A Selective Literature Review on Leadership and Some Personal Observations

Edward Erazo

Abstract

Leadership development is one of the most often discussed themes in library and management literature. It is no wonder: new leaders are always welcome and perpetually in short supply. This is as true among Latinos as it is for the rest of the library profession. While a lot has been written on leadership in general about traits, characteristics, skills and models of leaders, not too much has been written about library leadership and hardly anything from a Latino perspective. If the number of Latino leaders is in direct co-relation to the number of Latino librarians—estimated at less than one-half a percent of all working librarians—then the reason for this is easily explained. This chapter provides some definitions of leaders and leadership. It gives an overview of leadership qualities of leaders in general. It explores cultural differences that make Latino leaders unlike other leaders and makes some personal observations from one with two recent library leadership roles. Additionally, it will look at communication, why Latino leaders need to be culturally sensitive to both the majority culture and the Latino culture and act as cultural mediators and communication consultants when necessary between the two groups. The changing demographics of this country have made this critically important within our society and specifically library associations. Latino leaders also need to develop a personal philosophy of leadership that takes these factors into account and then must assume a moral and social responsibility within our associations to promote Latino library issues in our local, state and national library associations. It is a philosophy which is as important in our professional lives as it is in our personal lives. This perspective on Latino leadership will hopefully generate more perspectives as Latinos assume leadership roles for ourselves and identify future leaders.

Definitions of Leadership and Characteristics of Leaders

In *Leadership in the Library/Information Profession*, Alice Gertzog observes that the word "leader" can be traced in the English language back to 1300, but it was not until 1800 that the word "leadership" first appears; she adds that the definition of the latter word is problematic because it is "ambiguous, perceptual and contextual" (Gertzog, 1989: 59). This simple definition for leader from the *American Heritage Dictionary* (Boston, MA: Houghton Mifflin, 1980) illustrates the point: (1) one that leads or guides; (2) one in charge or command of others; (3a) the head of a political party or organization and (3b) one who has influence or power, especially of a political nature; (4a) a conductor, especially of an orchestra, band or choral group and (4b) the principal performer of an orchestral section or a group; (5) the foremost horse in a harnessed team.

Which is it then: guide, commander, political boss, orchestra leader, principal performer, or foremost workhorse? Another simple definition for leadership is from the *American Heritage Dictionary*: (1) the position or the office of a leader; (2) the capacity or ability to lead. Personal observation tells me the concepts of leadership and leader are complicated; they are all these definitions and then some.

Yet, despite the range of definitions, there are no shortages of attempts to define leadership nor to write articles and monographs on the topic. A keyword search on WorldCat identified more than 58,000 records—to say nothing of the related topics of managers and management—ERIC had more than 25,000 records on leadership or leaders. Yet, Library Lit only identified around 400 articles on leadership or leaders. Ten years ago, "Visionary Leaders for 2020" was Margaret Chisolm's 1988-89 ALA presidential theme and fortunately a number of articles and monographs on developing library leadership were one of the results. Interestingly, many of the observations at the time including the lack of leaders and the need to mentor future leaders are as true today as they were then. This discussion of library leadership begins with a review of the literature. Much of this literature centers on the traits and characteristics of leaders. Becoming a leader in the public arena is recognized as difficult (Bower, 1997). Elizabeth Martínez was interviewed (Riggs & Sabine, 1988: 122) and had this to say, "Most people want a comfortable existence. And it's not comfortable when you're out there on the front-line. You're the first one that's going to be shot at. Most people don't want that." These are the more telling discussions in the articles and books centered around the perceptions of leaders on leadership. Some of the themes were responsibility, leaders as doers and workers behind the scenes—not in the public eye, leaders as facilitators, and leaders as public performers.

There are probably hundreds of definitions of leadership, beyond the obvious definition that states that a leader must have followers. Many definitions of leadership list its traits. Here is one example (Albritton & Shaunessy, 1990: 30-31): vision, integrity, courage, judgment, understanding of others, persuasion, planning, optimism, and flexibility. Warren Bennis, the management guru, in his celebrated book, *On Becoming a Leader* (Bennis, 1989), lists the following ingredients shared by leaders: guiding vision; passion; integrity with candor, based in honesty of thought and action, and with trust as its basis; curiosity; and daring. He also draws some differences between managers and leaders, among them are: the manager administers, the leader innovates; the manager is a copy, the leader is an original; the manager focuses on systems and structure, the leader on people; the manager imitates, the leader originates, and (his most often quoted difference) the manager does things right, the leader does the right things. Leaders, then, are not just managers. Yet another list of characteristics of leaders is offered by authors Rosie Albritton and Thomas Shaughnessy in their book *Developing Leadership Skills: A Source Book for Librarians* (Albritton & Shaughnessy, 1990:19-20): (1) sense of responsibility, (2) technical and professional competence, (3) enthusiasm, (4) communication skills, (5) high ethical standards, (6) flexibility, and (7) vision. As we can see, some of the items on these lists begin to repeat themselves. There would seem to be a sort of consensus among researchers of these traits and characteristics. Most would also agree with the more comprehensive lists made by Normand Frigon and Harry Jackson, Jr., in *The Leader: Developing the Skills and Personal Qualities You Need to Lead Effectively* and their assessment that the prerequisites of leadership can be defined in terms of three categories: principles, traits and skills (Frigan & Jackson, 1996). These categories are broken down into their "building blocks" as follows. Their nine leadership principles are integrity; effective communication; responsibility, accountability, and authority; positive mental attitude; consideration and respect; constancy of purpose; teamwork; effective resources management; and fact-based decision making. Their ten traits are controlled emotions, adaptability, initiative, courage, determination and resolution, ethical behavior, sound judgment, endurance, dependability and desire. Finally, their fourteen skills are: planning, team leadership, fiscal responsibility, decision making, communication, situational assessment, communication, management, coaching, teaching, facilitating, effective meeting management, fact-based decision making, business knowledge, and technical knowledge. Several of these characteristics and traits repeat, among them, the need for communication skills. In "Leadership Language: Do We Say What We Mean and Mean What We Say?" a chapter in *Library Communications: The Language of Leadership* (Riggs, 1992), E. Anne Edwards laments the common complaint of many organizations: poor communication. This is lamentable, she explains, because good communication avoids misunderstandings, low morale, and feelings of mistrust. A review, then, of the literature of leadership would indicate that at least some of the leadership mystique is not so mysterious after all. The traits and characteristics of leadership would seem to be known. Can we, then, learn to be leaders? Can all these leadership traits be emulated to produce leaders? The questions are more complex than these, but the answers lie in part in the mix of characteristics and behavior, both of which can be learned by the emerging library leader.

Leaders Are Not Managers, or, Learning to Lead a Library Association

Several authors have made distinctions between library leaders and library managers, among them, Herbert White (White, 1997), who observes that leaders without management responsibility have far more freedom. One can be a leader without being a manager and be a manager without exercising leadership (Gertzog, 1989). Management guru Warren Bennis, who wrote *On Becoming a Leader* (Bennis, 1989), makes these distinctions. Lucile Wilson makes other differences between leaders and managers (Wilson, 1996: 110-111). Wilson states that leaders tend to stress relationships with others, managers tend to stress organization, coordination and control of resources. She also points out that leaders tend to create and articulate a long-term vision, while managers emphasize short-term objectives and goals. She also says that leaders tend to communicate the purpose of doing things, while managers focus on directives, policies and procedures.

Another list of how leaders differ from managers appears in Warren Blanks' *The 9 Natural Laws of Leadership* (Blank, 1995: 211): (1) managers have subordinates, leaders attract willing followers; (2) managers use influence based on formal authority, leaders develop influence beyond author-

ity; (3) managers operate within prescribed pathways, leaders outside of them; (4) managers are given a position, leaders take initiative to lead; and (5) managers rely on tradition and procedure, leaders, on consciousness. We have all heard that leaders are born and not made, but in most library associations, the leader is initiated when he or she agrees to be nominated and run for election or at least nominated and appointed under special circumstances. Opportunity knocks and, hopefully, the individual has several years of experience with the association, especially on the board of directors. Once the individual is elected or appointed to the role of leading the association, the vision as well as the nuts and bolts or mechanics of the role set in. Both the big picture vision (leadership) and the details of actually running the association (management) are involved. Many would argue that a leader should keep an eye on managing (possibly through delegation to various board members) while concentrating on leading. The association only moves forward with the big picture vision of the leader. Terrence Mech put it this way: "Leaders facilitate change and movement into unfamiliar areas. They do things: sometimes big things, but mostly a lot of little things" (Mech, 1996: 345). Fisher Howe puts the elements of an association president's role nicely: affirm values, agenda setting, motivating, institution building, clarifying and defining, coalition building and renewing (Howe, 1995). Fostering a culture that reinforces the mission and credo or philosophy (Bower, 1997), which are at the core of the association. This means shared values and the desire to meet the association's goals and objectives, the big picture vision part of it.

Few books on leadership have had the impact than those of Stephen R. Covey.

Beginning with *The 7 Habits of Highly Effective People* (Covey, 1989) and followed by *Principle-centered Leadership* (Covey, 1990). The first book is especially useful because of the balance it teaches and the mastery over self—the inner victory—necessary before the public victories can take place. This oversimplifies it, but the progression of the seven habits is in this order: (1) be proactive; (2) begin with the end in mind; (3) put first things first; (4) think win/win; (5) seek first to understand ... then to be understood; (6) synergize and (7) sharpen the saw. Covey wrote this book based on his review of the success literature in the United States from the last 200 years. What he found was that our forefathers had an emphasis on the character ethic that had been lost in our century. By going back to the important principles, those things we consider the most important in our lives and how we live them, first things first, we are able to achieve personal and professional success. This conviction that principles are essential elements of leaders was shared in an interview by Elizabeth Martinez (Riggs & Sabine, 1988: 112). Martinez said, "You can't be a leader without an inner strength, some inner characteristics. If you don't have those, you're not going to be a leader for long, or you're going to be a superficial one without any depth. They don't last long."

On the managing end, the board meetings can be public or private events, ceremonious and or chaotic, but be sure, this is where much of the real work of the association happens. Library associations may have one- to two-hour monthly board meetings (some state and regional library associations), or two- to three-hour meetings twice a year (most ALA divisions). Library associations often have multi-year board members, so appointments are a real opportunity for association leaders to bring in talented, hard-working members to work on the board. A word of caution, though, this is not without risks; the bottom line is that if one of the new people fails to perform his or her assigned tasks, these tasks become the responsibility of the association leader, who must do them or find someone else to do them. You want to fill the board with people who can be counted on to commit to a minimum term of office, one or two years, and who can be trusted to perform their assigned duties with little or no help from you. Maybe it is only bad luck, but the reverse scenario happens often enough, so it is worth mentioning to new association leaders.

Leadership Is Not Without Perils

Let us limit the discussion to three common perils, although by no means the only perils: (1) stress, (2) sleep disturbances (Caputo, 1991) and—in this age of technological advancement—(3) communication overload: e-mail, fax, voice-phone, snail mail and in person conversations. Stephen Fineman and Yiannis Gabriel, authors of *Experiencing Organizations* (Fineman & Gabriel, 1996), mention an often-overlooked part of a term or role of leadership: survival. Most association leaders, which in most of the library world means volunteer positions with no additional staff, will admit that getting through their term of office without too much suffering becomes an increasing consideration as the pressures of deadlines, returning daily telephone calls and answering daily bombardments of e-mail and snail mail mounts. The additional pressure of performance in a public role is also great: having association members and others both recognize and talk to you—people you do not know, but who now feel they know you from photos, name recognition, and association meetings. Other pressures entail preparing for public appearances and speaking engagements as part of the leader's expected role. For all of these pressures, leaders can only rise to the challenge of their newfound celebrity within and outside the association. These performance challenges make you want to get things right, and you only get one chance to do them right (Fineman & Gabriel, 1996). It adds to the pressures of leadership, nonetheless. There will always be limits of time and energy that association leaders face during their term of office. Ultimately, things must be ready to go, for better or for worse. The hard part is that we all want them to be for the better, never the worse; but time constraints dictate just how much better. Creating a balance of wanting to do what is best for the association and realistically doing what time and energy will permit is necessary and pragmatic. Do all you can, then move on, to survive your term of office.

Identifying Future Latino Leaders

So, just where are future Latino library leaders? If we take the time to look for them, we find that emerging library leaders can be found in local and state library associations already working on association committees and round tables. They are also a part of library networks that are active at conferences and on electronic mail lists. In most cases, these emerging leaders are active members of their chapter associations and were probably active in their student ALA chapter—if they were lucky enough to have one at their alma mater. Library association leaders obviously start out as library association joiners. The only drawback to their participation at national library association events in early career is the necessary travel funding to attend conferences and meetings. Emerging leaders are often just beginning their careers and are in positions that do not afford much travel money. The reality is that without institutional funding, the emerging leader must rely on personal funds to make these trips to professional conferences, a prospect that is enough to discourage most from any serious involvement in national associations. While they might get lucky one year and have a conference in their geographic area one year, the conference will likely be held across the country the next year. For this reason, library leaders as mentors are especially important: by assisting the mentee in furthering his or her career, the mentee can develop a career that will one day permit regular conference participation and with it, a greater participation in library associations as an emerging leader.

Leadership Through Team Building

Working effectively with the executive board is critical to the success of the association. It is the role of the leader as association president to encourage team building. The authors of *Light Bulbs for Leaders: A Guide Book for Team Learning* (Glacel & Robert, 1996) state that we can predict the stages of team building and learn lessons to see the board team through them: forming, storming, norming and performing. In another book, *Team Fitness: A How-To Manual for Building a Winning Work Team*, Meg Hartzel and Jane Henry compiled eight characteristics of effective teams (Hartzel & Henry, 1996). Here they are in abbreviated form: (1) teams produce results, (2) their purpose is clear and members feel it's worthwhile, (3) team members feel invested in the success of the team, (4) teams seem to be having fun working, (5) team members are clear on their roles, (6) nothing is under the table—members share issues and concerns openly, (7) team members are not afraid to surface a problem, and (8) the team does not lose sight of its goal and the higher purpose of moving closer to their vision of the shared mission. Another aspect of team building among board members is that of creating a culture of trust. This is what Gilbert Fairholm calls the leadership of trust, creating a trust relationship among board members that permits harmony, encourages participation, and facilitates working toward shared visioning (Fairholm, 1994). Leaders as board chairs should actively create a win-win atmosphere (Covey, 1989; Caputo, 1991). Team building and effective board management also often involves the art of compromise. Reducing role ambiguity for new board members is essential to increasing effective participation on the board (Howe, 1995). This is achieved by reviewing the policies and procedure manual outlining the responsibilities and expectations as soon into the presidential term as possible. These typically include reviewing the association's mission and the board member's general and specific role. Ideally, the board member is interviewed personally by the president to discuss these issues. This role of engaging and developing board members in particular is one of the greatest challenges faced by association leaders, along with the orchestration of running effective board meetings. In *Executive Leadership in Nonprofit Organizations*, Herman and

Heimovich identify six requisite skills of the board-centered leader (Herman & Heimovics, 1991): (1) facilitating interaction in board relationships, (2) showing consideration and respect toward board members, (3) envisioning change and innovation with the board, (4) promoting board accomplishments and productivity, (5) initiating and maintaining a structure for board work, and (6) providing helpful information to the board. While as association leaders, we would want all of the board members to attend all board meetings, the reality is that not all of them will—no reflection on anything other than the restraints of time and their level of involvement in other association meetings being held at the same time.

Mentoring Relationships

Mentoring has become a buzzword in the leadership literature in the past ten years and with good reason; it is an ideal way to match the novice with an experienced member of the association (Cubberley, 1996). Most leaders will acknowledge the invaluable assistance of a mentor or two during the development of their own careers. This age old practice of imparting knowledge to younger members of the profession is alive and well in librarianship. Brooke Sheldon's book, *Leaders in Libraries: Styles and Strategies for Success* (Sheldon, 1991) includes testimonials to the effect by several library leaders, from among others, a Latino, Kathleen (Heim) de la Peña McCook. While the benefits of a mentee finding a mentor are quite obvious, there are also many reasons that would explain why mentors are attracted to their mentees; one book offers fifteen (Albritton and Henry, 1990): intelligence, enthusiasm, ambition, loyalty, dedication, integrity, professional competence, a desire to learn, commitment to the organization, ability to accept responsibility, ability to take initiative, ability to work with others, ability to listen, ability to ask for guidance, and a willingness to speak up and at times disagree. While mentees can of course also search out their mentors, it is usually the mentor that takes the initiative. Ideally, as the mentoring relationship matures, the mentor one day accepts the mentee as a peer. The mentee may also one day surpass the mentor in the profession, something that could only make the mentor justifiably proud. Leaders should remember to act as mentors as they are able by providing opportunities for professional growth for association members—including members of the board and other association officers.

Latino Leadership and Cultural Differences

All of the previous discussion has been applicable for all leaders. However, Latino leadership involves a leadership strategy that generally is not discussed in the mainstream literature of leadership and applies to leaders who work with the various Latino minority populations. It is effective communication taking into account the social customs and recognizing that this is vital to our effectiveness as leadership in our communities. It is a consideration of that particular aspect of leadership involving our Latino community, lo nuestro. Latino leaders must be bicultural and bilingual to be able to relate effectively not only within our own community but also within the larger non–Latino community, and must be as comfortable in a professional or community group of Spanish speakers as in their English-speaking

equivalents. Philip Harris and Robert Moran in their book, *Managing Cultural Difference: Leadership Strategies for a New World of Business* (Harris & Moran, 1996), summarize some of the cultural differences that they have found both in the Mexican American and more inclusively in Latin American communities. Another great source—not only for Mexican and other Latin American cultural differences, but for sixty other countries—is *Kiss, Bow or Shake Hands* (Morrison, Conaway & Borden, 1994). While generalizations are often dangerous, some of their noted differences are presented here just the same. Latinos recognize the importance of shaking hands with each person in the room at meetings; recognize the different pace of Latino meetings (often slower with more discussion); accept a different idea of being on time (Latinos may often be late); exchange pleasantries, know the importance of personal relationships based on mutual trust or personalismo (Latinos do not like to rush into business), dress conservatively and are a bit formal (Harris & Moran, 1996). Personal space is also an important factor to consider since Latinos tend to speak from a closer distance than do North Americans. It is also important to add that many Latinos kiss on the cheek and often embrace at meetings; to do otherwise would be taken as an offensive. These greetings and farewells often have more to do with respect for the role of the leader than with any personal feelings on the part of the individual initiating an embrace or a kiss on the cheek.

Summary

Leadership as we have seen is a complex issue. Aspects of leadership such as traits and behavior may be learned, but this in no way insures the emergence of a leader. However, leadership development may permit library associations to recognize potential leaders early in their careers and encourage them to take opportunities that will provide experiences that will allow them to hasten their development as future leaders. This vital practice of mentoring may be the one thing that leaders can undertake to insure the future success of our associations. Communication, top down and bottom up are also important. It seems ironic that in an era when both technological and communication devices have advanced more than ever before, library associations still hear complaints of poor communication. Here the library association leader is torn: people should be kept in the loop so to speak, but not put in overload with trivial information. One example of this is the association electronic mail list(s). It would be inappropriate to distribute board-specific information using this medium, not because the information is necessarily privy, but because it constitutes "junk mail" to most of the subscribers. Sure they're interested, just not that interested in that much association detail. Save the detail for the association newsletter. More effective communication on an electronic mail list would be the announcements or brief summaries of events or action taken by the board. Discussions may also be had on electronic mail lists, but unless some of these issues are eventually brought before the board, all the electronic messages prove nothing more than the informal networking and sharing with our association colleagues. One of the best uses of an electronic mail list is to seek advice from other subscribers about something from their collective experience. Electronic ballots would also be an excellent use for electronic mail lists although

to date few if any associations are using them for this. Open communication insures that the association leader and the board do not isolate themselves from the concerns and wishes of the association members.

Mentoring is probably the single most important activity a library association leader can undertake outside of the big picture vision activity for the association that he or she leads. Nurturing new and experienced members of the association by providing professional advice and opportunities, we assure a strong contingent of emerging leaders for the association, assure a continuum of leadership from one term to another within the association. How do we get them involved? Former ALA president Barbara Ford suggests ten ways to get involved in ALA (Ford, 1997) and her list serves all library associations well. Mentors can start by sharing Ford's list with their mentees.

Allow me one last personal observation. My first mentor in the library profession shared a copy of a motto in Latin with me that an "old timer" at the New York Public had once shared with him: OMNIS VITA SERVITIUM EST (all life is service). This motto did not mean that much to me that day in my first year in the profession; nearly ten years later, its meaning is important to me. What is life about, if not service to our families, our communities, our profession? It is tacked up above the piles of papers on my desk as a reminder to myself of what we are all about in libraries. Every now and then, we all need reminding.

References

Albritton, R.L. & T.W. Shaughnessy. (1990). *Developing leadership skills: A sourcebook for librarians.* Englewood, CO: Libraries Unlimited, Inc.

Bennis, W. (1989). *On becoming a leader.* Reading, MA: Addision-Wesley Publishing Company.

Bennis, W. & B. Nanus. (1997). *Leaders: Strategies for taking charge.* 2nd. ed. New York: HarperBusiness.

Blank, W. (1995). *The 9 natural laws of leadership.* New York: Amacom.

Bower, M. (1997). *The will to lead: Running a business with a network of leaders.* Boston, MA: Harvard Business School Press.

Caputo, J. S. (1991). *Stress and burnout in library service.* Phoenix, AZ: Oryx.

Covey, S. R. (1989). *The 7 habits of highly effective people: Restoring the character ethic.* New York: Simon & Schuster.

Covey, S. R. (1990). *Principle-centered leadership.* New York: Summit Books.

Cubberley, C. W. (1996). *Tenure and promotion for academic librarians.* Jefferson, NC: McFarland & Company, Inc.

Fairholm, G. W. (1994). *Leadership and the culture of trust.* Westport, CT: Praeger.

Fineman, S. & Gabriel, Y. (1996). *Experiencing organizations.* London: Sage Publications.

Ford, B. J. (1997). "Voices and visions: 10 ways to get involved in ALA." *American Libraries, 28.*

Frigon, N. L., Sr. & Jackson, H. K., Jr. (1996). *The leader: developing the skills & personal qualities you need to lead effectively.* New York: Amacom.

Gertzog, A.. (Ed.). (1989). *Leadership in the library/information profession.* Jefferson, NC: McFarland & Company, Inc.

Glacel, B.P. & Robert, E. A., Jr. (1996). *Light bulbs for leaders: A guide book for team learning.* New York: John Wiley & Sons, Inc.

Harris, P.R. & Moran, R. T. (1996). *Managing cultural differences: leadership strategies for a new world of business. 4th ed.* Houston, TX: Gulf Publishing Company.

Hartzler, M. & Henry, J. E. (1994). *Team fitness: A How-to Manual for Building a Winning Work Team.* Milwaukee, WI: ASQC Quality Press.

Herman, R.D. & Heimovics, R. D. (1991). *Executive leadership in nonprofit organizations: New strategies for shaping executive-board dynamics.* San Francisco, CA: Jossey-Bass Publishers.

Howe, F. (1995). *Welcome to the board: Your guide to effective participation. San Francisco, CA:* Jossey-Bass Publishers.

Iannuzzi, P. (1992). *Leadership development and organizational maturity.* Journal of Library Administration, 17.

Jones, R. (1997). New technologies demand new roles: "Resistance is futile." *Computer in Libraries, 17.*

Kelly, J. & Robbins, K. (1996). "Changing roles for reference librarians." *Journal of Library Administration, 22.*

Kleiner, A. & Roth, G. (1997). "How to make experience your company's best teacher." *Harvard Business Review, 75.*

Lee, S. "Leadership: Revised and redesigned for the electronic age." *Journal of Library Administration, 20.*

Liu, C.F.L. (1994). "Cultural diversity: A conversation with the presidents of ALA's ethnic caucuses." *Library Administration & Management, 8.*

Martin, R.R. (1997). "Recruiting a library leader for the 21st century." *Journal of Library Administration, 24.*

Mech, T. (1996). "Leadership and the evolution of academic librarianship." *Journal of Academic Librarianship, 22.*

Morrison, T. Conaway, W. A. & Borden, G. A. (1994). *Kiss, bow or shake hands: How to do business in sixty countries.* Holbrook, MA: Bob Adams, Inc.

Riggs, D.E. (Ed.). (1991). *Library communication: The language of leadership.* Chicago, IL: American Library Association.

_____. (1997). "What's in store for academic libraries? Leadership and management issues." *Journal of Academic Librarianship, 23.*

Riggs, D.E. & Sabine, G. A. (1988).

Libraries in the '90s: What the leaders expect. Phoenix, AZ: Oryx Press.

Riggs, D.E. & Sykes, V. M.. (1993). "The time for transformational leadership is now!" *Journal of Library Administration,* 18.

Ross, S.M. & Offermann, L. R. (1997). "Transformational leaders: Measurement of personality attributes and work group performance." *Personality and Social Psychology Bulletin,* 23.

Sheldon, B.E. (1991). *Leaders in libraries: Styles and strategies for success.* Chicago, IL: American Library Association.

Sweeney, R. (1997). "Leadership skills in a reengineered library: Empowerment and value added trend implications for library leaders." *Library Administration & Management,* 11.

White, H.S. (1997). "Should leaders want to be managers and give up all that freedom?" *Library Journal,* 122.

Wilson, L. (1996). *People skills for library managers: A common sense guide for beginners.* Englewood, CO: Libraries Unlimited.

CHAPTER TWO

Recruiting Latinos to Librarianship: A Continuing Need

Tami Echavarria

As the twentieth century draws to a close, the rapidly changing demographics and politics of the latter years of the 20th century makes it imperative for libraries to respond to their changing constituencies. The country is fast becoming ethnically and culturally diverse. An appropriate response is concerted recruitment and retention of minority librarians to serve the growing minority populations' needs. But at the same time that the country's demographics are shifting toward more diversity, the political climate is shifting away from affirming the existence of a more diverse population.

Federal law recognizes four categories of underrepresented minority groups: Black or Afro-American, Hispanic, Asian and Pacific Islander, and American Indian or Native American.[1] The fastest growing groups of the American population are Asian and Pacific Islander and Hispanic. Since 1980 the growth rate of these groups has risen notably faster than the rest of the American population.[2] During the period 1990–1996 the Asian and Pacific Islander group increased by 42 percent and the Hispanic group by 37 percent.[3]

According to the United States Bureau of the Census, the United States population is expected to grow by an additional 50 percent from 1992 to 2050. Those projections on the ethnic composition anticipate that Hispanic and Afro-American women will continue the current trend of bearing children at higher rates than white women. The projected effect of such a trend will be that our nation's population which was 75 percent white and 25 percent minority in 1992 will be 53 percent white and 47 percent minority in 2050.[4] California, the most demographically diverse state in the nation, and having 12 percent of the U.S. population currently, will lead the nation. In 1990, California's population was 57 percent white and 43 percent minority, and is projected to be 32 percent white and 68 percent minority in 2040.[5] The trend is clearly toward greater diversification and a more pluralistic society.

A brief profile of the Hispanic population in the United States is helpful to begin understanding this important and rapidly growing sector of the U.S. population. According to the latest statistics of the U.S. Bureau of the Census, Hispanics number over 28 million, comprising just under 9.5 percent of the nation's total population.[6] The majority live in the states of California, Arizona, New Mexico, Texas, Colorado, Illinois, New York, New Jersey and Florida, although Hispanics live in every state. The overwhelming majority live in metropolitan areas. Nearly half are immigrants, coming from all Spanish-speaking countries. Overall they have a lower level of education, have more children, are younger, have higher unemployment, a lower level of voter participation, and lower income than the averages in America. They are united by a common Spanish language and similar cultural heritage. Many are English speakers, some are bilingual in Spanish and English, and others are learning English.

Within the Hispanic population there are subgroups based on the geographic origin in the Spanish speaking world from which each group comes. Latino, rather than Hispanic, is the term that has received the widest acceptance among all subgroups. They are divided by geography, country of origin, class, and the time and circumstance of their arrival to the United States. Latinos of Cuban background are concentrated in Florida, have higher incomes and education levels and are older than the profile for the other subgroups. Those of Puerto Rican background are concentrated in New York and New Jersey, have the highest proportion living below the poverty level, and are a non-immigrant population having citizenship from birth. Mexican-Americans, or Chicanos, are younger and less educated than the overall statistics and are concentrated in the southwestern states. Those of Central and South American origin are mostly immigrants, are not native speakers of English, and have a low percentage of unemployment.[7]

Many of the immigrants from Spain, the Canary Islands, Central and South America are highly skilled, educated professionals seeking career opportunities not available in their countries of origin. Distinct differences are evident in examining the major Hispanic, or Latino, subgroups separately, something which is necessary for libraries in order to respond appropriately to their communities.

Serving Latino Library Users

A strong connection needs to be made between the need for well-trained Latino librarians to serve the Latino community and the particular nature of that community's library and information needs. Traditionally library users were white, middle class Americans[8] but the demographics have shifted. The constituencies of libraries' in this country have changed dramatically since 1980. Library users in schools, public libraries and academic libraries are increasingly from underrepresented minority groups as well as white ethnic backgrounds. As different cultural groups use public, school and academic libraries, those libraries have the obligation to be responsive to user needs. Expanding populations and changing neighborhoods demand an appropriate, effective response to the obligation of service that libraries maintain. The libraries must change and adapt to serving the new populations and their needs.

Some of the needs of the various Latino subgroups are revealed readily when libraries become acquainted with the communities they serve. Variation exists according to the make-up of the community, but some needs are common within the Latino cultural context. All Latino subgroups demonstrate a high demand for materials that keep them informed about their homeland. Spanish language periodicals provide a lifeline to the Latino community that may not be available anywhere else but the library. A significant aspect of the reading habits of Latinos is the emphasis on poetry and short stories. These are read by Latinos of all education and income levels. Information is needed about survival to learn about and adjust to American society. Of paramount importance are materials relating to immigration policy and citizenship. Self-help books are sought on almost any topic. Materials are sought in Spanish as well as English, including basic materials for those learning English. For many Latin American immigrants who are well educated, their reading needs center around the career or course of study they are pursuing. The *fotonovela* is a familiar and popular source of recreational reading among many Mexican Americans. Romance novels are also popular but serious intellectual commentaries on social

and political issues, Mexican character and culture also have a readership.[9]

Internet instruction and library instruction is becoming increasingly important for the rising number of Latino students enrolling in higher education. Latino students' needs and learning styles tend to differ from those of the mainstream academic population due to different access to technology, different experiences using technology, linguistic patterns, and cultural aspects and expectations.[10] Bibliographic instruction librarians need to be knowledgeable about the learning style of Spanish language students in order to foster effective learning experiences for these students.

Latino communities are becoming more complex, diverse and more challenging for libraries to serve. The particular cultural ties between the local community, its people and their country of origin or heritage should be reflected in a library's collection. The community will use a library when they see library staff that are like themselves. The professional and support staff must be culturally knowledgeable and linguistically capable of serving the community.[11] It is important to have staff who reflect the racial and ethnic make-up, and share the language and the cultural values of the service community.[12] The professional and support staff must establish a relationship with the community. The resulting trust gives the library entry to the community,[13] which may not be accustomed to the services offered by American libraries. This is necessary so that the library will be accepted and used by the community.

The library science profession is faced with keeping up with the changing demographics of library user populations, and with the needs associated with these populations. Librarians, as well as parapro-

down a clear path to get there is mentoring. It is a complicated process.

There are few individuals who decide their life career as children. Most people are unaware of all of the options available and how to find out about them. Many follow role models they see frequently in their daily lives. Their choices are made from a limited amount of familiar information. As role models, minority librarians are in a unique position to be one of the influences in someone's life when they are making a career choice.

Librarians are often seen repeatedly by students in schools, colleges and in neighborhood public libraries. College students are a particularly good group to mentor because their time to select a profession is near at hand. Some college graduates have clear career goals but many do not and are searching for direction as they enter the workforce.

This is the perfect opportunity for a mentor to be present. Undergraduate students are a prime population from which to recruit because the accomplishment of a baccalaureate degree brings them to this point of decision in their lives. At this juncture, students are open to some suggestion and guidance. This is only possible if the student gets to know the mentor as a person who is trustworthy. For the mentoring to be effective, there must be an established relationship between the undergraduate student and the person who mentors him/her. The student must trust that the mentor has the best interests of the student at heart.

If an opportunity exists in which to work with a group of students, a combination of teaching and mentoring works well. Most undergraduates know little if anything about what careers in librarianship entail so instruction can be helpful. But instruction alone is insufficient. It is reminiscent of professors' lectures that students are accustomed to hearing in various subject disciplines, but which seldom provide personal career guidance. Mentoring bridges that gap and is the one-on-one interaction that takes into account the individual's personal circumstances and preferences. This is how a student can get his/her own questions answered as they arise during the process of choosing a career. Choosing a life path is not a decision to be taken lightly and the student must know that the mentor genuinely cares what happens to him/her.

The mentor becomes a confidant and role model for the students. "First hand acquaintance with a mentor takes on further value when the student and the mentor have enough cultural bonds in common so that the student can, without a great leap of imagination, picture him or herself doing that kind of work."[28] If the mentor is not a member of a minority group, students are likely to view him/her, as they do other members of the academy, as someone different from themselves, and fail to identify with the mentor. A mentor who is a minority member is more likely to be seen as someone like themselves, and is more readily accepted as a role model. They can see themselves in the mentor and thus in his/her shoes. Latino librarians and paraprofessionals are role models and they are well-positioned to serve as mentors for recruiting young Latinos to librarianship.

The process of mentoring a prospective librarian from undergraduate study to productive participation in the profession is a lengthy process. It includes not only the career decision, but also the selection of a library school, the application process to library school, application for sufficient financial aid to pursue graduate studies, library school education, first professional job search, participation in professional organizations and conferences, and often, transitioning to subsequent jobs. The mentor has to be willing to devote the energy, effort and time, albeit sporadically, and to be there when needed. It is a time-consuming process.

The time invested is well-rewarded. The gratification comes in the form of friendship and the network of colleagues that develops over time with the former students. The mentor's genuine personal regard for each student is returned as gratitude and trust. There is pride in watching the germination and growth of seeds long ago planted and watered, and so it is with protéges who have come up under one's wing. With time the protéges become colleagues with whom to network.

An example of a program based on these ideas was the Undergraduate Student Internship Program (USIP) at the University of California, San Diego. It began in 1989 [29] as a response to a need expressed in the journal literature of the profession between 1986 and 1989. The need was a call for more minority librarians to serve an ethnically broader based user population in libraries than previous decades had seen.[30] This need was well-documented in the professional literature then as it still is today.[31]

The purpose of the program was to recruit minority undergraduate students to librarianship and send them on to ALA accredited library schools to receive their M.L.S. degrees and from there into the profession at large. The objective with each participant was to give that student as much information possible upon which to make an informed decision as to whether librarianship was a viable career choice for him/her. Participants committed to the program for one academic year, beginning in 1989-1990 through 1995-1996. Because the USIP budget came from funds for affirmative action initiatives, non-minority students were not eligible to participate in USIP.

Sixty-one percent of the students chose to enter the field of library science as their chosen career. Of the 33 students who participated over the seven-year time span that the program was in operation, 22 chose to become librarians or chose para-professional library careers; six are Latinos. USIP was a successful recruitment tool.

The high rate of successful recruitment that was achieved indicates that the Undergraduate Student Internship Program met a need for the participants in a way that they responded to positively. The method of combining instruction with mentoring aided these students at a cross-road in their lives that made a clear difference. These young men and women are now part of the profession of librarianship as a result of their participation in this program.

But programs like USIP are threatened by political pressures. The Undergraduate Student Internship Program was discontinued, as were the funds earmarked for affirmative action initiatives that supported it in 1996. By 1995 the political environment in California had turned away from supporting affirmative action.

Despite the demographic trend toward a more pluralistic society, the decades of a political climate favorable to affirmative action in the United States seem to be waning. The political climate in California has seen a significant shift in recent years concerning affirmative action. Beginning with the landmark Supreme Court case, *Regents of University of California v. Bakke*[32] in 1978, affirmative action practices of the previous decade were successfully challenged. Nearly two decades later, affirmative action initiatives, in place for thirty years, have been overthrown in California.

On June 1, 1995, California Governor, Pete Wilson, issued Executive Order W-124-95 to "End Preferential Treatment and Promote Individual Opportunity Based on Merit"[33] throughout California public service, which was the beginning of the end of affirmative action in California. A month later, on July 20, 1996, the Regents of the University of California issued two resolutions, SP-1[34] and SP-2,[35] over the opposition and vigorous protest of faculty, administration, and students, to end affirmative action at the premier public university of the country's most demographically diverse state.

> At a stroke, the landscape of higher education had changed. Assumptions about race and ethnicity that had for decades guided policy were suddenly stripped of the armor of institutional inevitability. They were rent open, open to recuperation, revision, repudiation, whatever the newly emerging politics of a dawning era would decree.[36]

The University of California replaced its affirmative action policies with ones that are race-neutral. The effect was seen dramatically and almost immediately. The admissions rate for African American students at the Berkeley campus dropped by half of what it had been the previous year.[37] California became the proving ground for the nation in the political swing against affirmative action.[38] On November 5, 1996, California voters passed Proposition 209,[39] a constitutional amendment which banned racial and gender preferences in state and local government. Thus, came the end of affirmative action in California. Although California is wont

to be the nation's leader in political trends, the move to end affirmative action flies in the face of the demographic reality of the state.[40]

Affirmative action remains federal law in the United States and is still practiced in other states. Without support for affirmative action initiatives, formalized minority recruitment programs will not exist. But individual recruitment can still occur if each concerned librarian does his/her part to mentor promising young students. Latino librarians and paraprofessionals who work with Latino students are in the most advantageous position to recruit. Recruiting and mentoring over the years of one's career has an impact on the profession of adding quite a few new Latinos to librarianship.

The library and information science profession, as led by its professional associations, continues to support affirmative action.[41] Recruitment of excellent new librarians is essential for a graying profession's survival, and minority recruitment is essential to a profession in a multicultural society. Challenges face libraries in becoming multicultural centers for education. Multicultural staffing is one of those challenges that can be promoted if recruiting and mentoring is enhanced by promotions and role modeling. Together these efforts can move libraries toward institutionalizing diversity and meeting the information needs of a multicultural society of the next century.

Notes

1. "Revised Order No. 4," *Code of Federal Regulations*, 41, Pt. 60-4.3 (1996).

2. Cheryl Metoyer-Duran, *Gatekeepers in Ethnolinguistic Communities* (Norwood, N.J.: Ablex, 1993), ix.

3. U.S. Bureau of the Census. "Components of Population Change, by Race and Hispanic Origin, 1990 to 1996, and Projections, 2000," Table No. 20. *Statistical Abstracts of the United States: 1997* (Washington D.C.: GPO, 1997).

4. Sean R. Pollock, ed., *Statistical Forecasts of the United States,* 2d ed. (New York, Gale Research, 1995), 624.

5. James S. Fay, ed., *California Almanac,* 7th ed. (Santa Barbara, CA: Pacific Data Resources, 1995), 1,3.

6. U.S. Bureau of the Census. "Resident Population, by Race, Hispanic Origin, and Singles Years of Age: 1996," Table No. 22. *Statistical Abstract of the United States: 1997* (Washington, D.C., 1997).

7. Eugene Estrada, "Changing Latino Demographics and American Libraries," in *Latino Librarianship: A Handbook for Professionals,* ed. Salvador Güereña (Jefferson, N.C.: McFarland, 1990), 1–18.

8. David B.Carlson and others, *Adrift in a Sea of Change: California's Public Libraries Struggle to Meet the Information Needs of Multicultural Communities* ([Sacramento]: Center for Policy Development, 1990), 38.

9. Yolanda Cuesta, "From Survival to Sophistication: Hispanic Needs = Library Needs," *Library Journal* 115 no.9 (May 15, 1990): 26–28.

10. Lori S. Mestre, "Designing Internet Instruction for Latinos," in *The Challenge of Internet Literacy: The Instruction-Web Convergence,* ed. Lyn Elizabeth M. Martin (New York: Haworth, 1997), 185–199.

11. Rafaela Castro, "Assessment of Ethnic Library Collections," in *Developing Library Collections for California's Emerging Majority: A Manual of Resources for Ethnic Collection Development,* Conference held in San Francisco, September 22–23, 1990, edited by Katharine T.A. Scarborough (San Francisco: n.p., 1990), 40, 44.

12. David B. Carlson and others, *Adrift in a Sea of Change: California's Public Libraries Struggle to Meet the Information Needs of Multicultural Communities* ([Sacra-mento]: Center for Policy Development, 1990), 65.

13. Rita Torres, "Assessment of Community Needs" in *Developing Library Collections For California's Emerging Majority: A Manual of Resources for Ethnic Collection Development,* Conference held in San Francisco, September 22–23, 1990, edited by Katharine T.A. Scarborough (San Francisco: n.p., 1990), 48.

14. Stanley J. Wilder, *The Age Demographics of Academic Librarians: A Profession Apart* (Washington, D.C.: Association of College and Research Libraries, 1995), vii–x.

15. *Civil Rights Act of 1964, United States Statutes at Large* 78, 241–268 (1964).

16. U.S. President, Executive Order, "Equal Employment Opportunity Executive Order 11246," *Federal Register* (September 28, 1965): vol 30, p.12319. Microfilm.

17. "Revised Order No. 4," *Code of Federal Regulations,* 41, Pt. 60-2.1 (1996).

18. American Library Association, Office of Library Personnel Resources, *Academic and Public Librarians: Data by Race, Ethnicity and Sex* (Chicago: American Library Association, 1986), 7.

19. American Library Association, Office of Library Personnel Resources, *Academic and Public Librarians: Data by Race, Ethnicity and Sex, 1991* (Chicago, American Library Association, 1991), Table 1.

20. American Library Association, Office of Library Personnel Resources, "Degrees and Certificates Awarded by U.S. Library and Information Studies Education Programs, 1993–1994" (American Library Association, Office of Library Personnel Resources, Chicago, 1995), photocopied.

21. Kathleen de la Peña McCook and Paula Geist, "Diversity Deferred: Where are the Minority Librarians?" *Library Journal* 118 no.18 (November 1, 1993): 35–38.

22. Timothy W. Sineath, ed., *Library and Information Science Education Statistical Report 1996* (Raleigh, NC: Association of Library and Information Science Education, 1996), 143.

23. David B. Carlson and others, *Adrift in a Sea of Change: California's Public Libraries Struggle to Meet the Information Needs of Multicultural Communities* ([Sacramento]: Center for Policy Development, 1990), 66–71.

24. Carla J. Stoffle and Patricia A. Tarin, "No Place for Neutrality: The Case for Multiculturalism," *Library Journal* (July 1994), 46–49.

25. Evan St. Lifer and Corinne Nelson, "Unequal Opportunities" Race Does Matter," *Library Journal* vol. 122, no.18 (November 1, 1997): 42–46.

26. Mark Winston, "The Minority Librarian: Why Your Role is Different," in *In Our Own Voices: The Changing Face of Librarianship* eds. Teresa Y. Neely and Khafre K. Abif (Lanham, MD: Scarecrow, 1996), 396.

27. Khafre K. Abif, "Epilogue," in *In Our Own Voices: The Changing Face of Librarianship*, eds. Teresa Y. Neely and Khafre K. Abif (Lanham, MD: Scarecrow, 1996), 409.

28. Maurice B. Wheeler and Jacqueline Hanson, "Improving Diversity: Recruiting Students to the Library Profession," *Journal of Library Administration* 21 (3/4 1995): 143.

29. Tami Echavarria, "Minority Recruitment: A Success Story," *College and Research Libraries News* 51 (November 1990): 962–964.

30. Ann Knight Randall, "Minority Recruitment in Librarianship" in *Librarians for the New Millennium*, ed. William E. Moen & Kathleen M. Heim (Chicago: American Library Association, 1988), 11–25.

31. Veronica E. Nance-Mitchell, "A Multicultural Library: Strategies for the Twenty-First Century," *College and Research Libraries* 57 (September 1996): 405–413.

32. Regents of the University of California v. Bakke, 438 U.S. 265 (1978).

33. California. Governor, Executive Order, " Executive Order to End Preferential Treatment and to Promote Individual Opportunity Based on Merit," W-124-95.

34. Regents of the University of California, *SP-1: Adoption of Resolution: Policy Ensuring Equal Treatment—Admissions*, July 20, 1995. [http://www.ucsd.edu/campus/general/policy/regents/index. html]

35. Regents of the University of California, *SP-2: Adoption of Resolution: Policy Ensuring Equal Treatment—Employment and Contracting*, July 20, 1995. [http://www.ucsd.edu/campus/general/policy/regents/index.html]

36. Robert Post, "Introduction: After Bakke," *Representations* 55 (Summer 1996): 1–12.

37. William G. Bowen and Derek Bok, *The Shape of the River: Long-Term Consequences of Considering Race in College and University Admissions* (Princeton, NJ: Princeton University Press, 1998), 32–33.

38. Troy Duster, "Individual Fairness, Group Preferences, and the California Strategy," *Representations* 55 (Summer 1996): 41–58.

39. *California Constitution*, amend. "Prohibition Against Discrimination or Preferential Treatment by State and Other Public Entities," *California Ballot Pamphlet: General Election November 5, 1996.* [http://Vote96.ss.ca.gov/Vote96/html/BP/home.htm]

40. Richard Walker, "California's Collision of Race and Class," *Representations* 55 (Summer 1996): 163–193.

41. California Library Association, "Resolution Supporting affirmative action," August 26, 1996. Photocopied.

CHAPTER THREE

Battling the Adobe Ceiling: Barriers to Professional Advancement for Academic Librarians of Color

Rhonda Rios Kravitz

Do barriers exist for librarians of color desiring to enter upper level management positions? This question has been posed and answered anecdotally by librarians of color in the affirmative for many years.

Even though the profession, through its national and various state association mission statements, expresses a commitment to diversifying and recruiting a diverse workforce, librarians of color perceive they face an adobe or glass ceiling that limits their advancement to top management positions. Some librarians label it a cement or concrete ceiling as they cannot penetrate it. For others, the metaphor is even more drastic, a sticky floor.

Forget about reaching the ceiling, when you can't even get your feet off the ground.

Under the auspices of the Racial and Ethnic Diversity Committee of the Association of College and Research Libraries (ACRL) and with an ACRL Initiative Fund grant, a survey was conducted to identify the perceived barriers that have blocked the advancement of minorities into decision-making positions in the profession. Part of this survey was patterned after a 1987 survey of the barriers to upward mobility for 308 Asian Americans employed in the San Francisco Bay Area (Cabezas, 1989).

Data and Analysis

In August 1995, 600 questionnaires were mailed to academic librarians. Two sampling techniques were used. Surveys were sent to 300 randomly selected ACRL members. Surveys were also sent to the ethnic library organizations: 100 academic REFORMA (National Association to Promote Library Services to the Spanish Speaking) members; 100 academic APALA/CALA (Asian/Pacific American Librarians Association/Chinese-Americana Librarians Association) members; and 100 academic AFAS (Afro-American Studies Librarians) members. The survey design was a cross-sectional survey model to test the attitudes of a large number of librarians at one point in time, with a weighted sampling strategy to over-sample librarians of color. Due to the small number of academic American Indian/Native Americans, they were not included in this survey. This study does not imply that as a group, Native Americans/American Indians do not face the same the barriers as other librarians of color.

Eighteen surveys came back as undeliverable making the total sample size 582. 268 responses were initially received and 46 responses were received after a follow-up post card reminder for a total response rate of 314 (54 percent). The ethnic/racial breakdown was as follows (N = 299): African American: 14 percent (N = 44); Asian/Pacific American: 18 percent (N = 56); Chicano/Latino: 12 percent (N = 39); Caucasian: 51 percent (N = 160); Unknown: 5 percent (N = 15). The respondents worked at the following institutions (N = 313): University (including graduate): 60 percent (N = 187) College (4 year): 13 percent (N = 41); Junior/Community College: 11 percent (N = 33); Special Library 6 percent (N = 14); Library Science Faculty: 3 percent (N = 10); Other: 7 percent (N = 28). The salary range was as follows (N = 302): up to $34,999: 25 percent (N = 75)); $35,000–$44,999: 24 percent (N = 72); $45,000–$59,999: 31 percent (N = 93); $60,000 plus: 20 percent (N = 62). The age of the respondents was as follows (N = 306): 21–30: 5 percent (N = 16); 31–40: 19 percent (N = 59); 41–50: 40 percent (N = 122); 51–60: 27 percent (N = 81); 61 plus: 9 percent (N = 28). Females answering the survey = 207 (68 percent). Males answering the survey = 97 (32 percent). The perception of barriers and enhancers to professional advancement took on strong significance as 51 percent made $45,000 plus and 76 percent were 41 years or older. The respondents were not new to the profession nor were they making entry level salaries.

Employment Barriers

Respondents were asked to rank the impact of specific structural, societal, and family related barriers they had experienced over the last 5 years as related to their professional advancement. The structural barriers were: one's own values don't fit into management culture; management insensitivity; lack of informal networking; lack of mentors; lack of role models; shrinking opportunities; lack of training opportunities; and language deficiency. The societal barriers were: racism; sexism; and ageism. The family related barriers were geographic inflexibility and children/parent responsibilities. Tables 1–4 list the barriers cited by at least 40 percent of the respondents as very significant plus significant.

Table 1. Perceived Employment Barriers
African American/Black (N = 38–44, varies by barrier)

Barrier	Very Significant plus Significant (%)	Very Significant (%)
1. Racism	68	34
2. Management insensitivity	65	23
3. Shrinking opportunities	50	24
4. Values don't fit into management culture	49	21
5. Lack of mentors	48	12
6. Sexism	48	15
7. Lack of informal networking	42	17

Table 2. Perceived Employment Barriers
Asian/Pacific American (N = 52–55, varies by barrier)

Barrier	Very Significant plus Significant (%)	Very Significant (%)
1. Management insensitivity	67	24
2. Racism	66	29
3. Values don't fit into management culture	60	25
4. Lack of mentors	56	24
5. Sexism	51	20
6. Lack of informal networking	49	22
7. Lack of role models	46	16
8. Shrinking opportunities	44	17
9. Geographic inflexibility	42	17
10. Language deficiency	41	11

Table 3. Perceived Employment Barriers
Chicano/Latino Sample (N = 36–39, varies by barrier)

Barrier	Very Significant plus Significant (%)	Very Significant (%)
1. Management insensitivity	68	26
2. Shrinking opportunities	62	33
3. Values don't fit into management culture	59	26
4. Lack of mentors	51	21
5. Lack of role models	49	13
6. Geographic inflexibility	49	30
7. Lack of informal networking	46	10
8. Racism	41	31

Table 4. Perceived Employment Barriers
Caucasian (N = 147–155 varies by barrier)

Barrier	Very Significant plus Significant (%)	Very Significant (%)
1. Shrinking opportunities	52	23
2. Management insensitivity	47	19
3. Lack of mentors	40	15

Seven to ten barriers were ranked by 40 percent or more of the respondents from the various ethnic groups whereas only three barriers were ranked by 40 percent or more of the respondents from the Caucasian group. The most significant barrier for the Caucasian group, shrinking opportunities was ranked by 52 percent of the respondents as very significant plus significant. Whereas, two-thirds of the librarians of color, 67–68 percent, ranked their top barrier as very significant plus significant: management insensitivity for both Asian/Pacific Americans (67 percent) and Chicano/Latinos (68 percent) and racism for African Americans (68 percent). This is an important finding. The increased number of perceived barriers and the difference in percentage ranking, makes the road to advancement seem that much more unreachable for librarians of color than for Caucasian librarians. Deborah A. Curry echoes this finding in her article "Your Worries Ain't Like Mine" (Curry, 1994).

Management Insensitivity

Management insensitivity appeared in the top three barriers for all four groups. However, there was a significant difference by race. Two-thirds of the librarians of color perceived it as a very significant or significant factor whereas less than half of Caucasians perceived it as a barrier. By gender, Chicano/Latino males were more likely to perceive management insensitivity as an issue.

In informal discussion groups of the ACRL, Racial and Ethnic Diversity Committee, librarians of color have remarked that they need to learn techniques to avoid being misunderstood or evaluated inappropriately by their supervisors. They also felt they received less management and organizational support from the libraries in which they worked and that the relationship with their bosses was less supportive than their Caucasian counterparts. This discomfort is borne out by the perceptions of management insensitivity perceived by librarians of color.

Racism

Racism was in the top three barriers for African-Americans/Black and Asian/Pacific Americans, 68 percent and 66 percent respectively. Racism, as a barrier, is the most significant finding in the study (p = 0.000). Males were marginally more likely to rank racism as significant or very significant. However, African-American/Black females perceived race as a more significant barrier than African-

American/Black males (p = .06). Older respondents over 50 (39 percent) and younger, respondents 40 & under (32 percent) were marginally (p = .08) more likely to rank racism as significant or very significant vs. 41–50 year old (24 percent). It is interesting to note that Chicano/Latinos ranked Racism as the 8th most significant barrier (41 percent) when you totaled the rankings for very significant and significant. However, when you compare only the very significant rankings, racism is ranked very similarly for all three ethnic groups: Chicano/Latinos—31 percent, African-Americans—34 percent, and Asian/Pacific Americans—29 percent. This demonstrates clearly that racism is a very significant factor for all three ethnic groups, approximately one in three people of color perceive racism as a very significant barrier. Yet as a profession, because the causes are often not overt but rather subtle and institutionalized, we tend to downplay the impact of racism in our institutions.

Shrinking Opportunities/ Management Culture

Shrinking opportunities was in the top three barriers for Chicano/Latinos (62 percent) and Caucasians (52 percent). However for Chicano/Latinos it was a more significant barrier. "Values don't fit into management culture" was in the top listed three barriers for Asian/Pacific Americans (60 percent) and Chicano/Latinos (59 percent). African-American/Black females marginally (p = .06) were more likely to perceive management culture as a barrier than African-American/Black males.

Sexism

Asian/Pacific American and African-American females were significantly (p = .03) more likely to see sexism as a barrier than Chicano/Latino and Caucasian females and all males. The combined barriers of sexism and racism for African-American and Asian/Pacific American females makes the glass/adobe ceiling feel much more like a concrete ceiling, totally impenetrable. Asian/Pacific Americans (51 percent) and African Americans (48 percent) were statistically significantly more likely (p = .01) to see sexism as a barrier than Chicano/Latinos (31 percent) or Caucasians (29 percent). By age, 41–50 year olds feel significantly (p = .05) that sexism is a barrier. Middle age males also think sexism is a significant barrier.

Language

Language was perceived as a very significant factor for the Asian/Pacific American respondents. It's important to recognize that language differences, for example an accent, can readily victimize those who prefer to blame themselves rather than confront racism and other structural problems in the workplace. Intolerance of an Asian accent or a claim of a language "problem" by an employer can be a form of racism.

Changed Job Titles/ Place of Employment

Respondents were asked if they had changed job titles or place of employment in the last five years. 175 (56 percent) responded yes, 139 (44 percent) responded no. This question was highly significant by race. Asian/Pacific Americans were least likely to change (37.5 percent). Whereas, Caucasians (58 percent), Chicano/Latinos and African-Americans were two-thirds or more likely to move. Asian/Pacific American males, as compared to other males in the study were least likely to move (27 percent) as compared to African-Americans (86 percent), Chicano/Latinos (81 percent) and Caucasians (62 percent).

Job Satisfaction

On a five point scale, 1 (not satisfied) to 5 (very satisfied), respondents were asked to rank how satisfied they were in their current position (see chart below). The median score was 3.8. Only 12 percent of the survey respondents ranked any of the items less than 3.0. Asian/Pacific Americans were more likely to rank the satisfaction scale items with a number between 1–3 (56 percent) as compared to African-Americans (43 percent), Chicano/Latinos (36 percent) and Caucasians (33 percent). One is not satisfied and 5 is very satisfied. Interestingly, African-Americans and Asian/Pacific Americans ranked racism as a significant/very significant barrier, and one can perhaps relate the lower job satisfaction rankings with the significant ranking of racism as a job barrier. Job satisfaction will be lower for employees who feel they are the victims of discrimination. Respondents were also asked to rank their job satisfaction on a scale of 1 (not satisfied) to 5 (very satisfied) for a the following list of factors (N = 294–310):

Table 5. Job Satisfaction

1. Job is stimulating and challenging	4.0
2. Profession is rewarding	3.9
3. Encouragement to participate in state/national meetings	3.9
4. Commitment to affirmative action	3.5
5. Salary benefits package	3.4
6. Networking opportunities	3.4
7. Training opportunities provided	3.4
8. Participation in decision-making	3.3
9. Supervision/management by staff	3.3
10. Funding to participate in state/national meetings	3.1
11. Mentor relationships	2.8
12. Opportunities for advancement	2.6

It is interesting to note that the factors receiving the least satisfaction were those related to advancement: participation in decision-making; supervision/management by staff; funding to participate in state/national meetings; mentor relationships; and opportunities for advancement. This finding further substantiates that barriers exist to advancement. If one is unable to break through the adobe/glass ceiling, it is possible to hypothesize that one will find value in job factors not related to advancement, e.g., job is stimulating and challenging and profession is rewarding versus opportunities for advancement.

As was predicted, the satisfaction factor for commitment to affirmative action was highly significant by race (p = .01). Caucasians had a 3.7 average score, Chicano/Latinos (3.3), Asian/Pacific Americans (3.2), and African-Americans (3.0). African-Americans had the lowest ranking and predictably they also ranked

racism the most significant barrier to advancement. Asian/Pacific Americans rank the satisfaction factors the profession is rewarding and the salary package slightly less satisfying than the other ethnic groups.

Enhancers

The respondents were asked to rank four statements about their career advancement.

Table 6.   Career Advancement Abilities
(N = 308–312)
Mean score: ranking 1 (strongly disagree)—5 (strongly agree)

1. I have the ability to get needed resources and information	4.1
2. I have the ability to influence decisions and types of issues over which control may be exercised	3.7
3. I am adept at being aware of and using political skills	3.4
4. My talents, skills, and abilities are being fully utilized	3.4

The first statement, "I have the ability to get needed resources" was marginally significant (p = .098) by race with Asian/Pacific Americans feeling slightly less likely to have the ability to get the needed resources. 70 percent of Asian/Pacific Americans ranked this statement 4 or higher, 89 percent of African-Americans ranked it 4 or higher, 77 percent of Caucasians ranked it 4 or higher, and 85 percent of Chicano/Latinos ranked it 4 or higher.

The second statement, "I have the ability to influence decisions" was marginally significant by race (p = .03) with Asian/Pacific Americans feeling they did not have the ability to influence decisions. 45

percent of Asian/Pacific Americans ranked this statement 4 or higher, 61 percent of African-Americans ranked it 4 or higher, 66 percent of Caucasians ranked it 4 or higher; and 67 percent of Chicano/Latinos ranked it 4 or higher. Chicano/Latinos and Caucasians were very similar in their rankings.

The third statement, "I am adept at being aware of and using political skills," was highly significant by race (p = .0003). Asian/Pacific Americans felt they were less adept and Chicano/Latinos felt they were most adept at using political skills. 25 percent of Asian/Pacific Americans ranked it 4 or higher, 55 percent of African-Americans ranked it 4 or higher, 51 percent of

Caucasians ranked it 4 or higher, and 67 percent of Chicano/Latinos ranked it 4 or higher. This was the lowest ranking of the four statements by Asian/Pacific Americans. Gender was also highly significant (p = .017). 59 percent of Chicana/Latinas ranked it 4 or higher. 48 percent of African-American females ranked it 4 or higher; 47 percent of Caucasians ranked it 4 or higher, and 22 percent of Asian/Pacific American females ranked it 4 or higher. For males, this issue was not significant due to the small numbers.

The fourth statement, "my talents…are being fully utilized," was not significant by race. For all four statements, Asian/Pacific American rankings were lower than the other racial/ethnic groups, including Caucasians. This raises the question, do Asian/Pacific Americans tend to blame themselves rather than the structural barriers they are facing? The data seems to support this hypothesis. In further investigating career enhancers, respondents were asked to rank the following statements:

Table 7. Career Enhancers
(N = 291–305)
Mean score: ranking 1 (not important)—5 (very important)

Exceptionally competent at job	4.5
Gets things done and gets results	4.5
Takes career seriously	4.2
Able to take criticism	4.0
Important enough in the organization to move up	3.6
Develops connections with people who have power	3.5
Have a strong ego	1.9

Only the statement, "exceptionally competent by job," was marginally significant by race (p = .076) with Chicano/Latinos having slightly less agreement. 87 percent of Chicano/Latinos ranked it 4 or higher, 91 percent of Asian/Pacific Americans ranked it 4 or higher, 100 percent of African-Americans ranked it 4 or higher, and 95 percent of Caucasians ranked it 4 or higher. It is important to note that while Asian/Pacific Americans feel exceptionally competent at the mobs, they also feel their talents and skills are not being fully utilized.

Mentor

59 percent of the respondents (N = 181) statement they had a mentor, formal or informal. 41 percent (N = 128) stated they did not have a mentor. This response was highly significant by race (p = .0002). 79 percent of Latinos, 75 percent of African-Americans, 60 percent of Caucasians stated they had a mentor. Only 40 percent of Asian/Pacific Americans stated they had a mentor. Research has shown that mentors have a tremendous impact on the development and advancement of career skills for mentees. Given this important

impact, libraries should carefully assess how their Asian/Pacific employees can and do avail themselves of mentors in the workplace, either through structured or informal environments.

When respondents were asked if any of their mentors had been persons of color the response was as follows (N = 176): 82 percent of African-Americans, 77 percent of Chicano/Latinos, 48 percent of Asian/ Pacific Americans had mentors of color. Only about one in five Caucasians (21 percent) stated they had a mentor of color.

Conclusion

One of the strong values we hold as a profession and as individuals is the belief that everyone should have an equal right and opportunity in every aspect of life without prejudicial treatment because of her/his race, religion, personal beliefs, class, sex, age, disability, sexual orientation, political affiliation, etc. However, as the data in this survey makes clear, and as more and more librarians of color have been arguing, the perception of differential treatment in the workplace is radically different for librarians of color, everyone is not treated the same. One in three librarians of color in this study perceived racism as a very significant barrier. These perceived differences in treatment become more apparent as we become more diverse as a profession.

Clearly, as a profession we need to assess and re-evaluate management training opportunities that are available and how we include or exclude opportunities for librarians of color. We need to ask ourselves, are librarians of color clustered in middle management positions? Are people of color put in positions that lack career mobility? Does advancement require total assimilation and acculturation? Are people of color evaluated on white norms and standards? Although we acknowledge our cultural differences, do we only reward one cultural standard? The challenge before us is to promote "real" opportunities, not just a "positive" climate for diversity. If as a profession we want to continue to recruit and retain talented librarians of color, then we need to first acknowledge the barriers to advancement and second and most importantly, work to eliminate them.

The challenge before us is to create a system that supports and values a multitude of cultural styles. High level managers in individual libraries need to outline and follow through with specific plans to create a diverse multicultural workforce that values, seeks, and rewards diversity. Specifically, we need to be a profession with a career ladder to senior level management positions that includes people of color. Senior managers can help librarians of color by enabling opportunities for challenging assignments in the mainstream of the organization and reinforcing the authority of the people in these positions. Change will only occur when the highest level managers and directors advocate for change in the workplace and most importantly, act on those changes on a sustained basis. Managers must be committed to equal opportunities if change is to become permanently incorporated into the management environment. Interventions can and should be made in the areas of recruitment and advancement, evaluation, mentoring, and career development. Managers also need to critically examine the career ladders for people of color. As a profession, librarians must remember that racism is not just a minority problem.

As this data show, it is important to analyze each ethnic group's perceptions about the barriers they face in advancing their careers. Individual managers cannot erroneously generalize one set of perceptions to all ethnic groups. Each ethnic group has been the target of racism in similar and different ways. Each ethnic group has different positive and negative stereotypes thrust upon them. The diversity dialogue must also move beyond numbers and speak to the acceptance of differences. Multicultural values must be institutionalized. Managers need to be held accountable for creating goals and a supportive environment for people of color with an understanding that all people of color are not the same. Managers need to define, prioritize, and integrate their perceptions of the problems into their everyday workload. Further studies need to analyze the exodus of librarians of color from the profession. As a profession are we retaining our middle level librarians of color? Are they leaving librarianship for other career opportunities? Programs on race and the glass ceiling by the ACRL Racial and Ethnic Diversity Committee over the last several years saw librarians of color voice resentment and anger at the continuing racism they experienced in their professional careers and they felt that change would not come in their life time. It's in the self-interest of the profession to redress the barriers and to shift to a workforce diverse in all levels of positions from the line to the senior management levels. A multicultural workforce, diverse at all levels, can only enhance our productivity and creativity. It is time to un-weave the threads of racism that have too long been woven into our professional veneer. Only when the fabric of the organization changes, will effective change be made.

References

Cabezas, Amado, Tam, Tse Ming, Lowe, Brenda M., et al. 1989. Empirical Study of Barriers to Upward Mobility for Asian Americans in the San Francisco Bay Area. In *Frontiers of Asian American Studies* eds. Gail M. Nomura, Russell Endo, Stephen H. Sumida, Russell C. Leong. Pullman, Wash: Washington State University Press.

Curry, Deborah A. 1994. Your Worries Ain't Like Mine: African American Librarians and the Pervasiveness of Racism, Prejudice and Discrimination in Academe. *The Reference Librarian.* No. 45/46: 299–311.

Fact Finding Report of the Federal Glass Ceiling Commission. March 1995. *Good for Business: Making Full Use of the Nation's Human Capital*, Washington, D.C.

Jones, Edward W., Jr. 1986. Black Managers: the Dream Deferred. *Harvard Business Review.* No. 3, pp. 84–93.

Ray, Elaine. 1988. Black Female Executives Speak Out on: The Concrete Ceiling. *Executive Female.* 11, no. 6: 34–42 ,76.

Smith, Eleanor. Spring 1995. Upward Mobility: Black and White Women Administrators. *Journal of NAWDAC:* 28–32.

Yaffe, Jerry. August 1995. Latina Managers in Public Employment. *Hispanic Journal of Behavioral Sciences.* 17 no. 3: 334–347.

LANGUAGE ISSUES

Breaking Through the Linguistic Barrier: A Challenge for Initial Professional Education and Continuing Education of Librarians

Sonia Ramírez Wohlmuth

Cuando se siente uno rodeado de su mismo aire lingüístico, de nuestra misma manera de hablar, ocurre en nuestro ánimo un cambio análogo al de la respiración pulmonar, tomamos de la atmósfera algo, impapable, invisible, que adentramos en nuestro ser, que se nos entra en nuestra persona y cumple en ella una función vivificadora, que nos ayuda a seguir viviendo.
—Pedro Salinas, *La responsabilidad del escritor*[1]

Salinas' poetic explication is a far more compelling statement of the emotional, psychological, and physiological attachment to language than is a review of the literature on bilingualism, languages in contact, code switching behavior and the validity of a single national language as a tool of political unification. The identification of language as a natural, involuntary, vital function has as its concomitant the recognition that communication with the non–English speaking or limited–English speaking in "English only" will not only fail to convey sign and meaning, it will create an insurmountable psychological barrier.

Potential library users may deal with this barrier in several ways. The first is avoidance. If the initial contact with the library is negative, the client may rationalize that he or she does not need the services offered by the library. The second is a search for alternative avenues to satisfy needs for recreational reading or information/reference services. This may involve the purchase of books, the circulation of personal copies of reading materials among friends, relying on radio or television as a source of entertainment, and asking co-workers or the neighbors for information relating to any number of topics. The third, equally unfortunate alternative, is to accept reading materials or information offered in English out of a sense of embarrassment or shame caused by admitting that one does not understand or read English well. In this case, an attempt to decipher printed texts or other media may well lead to misunderstanding or confusion—"misinformation transfer."

To conclude that clients are best served in their own language or mother tongue seems a statement of the obvious. Yet, in today's political climate, it is also a statement charged with controversy. The chief antagonists in this struggle are nearly always embodied as "English only proponents" and "Latino activists." The English-Spanish confrontation is centuries old, dating back to the rivalry which followed the first European voyages to the New World. Today, this rivalry extends to the global arena. In terms of languages most spoken in the world today as first or native language, Spanish and English vie for third place with English forging ahead to second place only when non-native speakers are also included (*World Almanac* 1997, 444). Whether Spanish is ranked as the second or fourth most spoken language,[2] the fact remains that there are more than 300 million speakers of Spanish in the world, with a geographic distribution that includes North America, Central America, South America, the Caribbean, Spain (including the Canary Islands and the cities of Ceuta and Melilla on the Moroccan coast), and Equatorial Guinea. Like English, Spanish is truly a global language and its presence in the Americas predates the arrival of English.

Given the coexistence of Spanish and English in the same continent for nearly four hundred years and geographic proximity—the contiguous southwestern states and northern Mexico, south Florida and the Caribbean basin—resistance to the preservation and promotion of Spanish as a vehicle for providing public services is surprising. After all, little controversy has been generated by the use of Spanish in the private sector to sell products and services. Vendrell (1994) has examined the growth in Spanish language communication in the private sector and finds that it is increasingly necessary to provide a human interface in the form of a Hispanic public relations practitioner between the Spanish speaking public and an organization.

While English and Spanish are both viewed as global languages, it must be acknowledged that the resources of business, science, and technology tend to be published worldwide in English, even in those countries where only a small percent of the population speaks English and where historical ties to England or the United States are tenuous. Furthermore, access to information in the non-print age will require competence in English since a large portion of texts archived in machine-readable form are in English— reported by McCrum over ten years ago as 80 percent (1986, 20).

Does this imbalance extend to the printed medium as well? Twenty-five years ago the Bolivian essayist Baptista Gumucio (1973, 16) bemoaned the fact that Spain, a major publishing center for the Spanish-speaking world, produced fewer books than Poland or Yugoslavia, despite the fact that Spanish was the third-ranked language in the world in numbers of speakers. Today, Spain and Latin America tend to "export" through translation only the creative works of a handful of authors who have gained universal acceptance. On the other hand, scientific and technical texts are frequently written in English even when the authors are not native speakers of English. The editorial policy of many scholarly journals requires that articles be submitted in English. These impositions of English demonstrate that "The darker, aggressive side of the spread of global English is the elimination of regional language variety, the attack on deep cultural roots" (McCrum 1986, 44).

Studies of the assimilation of immigrant groups in the United States have shown that loss of language is followed quickly by loss of culture. The retention of Spanish in the U.S. borderlands, the West, and southern Florida is part of a struggle for cultural identity. Language is the only common thread among these diverse U.S. Latino populations. The "Hispanic" rubric of the U.S. Census bureau represents a very heterogeneous group, including persons of many national origins, of varying race and ethnicity, and with different linguistic skills—monolingual English speakers, bilingual speakers of both Spanish and English, and monolingual Spanish speakers. While the interests of the first two linguistic groups may not always be well represented by library holdings, it is only the last group that will be virtually excluded from library services by a language barrier.

The persistence of Spanish among U.S. Latinos has been the object of many sociolinguistic studies. Its survival is due in part to promulgation through family and community ties and a sense of language loyalty (Weinreich 1953). Only recently has the availability of Spanish language mass media become another vehicle for dissemination of the language. At the same time U.S. publishers have begun to respond to the small but growing market for Spanish language fiction and nonfiction. These conditions are propitious to the development of Spanish language services for users who would benefit most from materials in their mother tongue.

With resources now more accessible, the challenge to better serve Spanish speaking Latino clients is less daunting. Yet the title of this study begs the question, "Why should language learning/training be the responsibility of institutions of library education or continuing education for librarians?" In response, it must be noted that the United States is not a bilingual nation even on a regional basis, nor is Canada despite the political pressures of Francophone Québec. Second language instruction in the United States has been less than successful in endowing secondary students and college graduates with the ability to really communicate in another language even though there has been support for second language instruction through federal initiatives (America 2000 under the Bush administration and Goals 2000 in the Clinton administration). The stated goals of educational organizations such as the American Council on the Teaching of Foreign Languages (ACTFL) are a cogent exhortation for change: "The United States must educate students who are linguistically and culturally equipped to communicate successfully in a pluralistic American society and abroad. This imperative envisions a future in which all students will develop and maintain proficiency in English and at least one other language, modern or classical" (American Council 1993). The 1997 report from the Association for Library and Information Science Education (ALISE) indicates that only three of the 54 schools with programs accredited by the American Library Association (ALA) that reported have a foreign language entrance requirement. One school lists a certificate program in Latin American Studies for which one may subsume a requirement of language competency in one of the languages of Latin America. Several schools list joint degree programs, but there are only two with foreign languages (languages unspecified). A review of courses cross-listed with other academic units generates the following list of courses related to Latino librarianship: Information Resources for Hispanic Americans (University of Texas) and Latin American Research Resources (University of California-Los Angeles).

Although other educational opportunities may exist for students who wish to acquire the skills needed to serve Spanish speaking Latino populations, they are not reflected in the latest ALISE report. Informally (through electronic e-mail lists, professional meetings, etc.) there have been reports of classes or seminars with the purpose of fomenting Latino librarianship—with focus on collection development and acquisitions issues, adult literacy, children's services, and Spanish language instruction. However, these efforts seem not to have been formalized in the curriculum of most of the ALA-accredited programs.

In view of the above, it cannot be assumed that students enter postgraduate library and information science programs with the linguistic skills required to carry out a successful reference interview, to pose or understand simple questions, or even to produce minimal deictic utterances. Therefore, the responsibility for endowing library/information students with the language competencies they need has moved to the arena of initial professional education, that is the ALA-accredited programs. It is not suggested that language courses become an integral part of the curriculum of all programs of library education, but that it should be an option for those who wish to work with Latino communities upon graduation. It would be unthinkable to graduate a student without the requisite computer skills and on-line training if that student's expressed professional goal were to work in a highly automated special library. Similarly, it should be unthinkable to graduate a student who wishes to server the public at large, without the language skills and cultural sensitivity to do so successfully.

In further justifying the need to endow graduates of ALA programs with the linguistic and cultural competence necessary to serve Latino populations, it is illuminating to examine another source of potential librarians—members of the U.S. Latino community. The ongoing efforts of Kathleen de la Peña McCook (1993, 1997a, 1997b) to report on the diversity of graduates of ALA-accredited programs indicate that the numeric increases of minority graduates are heartening, but when compared as percentage of all graduates, it is evident that progress is painfully slow. According to McCook (1997a), minority graduates of ALA-accredited programs for the 1994-95 academic year— excluding Canadian institutions, Clark-Atlanta, North Carolina Central, University of Hawaii and University of Puerto

Rico—numbered 361. An examination of the latest ALISE report shows that a year later, 1995-96 minority graduates numbered 448 (Daniels 1997), but the percent increase from 8.63 percent in 1994-95 to 9.42 percent in 1995-96 is less than one percent. For graduates who identified themselves as Hispanic, the numeric change is from 80 in 1994-95 to 101 in 1996-97, but the percentage increase is minuscule—from 1.91 percent to 2.10 percent.

While any progress, however slight, should be lauded, it is clear that the recruitment of Latino students to ALA-accredited programs is an effort that has had limited success. The pervasive consequences of the failure to diversify enrollment in initial professional education are evident in a retrospective glance at the 1985 survey of academic and public libraries conducted by the Office for Library Personnel Resources of the ALA (Randall 1988, 20) which shows 1.8 percent of the total work force of professional librarians to be Hispanic. Furthermore, the assumption that "Hispanic" students will be better prepared to serve Spanish-speaking Latinos has many precarious assumptions. Self-identification as "Hispanic" on applications for work or school is not a guarantee of fluency in Spanish, nor of cultural sensitivity or empathy toward those outside one's immediate ethnic or national community (for example, Chicano, Cuban American, Dominican, Puerto Rican, Salvadoran).

Recruitment and retention efforts in allied professions such as education also demonstrate the difficulty of creating a cadre of minority professionals in sufficient number to reflect their representation in the population at large. A 1993 study of career choice of high school seniors (Mack 1993) found that 30 percent of students polled would select teaching as a career, yet at present Latino teachers account for only 3 percent of professional teachers. Further findings indicated that obstacles to pursuing this career path were lack of financial support, lack of career awareness and positive information about the teaching field, as well as lack of encouragement from significant others. These obstacles may also be present in the recruitment of minority students to librarianship. Clearly, as a discipline which requires post-graduate training, financial aid is a major obstacle. Library/information science as a career choice lacks a defined public presence. This may account for the lack of support by family members when a potential student announces his or her intent to continue post baccalaureate studies in a career which is not seen to enhance one's prestige in the community nor to bear promises of financial reward.

Recruitment of minority students to ALA-accredited programs as the sole effort to provide qualified professionals to serve the Spanish speaking Latino community will prove inadequate. Again, it is necessary to underscore the fact that this community is not insignificant numerically. In the 1990 census, those who code themselves as "Hispanic" account for only 10.2 percent of the population, yet 13.8 percent of the population—32 million persons—reports use of Spanish in the household (U.S. Bureau of the Census 1990). Of these, 21 percent categorize their ability to speak English as "not well" or "not at all." It should also be remembered that the question which elicits these responses is, "Does this person speak a language other than English at home?" If so, "How well does this person speak English—very well, well, not well, not at all?" Since the data here reflect oral/aural skills, true linguistic competency including the ability to read and write the language, is still an unknown. Weinreich's (1953, 76) seminal study on languages in contact suggests that "visual reinforcement in the use of a language that a bilingual gets by reading and writing it may put that language in a dominant position over a purely oral one." Therefore, those speakers who only use English as a sort of "lingua franca" in the context of work or other public or social activities, may, in fact, be quite unable to effectively use English to read for pleasure or to get information and would also benefit from the availability of materials in Spanish.

The selection and use of Spanish language materials in a library requires at least some knowledge of the language, but the introduction of language instruction in initial professional education of librarians and information specialists will not be an easy task. Due to the requirements of specialization within the library/information science discipline, many students will have little room for few electives. Therefore, a one semester three credit hour course is probably the maximum amount of time that students will be able to devote to a Spanish language elective. The details of course number and level will, of course, vary from one institution to another. The University of South Florida (USF) has offered an undergraduate course at the 4000 level which may be applied to total credits earned for the master's degree since the Graduate School permits a maximum of six semester hours at the 4000 level. Course content includes both basic language instruction and cultural information. Presentation of cultural information must achieve a balance between informing and "trivializing": "Ersatz celebration of diversity, 'progressive' first grade curriculums and phrases like 'gorgeous

mosaic' may ease fears about hatred, but they also subvert a cautious pluralism that soberly recognizes the passions inspired by cultural identities" (Hymowitz 1993). While it is tempting to engage students by references to the familiar, the familiar may also be the stereotype.

At the opening session of such a class, the following assignment is a way of broaching discussion of the historical ties with the Spanish speaking countries which are also part of the Americas. Ask students to:

(1) Find Spanish terms which designate U.S. geographical locations; search for the meaning of these words in a Spanish-English dictionary. An example would be the states Arizona, California, Colorado, Montana, Nevada, Texas.

(2) Find Spanish terms which have become common nouns in [American] English. What do the semantic fields of these words reveal, if anything, about Anglo-Hispanic relations? Examples would be the "cowboy" lexicon containing words like the following: barbecue, bonanza, bronco, buckaroo, canyon, chaps, desperado, lariat, lasso, mustang, pinto, rodeo, stampede, etc.

The purpose of this exercise is twofold: (1) It is a good reference hunt, and (2) It promotes awareness of a long-standing Anglo-Hispanic relationship, particularly in the American West and Southwest which begs the question, "Who are the immigrants?"

Other class exercises in the first phase of the class have the objective of getting students to view concepts in a new perspective. Advertising is a rich source of sociolinguistic material. The linguistic ascendance of English in the commercial context is readily apparent. While students may find enjoyable or amusing examples of advertising and mass media with intrusive English words or "Spanglish," this provides the instructor with an opportunity to discuss the question of linguistic, national, and ethnic identity. After all, the great fear of Latin America is the invasion, literal or cultural, by Anglo America. Nearly one hundred years ago, Rubén Darío posed the question in the poem "Los cisnes" in *Cantos de vida y esperanza*:

> ¿Seremos entregados a los bárbaros fieros?
>
> ¿Tantos millones de hombres hablaremos inglés?[3]

Other examples of cultural materials are books like Judith Noble and Jaime Lacasa's *The Hispanic Way* which also provide an opportunity to discuss cultural sensitivity and related issues. This small book contains useful information on many topics: Spanish names—given names and surnames; holidays—both religious and national; etiquette and customs; educational systems in Spain and Latin America; regional variations in Spanish and use of the term "American" both in English and Spanish. However, it is noteworthy that even here, the authors occasionally lapse into national stereotypes. This book containing barely over one hundred pages has four pages devoted to bullfighting and bullfighting terms and none to "fútbol," or soccer. There are also works of a more pensive nature. A point of departure could be the works of Mario Benedetti, Carlos Fuentes, Eduardo Galeano, and Roberto Fernández de Retamar, who have worked and reworked the theme of identity for Latin America and its relationship to Anglo America.

Humor and caricature are also an excellent means to view concepts of national identity and the often concomitant chauvinism or ethnocentrism of Western countries. The "non–Mafalda" work of the Argentine caricaturist Quino offers many insights into the economic and political chaos of Latin America.

Because students in such a class have a limited vocabulary, children's materials and materials for adult literacy, such as those produced by the Secretary of Public Education in Mexico, are also helpful. The link between libraries and literacy is undeniable. Salinas (1961, 91) eulogizes in biblical overtones the advent of literacy as an outcome of mandatory primary education:

> *En el principio fue el analfabetismo. Poco a poco, siglos arriba, se hizo la luz que hoy, gracias a Dios, nos ilumina: la enseñanza primaria obligatoria. En el consenso de la mayoría de las gentes … el analfabetismo … se tiene por una línea fronteriza tan clara y tajante, que divide a la humanidad en dos partes implacablemente distintas.*
>
> *Aquende esta línea el montón anónimo de los cuitados que no logran penetrar en los misterios de la letra impresa … Allende esa raya, las legiones de favorecidos por la suerte que alcanzaron ese estado venturoso, en que se sabe, sin vacilar, que c-o es co, que c-a es ca, y que gracias a esa sapiencia descifran sin pena los carteles por doquier nos cantan las palabras mágicas "Coca Cola."[4]*

Salinas' tongue-in-cheek reference to the ubiquitous presence of advertising does point to another source of readily available visual materials for the classroom. Depending upon resources available in the community, students should also be encouraged to do the following to bring them into contact with everyday language situations and the concerns of the local Latino community:

- monitor a Spanish language radio station, particularly for news of Latin America and public service announcements
- select one or two programs to view regularly on Spanish language television, especially news broadcasts, magazine format programs, or weekend variety programs
- search the Web in Spanish using local search engines such as Olé, from Spain, available http://www.oles.es, or multilingual search engines such as Digital's AltaVista, available at http://www.altavista.digital.com
- become familiar with the Hispanic yellow pages for the community, if available visit newsstands, bookstores, and music stores that have Spanish speaking clients
- find out what other community services exist for the Spanish speaking

These suggestions may seem trivial and obvious, but they provide a beginning to the training of a cadre of professionals "sensitized" to the needs of the Spanish-speaking community and with some fluency in the preferred language of that community.

Through the enlightened leadership of the director of the Tampa-Hillsborough County Public Library System, Joe Stines, the University of South Florida School of Library and Information Science has had the opportunity to replicate the above model in an off-campus setting as part of continuing education for professional librarians and paraprofessional staff. The practical aspects of the course, as opposed to grammar and vocabulary acquisition, have been the focus of the eight week thirty-two hour course offered for the public library system. This university-community collaboration has been a reinforcement of the School's stated mission: "Foster an understanding of the role of the library/information professional and information agencies in a multicultural society." (USF's mission statement is available at http://www.cas.usf.edu/lis/mission.html). Plans are now underway to create a mirror of the English web page for Tampa-Hillsborough County Public Library System in Spanish which will optimize access for the Spanish speaking patron while providing the library staff with an appropriate tool for better serving these users.

For these classes, introduction of vocabulary and grammar concepts have been tied to real life situations wherever possible. For example, learning the letters of the alphabet has a practical application in asking users to spell their name, if not immediately understand, to help locate records or fill out forms. Mastery of the numbers can also be used to verify user ID, fill out forms with address and phone number, or direct a user to a Dewey call number. The various forms of imperatives (formal, informal, impersonal "se," infinitives) have an immediate application in creating understandable, friendly signage for the Spanish speaking library user.

The presence of a bilingual/bicultural librarian at the reference desk of a library, or a librarian willing to expend the extra effort to communicate with someone who is unable to readily express his or her needs in English, is a tangible symbol of an institution's commitment to provide equal access. It is an overt invitation to the under-served, to the disenfranchised. While the suggestions for language instruction enumerated here may seem simplistic, they offer easy to implement changes, in terms of human and fiscal resources, in the initial professional education of future librarians and in the continuing education of librarians and library paraprofessionals already active in the field.

REFORMA and other organizations dedicated to the empowerment of the Latino community through information access and education may well continue to ask "Where are the Latino librarians? Where are their mentors? Where are the Spanish speaking professionals?" The discrepancy between representation of Latinos in the public at large is great. This is an indisputable fact. The number of graduates of ALA-accredited programs shows imperceptible gains. Their mentors are sadly lacking. Doctoral programs in library and information science in the United States produced only one Hispanic graduate in the 1995-96 academic year (Daniel 1997). Language proficiency has been eased out of the curriculum of graduate library and information science programs. Yet individual stories ofd success, transmitted both formally and informally, increase in number. Commitments for language training, and its inseparable cultural component, from institutions of library education and public library systems offer a partial answer to the plaintive literary topos "Ubi sunt?"

Works Cited

American Council on the Teaching of Foreign Languages. [1993]. *Standards for foreign language learning: Preparing for the 21st century*. Available at http://www.actfl.org/htdocs/pubs/standards.htm.

Baptista Gumucio, Mariano. 1973. *La cultura que heredamos*. La Paz: Ediciones Camarlinghi.

Daniel, Evelyn H. and Jerry D. Saye, eds. 1997. *Association for Library and Information Science Education Statistical Report*. Arlington, VA: Association for Library and Information Science.

Hymowitz, Kay S. "Multiculturalism is anti-culture." *New York Times*, 24 March 1993.

Mack, F. R. Poncefonte and Thomas E. Jackson. 1993. *Teacher education as a career choice of Hispanic high school seniors*. ERIC, ED 358087.

McCook, Kathleen de la Peña and Paula Geist. 1993. Diversity deferred: Where are the minority librarians? *Library Journal* 118 (November 1): 35-38.

McCook, Kathleen de la Peña and Kate Lippincott. 1997a. *Planning for a diverse workforce in library and information science professions*. ERIC, ED 402948.

McCook, Kathleen de la Peña and Kate Lippincott. 1997b. Library schools and diversity: Who makes the grade? *Library Journal* 122 (April 15): 30-32.

McCrum, Robert, William Cran, and Robert MacNeil. 1986. *The Story of English*. New York: Viking.

Randall, Ann Knight. 1988. Minority recruitment in librarianship. *Librarians for the New Millennium*. Eds. William Moen and Kathleen M. Heim. Chicago: American Library Association, 11-25.

Salinas, Pedro. 1961. *La responsabilidad del escritor*. Barcelona: Seix Barral.

U.S. Bureau of the Census. *1990 U.S. Census of Population and Housing*. Available http://www.census.gov/population/socdemo/language/table5.txt.

Vendrell, Ignasi B. 1994. What is Hispanic public relations and where is it going? *Public Relations Quarterly*, 39(4): 33-35.

Weinreich, Uriel. 1953. *Languages in Contact*. The Hague: Mouton.

The World Almanac and Book of Facts. Mahwah, N.J.: World Almanac Books, 1997.

Notes

1. Translation of the text of Salinas (1961, 15) follows: When we are enveloped by our same linguistic air, by our same way of speaking, a change takes place in our soul, analogous to breathing — we take in some-

thing, impalpable, invisible from the atmosphere, which enters our being and effects in it a vitalizing function, which permits us to continue living.

2. The figures given in *The World Almanac* for 1998 (based on 1997 data) are as follows: Native Speakers, in rank order, in millions: Mandarin 863, Hindi 357, Spanish 352, and English 335; All Speakers, in rank order, in millions: Mandarin 1,025, English 497, Hindi 476, Spanish 409.

3. Translation of the text of Darío: Shall we be given over to the fierce barbarians? Shall our many millions speak English?

4. Translation of the text of Salinas: In the beginning, there was illiteracy. Little by little came the light which today, thank God, illuminates us: obligatory primary schooling. It is the consensus of most people that illiteracy is a boundary, so clear and cutting, which divides humanity into two parts, irreconcilably different. On one side of that line is the anonymous rabble of poor souls unable to penetrate the mysteries of the printed word.... On the other side are the legions of those favored by fortune who have attained that happy state in which they know without faltering that c-o is "co" and c-a is "ca," and thanks to that knowledge they can decipher effortlessly the ubiquitous billboards which sing to us the magic words "Coca Cola."

CHAPTER FIVE

Cross-Cultural Communication: Identifying Barriers to Information Retrieval with Culturally and Linguistically Different Library Patrons

Graciela Berlanga-Cortéz

The purpose of this report on cross-cultural communication is to identify barriers to information retrieval and to discuss cultural differences that can lead to communication problems when culturally and linguistically different library users access information in libraries. Recommendations to removing cultural and linguistic barriers are discussed and presented. This paper addresses four main issues that are perceived as barriers to effectively serve the information needs of such users.

• Cultural differences in verbal and nonverbal communication styles among library professionals and culturally diverse groups

• Cultural awareness of ethnic minority groups in the U.S. on the part of practitioners of information services

• Cultural sensitivity training for library professionals serving culturally and linguistically diverse patrons

• Training on the use of information technology for culturally and linguistically diverse library users.

As our society becomes more multicultural and multilingual, information specialists are faced with the challenge of learning how to communicate more effectively with an emerging culturally and linguistically diverse library user. As we enter a new millennium characterized as the information-age era, library and information technology specialists should be cognizant of the need to communicate effectively in various forms and with various cultures locally, regionally, as well as globally.

Factors such as immigration, the North American Foreign Trade Agreement (NAFTA), the concept of a unified Europe, and the Internet make cross-cultural communication today more important than ever before.

U.S. Demographics

Many of today's U.S. citizens trace their roots to Africa, Asia, Mexico, Latin America, the Pacific Islands, and Europe. Because the population of ethnic minorities in the U.S. has grown dramatically and is continually increasing, libraries and library professionals should proactively prepare to meet the information needs of this culturally diverse citizenry. According to the U.S. Bureau of the Census, the minority population has experienced a noticeable increase during the 1990s. At the national level, the 1990 U.S. Census reports that:

- By the turn of the century, ethnic minorities will comprise approximately 30 percent of the United States population.
- By the early part of the 21st century, Hispanic Americans will become the country's largest group.
- Twenty-five and one half million adults and 6.3 million children between the ages of 5 and 17 in the U.S. speak a language other than English at home.

Current statistics show that the African American population increased from 30.62 million in 1990 to 34.48 million in 1998. The Hispanic population increased significantly from 22.57 million in 1990 to 30.68 million in 1998; the Asian and Pacific Islanders also experienced a sharp increase from 7.55 million in 1990 to 10.47 million in 1998. The American Indian, Eskimo, and Aleut population doubled from 1.8 million in 1990 to 2.0 million in 1998 (U.S. Census 1998). As the ethnic minority population increases, libraries across the country must prepare themselves to address the information needs of a culturally and linguistically diverse population.

Definition of Key Terms

- *Cross-cultural communication* occurs when communicating across various cultures with a clear understanding of values, customs, traditions, history, and linguistic knowledge of a particular ethnic minority group as well as having a clear knowledge of one's own.
- *Culture* is defined as all the accepted and patterned ways of behavior of a given people. It is also largely unconscious. Physical manifestations of culture include diet, dress or costuming, customs, traditions, language, and technology. Cognitive manifestations of culture include ethics and values, religion, and aesthetics (Glover 1998).
- *Cultural group* is a group of people who have common understandings about an organized way of thinking, feeling, and acting. Its members have common values, cultural heritage, and language (Glover 1998).
- *Diversity* is a democratic ideology/social reality that recognizes and respects indi-

vidual cultural groups' worldviews, values, traditions, language, and behaviors (Banks 1994). It means inclusion of culturally diverse individuals in the structure and institutions of our society.

• *Monoculturalism* is a set of beliefs that ignores the existence of the values and heritage of other cultural groups and is based on only one reality biased toward the dominant group (Nieto 1992).

• *Multiculturalism* is a set of beliefs and explanations that recognizes and values the importance of ethnic and cultural diversity in shaping lifestyles, social experiences, personal identities, and educational opportunities, of individuals, groups, and nations. It is a framework where individuals co-exist peacefully, productively in a pluralistic and democratic society (Trueba 1992).

Cross-Cultural Communication Issues

Understanding cultural diversity and realizing its importance in the library profession will help facilitate retrieval of data by information seekers from diverse cultural and linguistic backgrounds. In most cases, education and service-oriented institutions tend to reflect primarily the norms and values of the majority culture reflecting a mono-cultural society, at the expense of not affirming the norms and values of the many cultural groups who make up our present society. Consequently, such institutions are not only creating cultural misunderstandings and misconceptions, limiting outreach to culturally and linguistically diverse potential clientele, but also are negligent in providing responsive information services to library users representing all walks of life, particularly ethnic minorities.

How are they negligent? They are neglectful by not being culturally sensitive, by being unfamiliar with verbal or nonverbal communication styles of different populations, by lacking knowledge of and skills to understand other languages other than English, and by their inattentiveness to provide training on the use of information for the culturally and linguistically diverse users.

Verbal and Nonverbal Communication Barriers to Information Retrieval

The act of communication involves a variety of behaviors, processes, or technologies through which meaning is derived or transmitted from a sender to a receiver. Some factors affect the quality of interface between the user and information intermediary, such as differences in communication styles, cultural background, and language. Verbal and nonverbal communication can have a major impact on library users, especially culturally and linguistically different patrons such as Latinos, who may have specific type of information needs. Generally, users vary greatly in their knowledge about the subject, the system, and the language. Language-wise, there is a tendency on the part of information systems to concentrate on the use of the English language (Florian 1991), therefore, a cultural and language barrier is encountered by non–English speaking library users. It effects the Spanish-speaking user in greater numbers since they comprise the largest language minority group in the U.S. Globally, there are approximately 352 million Spanish-speakers. The problem of retrieving information by the Spanish-speaking or speakers of other languages is compounded by the scarcity of library professionals who can communicate in another language other than English. For many Latinos, whose primary language is Spanish, this task becomes increasingly more difficult as more information is being stored electronically and requires the assistance of trained information specialists in technology who are bilingual.

Frame of Reference Affects Information Storage and Retrieval

As in all systems, information has to be stored as data before it can be retrieved. In most cases, the task of information storage and retrieval is performed on machines by individuals who have different perspectives that are commonly outside the user's competence (Florian 1991). It can create problems for limited English speakers and for the culturally different who have little or no training in accessing information, especially electronic data. Consequently, the issue of understanding people and systems is crucial in different social, educational, and cultural settings. As a result, the role of a culturally sensitive, bilingual information specialist becomes central to meeting the information needs of such library users.

The task of retrieving information becomes a complicated process due to the differences of systems, people, and cultures. Systems include the availability of information to be handled, technology to support the necessary tasks, and sufficient funding to provide these resources (Florian 1991). The process of information retrieval becomes more complex when the information specialists lack familiarity with certain cultural differences relating to *verbal and non-verbal communication*

styles which can create communication barriers between members of the dominant culture and those who are culturally different.

Nonverbal Communication Impacts Communicating Cross-Culturally

The nonverbal aspects of our communication often carry the strongest sensory messages, particularly our sense of feeling, sight, and hearing, and leave the most powerful impressions. For example, some Anglos typically consider raised voices to be a sign that a fight has begun, while some African Americans, Jewish and Italian Americans often feel that an increase in volume is a sign of an exciting conversation among friends. Hence, some Anglo Americans may react with greater alarm to a loud discussion than members of an American ethnic group (DuPraw; Axner 1998). Other aspects of nonverbal communication that may impact communicating cross-culturally are *proxemics*. Proxemics refers to *fixed space* such as the shapes and physical appearance of buildings that can affect individuals. For example, a study conducted by social psychologist Maslow found that subjects who sat in a beautifully decorated room and looked at pictures of faces saw them in a significantly more positive light than those who looked at them while sitting in a drab, ugly room. *Semi-fixed space* refers to spatial arrangements of movable objects within a room which can be arranged to encourage face-to-face participation; and *personal space,* which is culturally related, involves intimate zone, personal zone, social zone, and public zone. For example, the *intimate zone* encompasses a distance of up to eighteen inches for North Americans and is a zone reserved only for very close, intimate relationships. The *personal zone* ranges from one and a half to three and a half feet and is used for confidentiality. The *social zone* is the normal conversational space for North Americans and includes space from about four to twelve feet. The *public zone* is used for talking across a room and for public speaking. It includes distances of twelve feet and larger. These social norms generally apply to all cultural groups in North America that ought to be acknowledged by information providers when assisting information seekers.

Kinesics, commonly known as body language, is perhaps the most frequent form of nonverbal communication which can become a cultural barrier when seeking and obtaining information. Kinesics refers to gestures, facial expressions, eye contact, body positions and movement, and forms of greeting. Problems may arise from differences in communicating cross-culturally due to inappropriate facial expressions, eye contact, body movement, and forms of greeting. For example, eye contact carries different meanings in different cultures. In the African American, Hispanic, and Asian cultures some members believe listeners of a conversation are expected to avert eyes to indicate respect and attention. On the other hand, in the Anglo American culture *listeners* are expected to look at a speaker directly to indicate respect and attention. While, in the African American, Hispanic, and Asian cultures *speakers,* rather than the listeners, are expected to look at listeners directly in the eye. Conversely, in the Anglo American culture speakers are expected to avert eye contact, especially in informal speaking. This can have significant consequences when the information provider is trying to ascertain the specificity of the information sought by the information user in order to fulfill the unmet information need.

Respecting Linguistic Differences Will Enhance Communicating Cross-culturally

Negative non-verbal behavior toward individuals with linguistic differences can result in turning away users with unmet information needs. Stereotyping and pre-judging based on language dialect and language accent in speech patterns can lead to improperly serving the information needs of such users. A nonverbal cross-cultural communication act occurs when, for example, someone approaches the reference desk speaking French, a language widely accepted in the Anglo culture, and the patron readily receives assistance. On the other hand, when a speaker of Black English comes to the same desk requesting assistance, the patron may be received with reluctance because of the pejorative stigma surrounding Black dialect (Hall 1992). More noticeable, however, is the linguistic bias against individuals with Spanish accents as opposed to other groups with various European accents (Korzenny; Schiff 1986). It is extremely unfair to equate speech or pronunciation difficulties and a limited English language proficiency with lack of intelligence. Equally unjust is showing a bias against members of certain ethnic groups due to linguistic intolerance by the dominant cultural group (Hall 1992).

Recommendations to Eliminate Communication Barriers Across Different Cultures Within Library Systems

Though we may think we understand each other because we speak the same language and may possess some knowledge about each other's culture, communicating successfully can still be very difficult. Learning to work with and serve a multicultural population becomes the responsibility of information systems and information specialists. They must collaboratively embark on a multicultural-learning journey. Learning about people from other cultures and language backgrounds will empower library professionals to connect positively with users from various cultural backgrounds. How can this learning occur? Librarians can assist the culturally and linguistically different user more effectively if they are:

• culturally sensitive
• familiar with the values, traditions, customs, and history, of major ethnic groups in the U.S.
• able to communicate in the users' native language
• knowledgeable of the varying communication styles
• familiar with the high-context and low-context cultures

Similarly, library institutions can be responsive in meeting the information needs of the culturally diverse patrons by providing training on the use of information technology.

Cultural Diversity Training for Library Professionals

The training of library professionals and staff can be achieved by using the "ASK" model that emphasizes three major components: Awareness, Skills, and Knowledge (Sue, Arredondo & McDavis 1992). This model offers a comprehensive and integrated "paradigm shift" in training service-oriented professionals about valuing diversity and multiculturalism. The model begins by emphasizing awareness that involves professionals examining their own values, myths, stereotypes, and world view. Professionals must first understand and become aware of their own value system, traditions, eccentricities, and in general be more aware of self, before they learn about others in a more objective manner. For instance, by understanding one's own values, traditions, and customs better, it becomes easier to acquire an awareness and knowledge about the values, traditions, and customs of culturally diverse library users.

The second component focuses on skills important to developing cultural sensitivity towards others who are different. It includes learning about the varying communication styles within different cultural groups and how others view their own world and that of the dominant culture. For example, cultural values of Hispanic Americans and Asian Americans (Feng 1994) have similarities inasmuch as these cultures value and respect elders greatly, are taught to respect authority, value educational achievement, have a strong commitment to family, and tend to be more dependent or more closely tied to family. In addition, their quiet behavior is often mistaken by the dominant culture as lacking knowledge or shyness rather than what it truly represents: a sign of respect toward others. These cultural traits may work against ethnic populations when seeking library services and information, since their passive demeanor may stand in the way of receiving the attention and assistance they may need in accessing information and resources. It's important to note that some of these traits discussed here are generalizations and are often associated with the older generation within an ethnic population.

Knowledge is the third component of the "ASK" diversity training model. It entails developing a non-stereotyping, flexible understanding of cultural, social, and family dynamics of diverse groups as well as a comprehension of the sociopolitical, historical, and economic contexts of the multiculturally diverse groups (Sanchez 1995). Knowing about the culture of library patrons will guide the information professionals to effectively communicate with them. Gaining cognitive knowledge about different cultures, cultural values, current culture related issues and how they impact individual perceptions and world views may be the most important thing in becoming a more effective intercultural communicator (Wittmer 1992).

Cultures Are Generally Divided Into Two Types: High Context and Low Context

There are unique factors distinguishing various cultures from one another. These factors may have an impact on how well we communicate cross-culturally. It is important to know cultures are divided into two types: those that are *high-context* and those which are *low-context* (Huang 93).

In general, high context cultures, such as Hispanic American/Latino and Asian American, place great importance on:

- ambience
- presumptions shared by people
- non-verbal signals such as body movements
- decorum
- establishing a rapport or relationship
- the manner and attitude of a message's delivery

- unwillingness among some to use the word "no" even when they disagree with others

Whereas, *low-context societies*, such as the Anglo American culture, place more importance on the content of the communication, ignoring the features important to a high-context society. Low-context cultures tend to exhibit an attitude that indicate a "let's get to the point" approach. Low-context cultures generally:

- tend to ignore things that are important to high-context societies
- emphasize the content of a communication with elaborate expressions
- disregard cultural considerations
- ignore nonverbal communication
- accepts smiles and verbal approval as clear indication of consent

Consequently, it behooves library professionals to learn about the differences in the high-context and low-context societies in order to avoid misconceptions, misunderstandings, and to eliminate cross-cultural communication barriers. Acquiring basic communication skills in a second language other than English will facilitate meeting the information needs of limited English speaking library patrons. One suggestion for learning to speak a second language such as Spanish is to establish a conversation group. For example, a Spanish language conversation group could meet on a regular basis to practice listening and speaking the language under the tutelage of a colleague who is fluent in that language. The group may also plan site visits to supermarkets, retail stores, bookstores, and community centers preferable located in a community where Spanish is spoken. This will provide a "hands-on" activity for language building and will provide for a culturally rich experience for the participants.

Reassessing the Library's Role in Reducing Barriers

Does the library's personnel interface well with users? Does its technology assist or hinder serving the information needs of the culturally and linguistically different? Does the library provide easy access and availability of resources and materials to under-served multicultural clientele? These are important current issues that librarians must address. Just as language is crucial to interfacing with users, the tone or cultural climate, and the physical environment play an important role in attracting and maintaining the interest of library patrons. Certain aspects of a library can set the tone and be a decisive factor as to whether first-time library users, particularly African Americans and Latinos, will continue to use the library. For example, being helped by a culturally sensitive library professional can and will immediately make a positive impression. The physical environment can also contribute to how well the users feel toward the library, or conversely, it can also determine how out of place they feel they are. Overly ostentatious surroundings can make them feel intimidated. Likewise, poorly maintained or outdated resources such computers can be a disservice. Literacy programs to assist with improving literacy skills and ESL instruction can be offered. Developing special collections with materials authored by ethnic minorities and materials reflective of specific cultures such as the Latino culture play an important role in meeting the needs of the Latino and Spanish-speaking community. Libraries should include materials that reflect the history, customs, language, values, beliefs, and major contributions made to this nation by ethnic minorities. The library will be viewed as a place where the patron's culture is respected and valued if it provides a wide variety of reading material and other resources in the library patron's first language, the library will be viewed as a place where the patron's culture is respected and valued.

Effective communication is indispensable to serve the needs of language minority patrons and promote their use of the library. Positive interactions between library employees and library patrons are crucial when assisting under-served ethnic groups who are seeking information. Library professionals can reduce the patrons' anxiety or apprehension by introducing them to a positive, user-friendly environment. The information intermediary may make the users feel less confused by giving them a brief tour of the area, supplying a diagram of the library, and providing hands-on activities relevant to accessing information (Dame 1995).

Training Culturally Diverse Patrons How to Use Information Technology

The library should bear the responsibility of training the culturally diverse library patrons on how to use successfully information technology. While retrieving information manually may still present a challenge to some, attempting to obtain information through on-line methods presents even a greater challenge to those unfamiliar with on-line information environments (Huston 1989). The rapidly changing information age deems it necessary to bring all library users, particularly the traditionally under-served patrons, on board before they are left behind on learning how to access the information superhighway. Library professionals must be the forerunners in introducing the culturally and linguistically different users to the World Wide Web and to the virtual communities being created continually. The virtual communities consist of diverse individuals who are located in a variety of places, but who share common interests, and even a common language (Skrozeszewski 1997). Information technology and the Internet can in fact become the great equalizers both in global communication and acquisition of knowledge by all regardless of the language they speak or the personal values they possess. Technology can enhance communication between members of virtual communities and provide opportunities to increase understanding between and among ethno-cultural groups, no matter where they live, or how large or small the ethno-cultural community is (Skrozeszewski 1997). Society certainly would not benefit from having a generation made up of culturally different groups become information technology "dropouts" due to lack of learning opportunities. Libraries should capitalize on this need by providing appropriate training for these users and in the process gain lifelong library patrons.

In conclusion, libraries and library professionals must take a leadership role in initiating a process which would focus on serving the information needs of culturally and linguistically diverse library users. We need to remove communication barriers that may prevent successful retrieval of information by African Americans, Asian Americans, and Hispanic Americans/ Latinos. Learning how to relate to others in a multicultural society should be a priority. When library professionals and library systems truly become culturally

sensitive, they will undoubtedly be fulfilling their role to our multicultural society. Likewise, understanding the existing cultural differences between high-context and low-context cultures will certainly enhance the ability for library professionals to relate positively with the culturally and linguistically diverse library patron. The information presented in this paper will hopefully be viewed as useful material for library professionals planning to embark on the task of embracing multiculturalism for the purpose of better serving the information needs of an increasingly culturally diverse society. Indeed, it is a challenge to find ways to convey the spirit and nature of one cultural group to another and to learn how to better communicate cross-culturally. ¡ Si se puede, it can be done!

References

Banks, James A. 1994. *Multiethnic education theory and practice.* Needham Heights, MA:. Allyn and Bacon.

Dame, Melvina Azar. 1995. *Serving linguistically and culturally diverse students: strategies for the school librarian.* Washington, D.C.: ERIC Clearinghouse on Languages and Linguistics, ERIC, ED 390283.

Denbo, Sheryl. 1990. *Cross-cultural communication: an essential dimension of effective education.* The Mid-Atlantic Center. Chevy Chase, MD. Web: www.maec.org/cross/9.html

DuPraw, Marcelle E., and Marya Axner. 1998. *Toward a more perfect union in an age of diversity: working on common cross-cultural communication challenges.* Web: www.wwcd.org/action/ampu/crosscult.html

Feng, Jianhua. 1994. *Asian-American children: what teachers should know.* Urbana,

Ill.: ERIC Clearinghouse on Elementary and Early Childhood Education. ERIC, ED 369577.

Florian, Doris. 1991. *Understanding and overcoming cultural barriers in information systems. Proceedings of the 54th ASIS annual meeting in Washington, D.C., October 27-31, 1991* by the American Society for Information Science, 60-67.

Glover, Clarence. 1998. *Educating one race, many cultures: reaching to teach in a multicultural world.* Dallas, TX: Dallas Public Schools.

Hall, Patrick A. 1992. *Peanuts: a note on intercultural communication. Presented at the conference Linking libraries with instruction* held in Olympia, WA, December 1988.

Huang, Gary. 1993. *Beyond culture: communicating with Asian American children and families.* New York: ERIC Clearinghouse on Urban Education. ERIC, ED 366673.

Huston, Mary M. 1989. "May I introduce you: teaching culturally diverse end-users through everyday information seeking experiences." *Reference Services Review* Vol. 17 no. 1: 7-11.

Nieto, Sonia. 1992. *Affirming diversity the sociopolitical context of multicultural education.* New York: Longman.

Office of Ethnic Minority Affairs. 1995. *Communiqué.* Washington D.C.: American Psychological Association.

Pinal, Jorge del. 1997. *Diverse Hispanic population to become largest U.S. minority.* Population Reference Bureau, Inc., http://www.prb.org/media/pressrel/hispanic.htm

Sánchez, William. 1995. *Working with diverse learners and school staff in a multicultural society.* Washington, D.C.: American Psychological Association. ERIC Clearinghouse on Counseling and Student Services, Greensboro, N.C. ERIC, ED 39001895.

Skrzeszewski, Stan. 1997. *A vision for the future: exploring new roles for multicultural library services.* IFLA satellite meeting on library service in a multicultural society in Aarhus, Denmark, August 28, 1997, by the International Forum of Library Associations.

Sue, D. W., Arredondo, P., & McDavis, R. J. 1992. "Multicultural counseling competencies and standards: a call to the profession." *Journal of Counseling and Development* Vol. 70, No. 2: 477-486.

Trueba, Enrique T., and Lilia I. Bartolome. 1997. *The education of latino students: is school reform enough.* New York, NY: ERIC Clearinghouse on Urban Education. ERIC, ED 410367.

U.S. Bureau of the Census 1998. Web:.

Wittmer, Joe. 1992. *Valuing diversity in the schools: the counselor's role.* Ann Arbor, Mich.: ERIC Clearinghouse on Counseling and Personnel Services. ERIC, ED 347475.

CHAPTER SIX

Use of the Spanish Language in Organizing Library Materials for Latinos

Danelle Crowley

Studies of Spanish used in the United States and assessments of Latino demographics emphasize the great diversity found among Latinos.[1] The library system that plans to improve its services to Latinos must take this great diversity into consideration. Personnel with adequate Spanish language abilities and cultural sensitivities should be recruited. Outreach should be planned to contact all segments of the population. Collection development should expand the collection for those users and potential users who read primarily in Spanish as well as for those who speak Spanish but read mostly in English. Technical services can then play a role in facilitating Spanish-reading patrons' access to materials.

Use of Spanish language in organization of Spanish and bilingual materials is the focus of this article. Issues of Spanish vocabulary usage in call label production, cataloging, and development of bilingual on-line catalogs will be discussed. Library decision-makers need to take into consideration not only their present local population but also past demographic trends and future likelihood of change. Some locations have a consistent history of attracting immigrants, but the national or ethnic origin of immigration sometimes changes rapidly. Others may have communities that experience little change in ethnic base.

A wide range of opinions in the ongoing debate about Spanish usage will most likely surface during the process of deciding what Spanish vocabulary and grammatical structures to use in library settings.[2] There are those who think that the dictionary compiled by Spain's Royal Academy of Language in Madrid is the international authority on Spanish and should be the primary source of the vocabulary we use.[3] Some feel that the Spanish language is threatened by the influence of English and other languages, and that by use of the Academy reference, we participate in the preservation of Spanish. Meanwhile, the Spanish in common usage in the Americas is constantly being infused with words from English, Native Indian languages of the Americas, and others, not to mention new usage of old Spanish words and creative slang. From the perspective of libraries in the United States, language terms of common usage in the Americas would provide easier access for most of our Spanish-reading patrons, however, some of these terms vary greatly from one region of the Americas to another. At the other end of the continuum are those who think that the Spanish vocabulary we use should be as close to English as possible in order to facilitate learning English terminology or to adapt to tendencies to anglicize in common usage. However, as will be noted later, there are differences in meaning between very similar appearing English and Spanish words that we commonly use in libraries.

The manner in which Spanish materials will be organized is related to policy decisions as to whether or not the Spanish collection will be separate, i.e., shelved in an area apart from, or inter-filed with the general collection. Separate collections facilitate browsing, save users' and public service staff's time, and give the impression that the library is taking into consideration the population's needs. In large public libraries, advantages of a separate

Spanish collection far outweigh inconveniences experienced in cataloging, processing and shelving departments. If Spanish materials are shelved separately but bilingual materials are not, catalogers will need to make item-by-item decisions in placement of bilingual or multilingual items. Authors and publishers are infinitely creative in combination of languages. OCLC's MARC record format gives the cataloger some guidance in assigning language code by defining the item as "the principal work, including legends, accompanying text, singing, or spoken text, and excluding preface, introduction, foreword, and appendixes."[4] However, at the local level, criteria other than predominant language (more one language than the other) of the principal body of the work may be set for deciding where a particular work will be shelved, especially for items whose predominant language is very difficult to choose. These local criteria might include the following:

1. shelved where it is most needed (may depend on relative size of general and separate collections or on informational content);

2. shelved by language of apparent intended audience (Proponents of this shelving arrangement believe that the language used in the introduction, prologue, notes, cover, etc. indicates an intended audience. This arrangement contradicts language code assignment guidelines, however, and probably should be utilized only for materials designed for second language instruction);

3. shelved where it will get the greatest amount of use (popular argument among those concerned with circulation statistics);

4. shelved by language of first or most

prominent part of the title (works well in collections where the objective is to have bilingual materials mixed in with both the general and the separate Spanish collections);

5. materials by and about Latinos shelved in a separate Latino Collection regardless of language (solves many of the most difficult and subjective decisions of language designation). Non-Latino Spanish/English materials may be shelved in the Spanish (or general) collection. Materials which are a combination of Spanish and some other language (e.g., Nahuatl, Latin, etc.) may be shelved in the Spanish collection with classification either by subject or by non–Spanish language literature number;

6. last but not least, shelved in a section for which it was ordered by collection development personnel.

Videocassettes are notorious for being packaged and labeled with various language combinations. For Spanish-speakers Spanish videos packaged in English are virtually lost in a large general collection. A policy for a separate Spanish video collection might state:

Regardless of the language used on their cases and labels, the following types of videos will be added to the Spanish collection:

- original dialogue in Spanish;
- dialogue dubbed in Spanish;
- original dialogue in Spanish, subtitles in English;
- original dialogue in English, subtitles in Spanish;
- most of dialogue or commentary is presented both in English and Spanish;
- materials designed for teaching English or other languages to Spanish speakers.

Whether the collection is separate or not, use of Spanish language in labeling, cataloging, and on-line user instruction will improve the patrons' access to the materials and increase their level of independence in library use. Below is an elaboration on labeling materials, enhancing bibliographic records for greater accessibility, and providing on-line instructions.

Labeling for the Spanish Materials Collection

The objective of using Spanish words in labeling of materials for the Spanish collection is to make the collection self-serviceable and user-friendly. Labels of Spanish materials should be as descriptive and understandable as possible within the confines of the classification system.

Decisions about the labels of Spanish and bilingual materials should take into consideration not only users but also shelvers. Materials not shelved correctly are not easily accessible regardless of the hard work put into selecting, cataloging, and processing them. Shelvers should be frequently reminded of their importance and adequately trained to recognize the difference between separate and general collection items. Materials for separate collections should be labeled in such a way that they are recognizable at a quick glance.

With Spanish-reading users and shelvers in mind, it is recommended that materials for separate Spanish collections be labeled bilingually with both a brightly colored sticker, ideally those with the word "SPANISH" printed on them, and also with a call number label displaying the word "ESPANOL" or vice versa. It helps to have the language designation on the label underlined with a yellow highlighter.[5] Regardless of where they are shelved, bilingual materials should have a sticker which says "Bilingual" and/or "Bilingüe."

Before technical services plunges into processing separate collection materials, written policies and procedures should be established for consistency and clarity. Specifics include a hierarchy of call number elements, vocabulary to be used on call number labels, and designation of type of author or other main entry mark or number.

The hierarchy of call number elements refers to the order of the parts in enhanced call labels. The best order is debatable and depends on how the collection is arranged. If all the Spanish materials are shelved together, including adult and juvenile, print and media, circulating and non-circulating, then it is probably best to have language designation first or last on the label.

On the other hand, if Spanish materials are shelved separately but in various departments such as juvenile works in the children's section, videos in a media area, etc., it might be more practical to put a location designation first. What matters most is that the order be set in writing and adhered to consistently. The following hierarchy of call number elements used at the San Antonio Public Library is an example, not meant to be a general recommendation:

1. Latino collection designation, if appropriate (e.g., "LATINO")
2. Intellectual level if not adult (e.g., "JUVENIL")
3. Language if not English (e.g., "ESPANOL"; language designation is not used on Latino collection materials)
4. Format or location as needed (e.g., "VIDEO" or "CONSULTA")
5. Classification (e.g., Dewey Decimal number or "FICCION")
6. Main entry mark (e.g., the full surname of author or first word of title of works with multiple or corporate authors).

Even more debatable than hierarchy of call number elements is Spanish vocabulary to be used on call labels. Agreement on this list of words may involve a number of compromises. One person might want to use vocabulary which most closely reflects that used in authority files of Spanish cataloging, another person might want to use words in most current usage among patrons, while another might want to use those words closest to English in appearance. The following is a partial list of terminology used at the San Antonio Public Library with *Bilindex*[6] subject headings listed for comparison:

English	Spanish	
Bilindex		
FICTION	FICCION	Novela
YOUNG ADULT	JOVEN	[unclear; not specifically provided as adjective]
JUVENILE	JUVENIL	Literatura infantil or Literatura juvenil
READ ALONG	AUDIO CON LIBRO	[not provided]
CASSETTE	CASSETTE	[not provided; pattern from videocintas would be audiocintas]
VIDEO	VIDEO	Videocintas
REFERENCE	CONSULTA	Libros de consulta

Examples of discussion over these terms might include the following points:

- "NOVELA" means fiction in the standard subject headings, but is too close to the English word "novel" which does not imply inclusion of short stories. "FICCION" is closer to the English word "fiction" and is inclusive of novels and short stories, but in some cultures it is used to mean "lies."
- In some places the word "JUVENIL" is used to describe adolescents or youth. However, it is too close to the word "juvenile" in English which is generally used in libraries to mean materials for preadolescent children. *Bilindex* is not very clear in the intended meaning of "Juvenil." At any rate, what goes into young adult collections needs to be clearly defined by policy before a descriptive word is chosen for the labels.
- In Spanish "INFANTIL" often describes preadolescent children but is too close to the English word "infantile" which usually relates to infants and is even used in a derogatory way, "infantile behavior" to label immature behavior of adults. Thus the label "JUVENIL" is sometimes chosen for children's Spanish language materials in U.S. libraries.
- "CASSETTE" is actually a French word also used in English. By Spanish spelling rules it should be "Casete." However, both words are listed in some Spanish dictionaries. Neither are in *Bilindex*. The label "AUDIO" is another possibility, but it may be understood to have a broader meaning than intended. "Audio-libros" is a term publishers sometimes use for books on tape, but it does not work well as a label term if books on tape, music, and instructional tapes are shelved together. "REFERENCIA" is a possible alternative to

"CONSULTA" but may be confusing since it has so many different meanings, e.g., "persons whom one asks for recommendations."[7] It is also too long to fit comfortably on a label.

Although Cutter numbers have practical purposes as author marks in libraries, they add to patrons' disorientation. In public library settings, the most straightforward author mark is entire surname or surnames as they are presented in the author entry of the bibliographic record or whole name if a direct order entry. Some authors have several surnames, and shelvers will need to be trained to file them correctly by first surname first.

Understanding classification numbers is a challenge for almost everyone including catalogers. One way to help Spanish-reading patrons who want to orient themselves to the classification system is to provide Spanish or bilingual fliers which summarize the system. In the case of Dewey Decimal Classification, a reference copy of the Spanish edition of Dewey, and/or a photocopy of the third summaries of the same,[8] should be kept on hand. Alternately, a bilingual hand-out combining the English and Spanish versions of the summaries could easily be typed. For catalogers of Spanish and bilingual materials Dewey Decimal Classification presents special problems not within the scope of this article.

Cataloging for the Spanish Materials Collection

Whether bibliographic records are on cards or are on-line, the Spanish reader will feel less overwhelmed by them if they are in Spanish. All bibliographic records of Spanish and bilingual materials in the catalog should be updated with subject headings and notes in Spanish and name authority corrections. If resources do not allow, then at least the records of new acquisitions should be enhanced with Spanish.

Bilingual cataloging offers the best results. The highest quality record is one that can be accessed by library personnel or users who type word searches in either English or Spanish. Once the record is accessed, the patron should be able to understand what the material is and what it is about. When circumstances do not permit this optimal level of cataloging, a minimal level is bilingual records for bilingual materials and Spanish records for Spanish materials. All original cataloging of Spanish and bilingual materials which is added to cooperative databases such as OCLC should be as enhanced as possible with the Spanish language so that untold duplication of effort can be avoided. When available, keyword access through automated catalogs greatly simplifies access and overrides much of the confusion in subject heading and subdivision order present in both English and Spanish cataloging. Since some on-line systems will keyword access MARC record fields which others will not, the cataloger needs to adapt to the local system and add the Spanish terms where the system can access them.

Spanish Language Subject Headings

When Spanish language subject headings are present in the bibliographic records of Spanish and bilingual materials, Spanish-reading library patrons can attain a higher degree of independence in accessing materials and information. The addition of subject headings is especially important since we have no complete thesaurus in Spanish to Library of Congress Subject Headings. Even if we had a complete thesaurus to hand to patrons, ease of access would be unequal for Spanish-reading users without Spanish subject headings in the actual catalog.

The use of Spanish subject headings is not as difficult and time-consuming as it may seem initially. Many of the bibliographic records purchased on cards or copied from cooperative catalogs such as OCLC will already contain Spanish subject headings or only English headings which can be translated easily with English/Spanish subject headings lists. Headings not found on the lists will require more time since a local subject authority file needs to be constructed. Some records contain no subject headings and ideally should have both English and Spanish subject or genre headings added.

Mowery[9] has published useful suggestions for subject cataloging to make Latino materials more accessible. Records of Latino materials, both English and Spanish, often need to be enhanced with the suggested English headings and their Spanish equivalents. At present one of the biggest problems in the use of Spanish subject headings is the much discussed lack of an easy-to-use, up-to-date, broadly inclusive, English/Spanish, Spanish/English standard list of subject headings. For those small libraries which use Sears subject headings there is an equivalent list in Spanish, the Sears *Lista de Encabezamientos de Materia*.[10] It has an English to Spanish index but no Spanish to English one. At any rate it is long out-of-date. Many larger libraries use *Library of Congress Subject Headings* in English and would prefer an equivalent in Spanish with extensive "used for" references from those terms which vary greatly from country to country or region to region. While *Bilindex* I is widely used and is extremely helpful, it is a highly abridged list. The basic work was published in 1984. The two bound supplements in are dated 1985 and 1986, and 1987–1990. Supplement II is not English/Spanish indexed except for the free-floating subdivisions which are fairly complete. Further supplements are in loose-leaf format including Supplements III (1991), IV (1992), V (1993), and VI (1993). Supplements I–VI have been placed on three diskettes called *Bilindex* Online. The original basic work is not included in it. A paper edition of these merged supplements is not available. *Bilindex* would obviously be much easier to use if all volumes were combined in a single alphabet, extensively cross-referenced, both English/Spanish and Spanish/English indexed, and updated. Nonetheless, *Bilindex* remains an invaluable tool. *Bilindex* also contains children's subject headings, but many more are needed. A book of Spanish subject headings for children's materials was published in 1994.[11] Señor Alberto Villalón, the compiler, used lists and reference books from several countries as sources for his work. The print is easy to read. However, there is no cross-indexing with English and more terms need to be added.

Occasionally supplemental lists are shared through the Internet, such as the Commission for Environmental Cooperation (CEC) Resource Center list of English, French, and Spanish subject headings pertaining to the environment[12]; Oakland Public & San Francisco Public Libraries Spanish equivalents to Library of Congress subject headings[13]; Yolanda M. Rivas' list of English CyberSpanglish, and Spanish vocabulary.[14] Sharing of lists creates dialog among interested persons.

Hopefully this dialog will contribute to future standardization and further cooperation.

In Mexico, Gloria Escamilla González, Reynaldo Figueroa Servin, and others are working on updates of the Escamilla subject headings,[15] but it is a massive project which will require time. Some libraries may not find the Mexican standard list adequate for their population, but it will nonetheless serve as a very important reference from which we can all work in devising our local headings and our national standards for the U.S. Construction of standard subject headings in Spanish for the United States population is an especially difficult matter due to the great diversity of Spanish vocabulary usage among Latinos and the strong influence of English on spoken vocabulary. Subject heading lists need to be extensively cross-referenced or many local subject headings added. Spanish used in these headings should be found in most commonly-used, available dictionaries. Meanings and connotations need to be checked in Spanish/Spanish dictionaries.

In translating *Library of Congress Subject Headings* into Spanish, we should also take into consideration that some of the headings are nationalistic, ethnocentric, biased, or insensitive; and should be reworked in their Spanish version to be more informed and global in expression.[16] Some of these terms in English are so deeply entrenched in United States culture that they may never be revised. The use of the word "American" to refer to things pertaining to the United States is an example. Many Europeans and Latin Americans use "American" in referring to things and people from all of the Americas. Indeed this English use of "American" to mean "of the United States" deprives us of the adjective we need in referring to the

Western Hemisphere. On the other hand we do not have a commonly used term like "U.S.ian" or "United States-siders" to refer to ourselves.

Whether Spanish language subject headings are being constructed for international, national, or local use, certain types of terms create a challenge. For example, words borrowed from other languages are often spelled in several ways even in the reference books. One spelling might be the same as in the lending language, in which case the phonetical pronunciation may differ; or, the spelling may appear to be a phonetical one of the pronunciation in the lending language. One example comes from a cataloger's attempt to construct a Spanish subject heading equivalent of the Library of Congress heading "Cherokee Indians." Using *Bilindex* headings for Mexican Indians like "Huicholes," "Otomíes," and "Aztecas" as a pattern, we find several options in the dictionaries:

"Cherokees" (not standard Spanish spelling; pronunciation and syllable of stress differ from English), "Cheroquis," (written without an accent automatically puts the accent on the "o") "Cheroquís" (with the accent on the "i" breaks the spelling rules for plurals with accent on final "i" or "u"),[17] or "Cheroquíes" (follows the spelling rules). One option not found in the references at all was "Chéroquis" with the accent on the "e," which would be the Spanish phonetical spelling closest to the English pronunciation.

In both English and Spanish common names for things such as animals and plants sometimes vary greatly from one area to the next. Also the same word may be used for something completely different. Confusion of these terms can even be dangerous as in the case of a plant which is poisonous having the same name as an edible plant from a different area. The names of similar species can also be complicated by colloquial usage. For example "grillos" is used for grasshoppers in some places, for crickets in others.

If the library has a small Spanish collection which is inter-filed in the general collection and there is no administrative support for enhancement with Spanish language of call labels or catalog records, minimal addition of the subject heading "Spanish language materials" or "Spanish language materials—Bilingual" can be used as a genre heading for each record. Thus records can be brought together in one place in the card catalog or on-line public access catalog. Then at least public service personnel can point the way to the Spanish holdings. When one becomes available, it would be good to have a Spanish-to-English Library of Congress subject heading thesaurus for use by patrons.

Other Enhancements of the Catalog Record

In addition to subject and/or genre, records should contain those features which enable patrons and reference librarians to find what they are looking for in specific formats and translations; for example, bilingual editions with parallel texts, translations into Spanish of specific titles or authors, and materials by authors of a specific nationality. In the case of bilingual materials, it is helpful to both technical and public services staff to have a written statement defining what materials are designated as bilingual. The following is an example of a statement modeled after OCLC's MARC record format assignment of language code mentioned above:

Only those materials in which the principal body of the work is presented completely in each language will be classified as bilingual. Preface, introduction, foreword, appendixes, etc. may be in only one language. In the case of Spanish and English bilingual materials, "Bilingual books" and "Libros bilingües" subject headings will be added to records as genre headings or used as patterns to formulate other headings such as "Videocintas bilingües." A bilingual sticker will be placed on the cover or case. A bilingual Spanish/English note in the catalog record will clarify the language arrangement of materials containing significant amounts of both languages. Whether policy defines a material as bilingual or not, it is preferable that bibliographic records of all materials containing significant amounts of both English and Spanish have a bilingual note describing the language arrangement of the material. Examples of notes which clarify language content are as follows: "En español con subtítulos en inglés = In Spanish with subtitles in English" "Textos paralelos en inglés y español = parallel texts in English and Spanish" "Inglés y español mezclados = English and Spanish mixed."

Materials which are titled in a language different from the principal body of the work especially need a note clarifying language. It is not uncommon to find works all or almost all in English but with Spanish titles and vice-versa. These materials have a tendency to be incorrectly shelved, especially if they are not labeled very conspicuously. Materials which are translations are accessible through a uniform title entry with designation of the language of translation. Genre headings such as "Novela estadounidense—Autores mexicanoamericanos—Traducciones al español" may be added to assist Spanish-readers in locating specific translations. Although a note is repetitious, it adds clarity to the record, e.g., in the case of La casa en Mango Street by Sandra Cisneros, the note would read thus: "Traducción de = Translation of: The House on Mango Street."

Some patrons want to read authors of a specific nationality. The nationality of an author, however, is sometimes difficult to define. Many have spent large portions of their lives outside the countries of their birth. Biographic sketches usually tell their birth places but seldom denote citizenship or preference of national identity.

Materials on the history and criticism of the literatures of U.S. Latinos and of the literatures of each Latin American country should be a minimum addition to our collections. General references like Diccionario de literatura española e hispanoamericana are very useful to public and technical services personnel as well as to patrons.[18] Catalogers can use this type of reference and biographical information in the item being cataloged to formulate genre headings based on the author's nationality. Adding summary notes in Spanish and contents notes to the bibliographic record is another way to improve the patrons' chances of accessing the information they seek, especially when the on-line catalog in use can provide keyword access from these notes. In original cataloging of children's materials for cooperative databases, the summary note is an important addition to the record. It is one of the most time consuming parts of the cataloging but is a field that is prominently displayed in some of the graphic user interfaces for children's catalogs. Summary notes also offer the opportunity for the cataloger to add words which are not the standard subject heading term but are in common usage. The note can also be used to reinforce the meaning of standard subject heading words by presenting them in context.

While content notes in MARC records are primarily designed to list the titles of separate works or parts of an item,[19] at the local level they can be used to list all or part of the table of contents of an item. If a library's collection of Spanish materials is small, this type of record enhancement will provide the Spanish-reader quicker access to information which might not be enough to warrant the addition of a subject heading in the record of any of the materials in the collection. Additionally, the table of contents might use words more familiar to users than the standard subject headings.

A few other considerations are specific to Spanish cataloging. One common error is the presence of a note that says "Includes index" when the material does not actually include the alphabetical, analytical list referred to by the English word "index." The word "índice" used in Spanish does not always mean the same thing as "index" in English. When used alone it usually means "table of contents." In Spanish, index as it is understood in English, will be called "índice" with some type of qualifying adjective, e.g., "índice alfabetico." If the material does contain an index the note might read as follows: "Includes index = Se incluye "índice alfabetico."

Bilingual on-line user instructions:

On-line instructions are often quite difficult to understand and follow even in one's own first language much less in an unknown or second language. If we expect our patrons to use on-line catalogs, periodical indexes, and other on-line information sources, they need to be provided with appealing, inoffensive, and understandable instructions ideally in person, in writing, and on-line. The amount of time,

energy, and money spent in these endeavors is repaid many times as users become increasingly confident and adept in using resources without the assistance of library personnel.

On-line instructions will ideally be composed of language and/or graphics that are clear to the user but also gradually introduce them to jargon and other technical vocabulary that they will be encountering as they become more skillful in the use of computers. The language used should also be culturally sensitive. Spanish adds the choice of whether to use formal or informal address in commands. While many Spanish-speaking adults come from extremely polite and formal environments where they expect to be addressed with formal grammar except by close friends and family peers, other adults may find the formal address too rigid. Children may be addressed informally but are expected to respond to adults in a formal manner.

The addition of Spanish language instructions to on-line catalogs and databases involves programming expertise and access to necessary technology for the particular system being enhanced. It can become very complicated. Fortunately there are Spanish interfaces on the market and others being developed which can be purchased and adapted to many different systems. CARL Corporation's graphic user's interface in Spanish for Kid's Catalog is one example.

If a library purchases an interface in Spanish, it is preferable that it be one which can be modified locally. Technical services personnel need to be provided with adequate training for making these changes. The person or committee who is authorized by the administration to make decisions about what modifications will be made to the interface should know

Spanish, be well acquainted with local language usage and cultural sensitivities, and have some knowledge of education principles.

Conclusion

A library's primary concern is providing equal access to information for all its users. In addition to expecting this access, the public, especially children, expect the library to be a model of excellence. Patrons may study the translations they see on bilingual signs posted in the library and assume that they are correctly done. A child may check the spelling of a word by looking at a subject heading in the catalog rather than search for a dictionary. Subconscious as well as conscious learning takes place in the library environment. In the United States a few patrons may object to the use of anything except English. Others will enjoy being in surroundings where there is an awareness of diversity and will be interested in learning more about the unfamiliar languages they see and hear. The library's responsibility to its users is enormous. However, lack of agreement and insecurities about what we do should not stop us from trying to improve our services to the best of our abilities. Most of the commentary in this article was not based on research but rather on my personal observations, work experience as Spanish language materials cataloger at the San Antonio Public Library, and suggestions of other librarians. There is much research to be done in the area of Latino library user studies, information needs, and effectiveness of services. In the meantime we can experiment, trust that what we attempt is better than nothing, and hope that later research will indicate that our services have a positive impact.

Notes

1. See Eugene Estrada, "Changing Latino Demographics and American Libraries," in *Latino Librarianship: A Handbook for Professionals*, ed. Salvador Güereña (Jefferson, North Carolina: McFarland & Company, 1990), 1–16; Juan M. Lope Blanch, *El Espanol Hablado en el Suroeste de los Estados Unidos: Materiales para su Estudio* (Mexico, D. F.: Universidad Nacional Autónoma de Mexico, 1990); and M. Isabel Valdes and Marta H. Seoane, *Hispanic Market Handbook* (New York: Gale Research Inc., 1995), 215–249, 361–364.

2. *New York Times* (New York City, N.Y.), 28 March–16 April 1997.

3. *Diccionario de la lengua española* (Madrid: Real Academia Espanola, 1992).

4. *Bibliographic Formats and Standards*, 2nd ed. (Dublin, Ohio: OCLC Online Computer Library Center, Inc., 1996), FF:53.

5. Suggestion from Sally Gray Miller, librarian at the Lexington (Kentucky) Public Library.

6. *Bilindex: A bilingual Spanish-English subject heading list: Spanish equivalents to Library of Congress Subject Headings* (Oakland, Calif.: California Spanish Language Data Base, 1984). Bilindex. Supplement I 1985–1986 (Berkeley, Calif.: Floricanto Press, 1986). Bilindex. Supplement II 1987–1990 (Encino, Calif.: Floricanto Press, 1992).

7. Marta Stiefel Ayala, Reynaldo Ayala, and Jesus Lau, *Technical Dictionary of Library and Information Science : English/Spanish, Spanish/English = Diccionario Técnico de Bibliotecología y Ciencias de la Información* (New York: Garland Publishing, Inc., 1993) 590–591.

8. *Sistema de Clasificación Decimal Dewey*, traducción de la ed. 20 en ingles (Santafe de Bogota: Rojas Eberhard Editores, 1995) v.2, xi–xx.

9. Robert L. Mowery, "Subject cataloging of Chicano Literature," *Library Resources*

& Technical Services 39, no. 3 (1995): 229–237

10. *Sears: Lista de Encabezamientos de Materia.* Traducción y adaptación de la 12a. edición en inglés (New York: H. W. Wilson Company, 1984).

11. Alberto Villalon, *Encabezamientos de materia para libros infantiles y juveniles* (Madrid: Fundación German Sanchez Ruiperez, 1994).

12. Oakland Public & San Francisco Public Libraries Spanish Equivalents to Library of Congress Subject Headings," [list on-line]. (Oakland, Calif.: Oakland Public Library; San Francisco, Calif.: San Francisco Public Library, 1997, accessed 7 December 1997); available from http://clnet.ucr.edu/library/bplg/sujetos1.htm; Internet.

13. Yolanda M. Rivas, "CyberSpanglish," [list on-line] in Yolanda's Website [on-line] (Austin, Tex.: accessed 7 December 1997); available from http://www.actlab.utexas.edu/~seagull/spang-b.html; Internet.

14. Gloria Escamilla González, *Lista de Encabezamientos de Materia* (Mexico: Universidad Nacional Autónoma de Mexico, 1978).

15. Gloria Escamilla González, *Lista de Encabezamientos de Materia* (Mexico: Universidad Nacional Autónoma de Mexico, 1978).

16. See Lois Olsrud and Jennalyn Chapman, "Difficulties of Subject Access for Information About Minority Groups," in *Multicultural Acquistions*, ed. Karen Parrish and Bill Katz (New York: Haworth Press, 1993) 47–60; and Marielena Fina, "The Role of Subject Headings in Access to Information: The Experience of One Spanish-Speaking Patron," *Cataloging & Classification Quarterly* 17, no. 1–2 (1993) : 267–274.

17. Marion P. Holt and Julianne Dueber, *Barron's 1001 pitfalls in Spanish* (Hauppauge, New York: Barron's Educational Series, Inc., 1986), 53.

18. Ricardo Gullon, ed., *Diccionario de literatura española e hispanoamericana* (Madrid: Alianza Editorial, 1993).

19. Bibliographic Formats and Standards, 5:11.

LIBRARY SERVICE TO CHILDREN

CHAPTER SEVEN

Developing the Spanish Children's Collection

Oralia Garza de Cortés

Historical Background

Developing Spanish children's collections in school and public libraries in the United States has been a significant challenge for librarians ever since the passage of the Bilingual Education Act in 1968. Since then, school and public libraries have struggled with mixed success to obtain the necessary materials to meet the demands of bilingual and Spanish-speaking students in their schools and communities. Reference tools developed by bibliographers Duran (1978) Cruger Dale (1985) and Beilke (1986) served a useful purpose in helping librarians identify and select the materials suitable for their collection needs. These materials, however, tended to document primarily bilingual titles or English titles with Hispanic themes. The works of Isabel Schon in her many volumes on Spanish children's bibliography, however, have provided the most comprehensive source for the development of a Spanish children's literature collection.[1] The Reagan years and the resulting diminished federal funding for books in school libraries, however, have made it difficult for librarians to make book budget choices. For the conscientious librarian committed to providing books in Spanish, the book budget indeed posed a serious dilemma. For the librarian who found the process of Spanish book selection in general to be difficult, tedious, cumbersome and bothersome, the budget cuts served as a welcome acknowledgment to return to business as usual. Studies of

Spanish book buying practices among school and public librarians have well documented the resistance to Spanish books among school and public services librarians (Artola Allen, 1992, Schon, Hopkins, Main and Hopkins, 1987).

As the Hispanic population in the U.S. continues to grow, so too will the demand for books in Spanish.[2] Unfortunately, neither the need nor the demand for books in Spanish has easily transferred into a serious commitment by children's book publishers in the United States to launch into the U. S. Spanish market. There has always been a presence of Spanish-speaking children in the United States, yet it was not until the late 1980s and early 1990s, almost twenty years after the Bilingual Education Act became law, that the "boom" for Spanish children's book really took place. While one would hope that the production of books in Spanish published in the United States occurs because publishers recognize the linguistic needs of Spanish-speaking children, the sad reality lies in the fact that the publication of these materials is market driven, and publishers respond to the needs of a market.

The recognition of "new" audience of a Spanish-speaking children in the United States is the impetus for a body of work that more accurately reflects the mainstream of children's literary experience translated into Spanish. The current development in Spanish children's books publishing is primarily an attempt by publishers to reproduce best selling and award winning English titles to new Spanish markets (Lodge). For all practical purposes, then, selecting books for children in Spanish that are published in the United States is a pre-selective process if one considers that the decision of what to buy in Spanish is pre-determined in the board rooms of American publishing

houses that first and foremost must assure that the materials in question will sell and produce a profit. Yet in spite of this market-driven self-interest, various factors account for the cautious approach that publishers have taken in their attempt to publish in Spanish, among them issues of translation, sales, and markets (Lodge). Many publishers have found themselves easy target for criticism from librarians who decry the poor quality of translation (Carlson) as well as the lack of editorial attention that Spanish language publication requires.

Decision-making in the board rooms of American children's publishing houses are devoid of a Spanish children's literature base, and drive the market for the publication of Spanish works away from the classic of Spanish children's literature to works that are first and foremost 'American'. It is no surprise, then, that classic children's works such as *Platero y Yo* by the Spaniard Juan Ramón Jiménez remains unpublished in English in a children's edition in its entirety.[3]

Librarians, too, have conspired with publishers in establishing the framework which has driven the Spanish children's publishing market. Unfamiliar with Spanish children's literature, librarians have opted for the fast track, purchasing Spanish translations of titles that they themselves are most familiar with. Additional factors that researchers have documented as driving librarians' decisions stem from issues related to easy access to U.S. materials; cost; built-in cataloging, and easy access to reviews (Artola Allen, 449). What librarians have not taken into consideration, however, are the effects that their selection practices have on the children that they are meant to serve. What are the effects of children's readings of dissimilar life experiences of Anglo children, books where the protagonists are not Hispanic children like themselves, books that are devoid of a Hispanic cultural background, and books that basically deny a child acquaintance with his or her Hispanic literary heritage? (Artola Allen, 449).

It is only in the last decade of this century, however, that publishers have finally begun to recognize the importance of producing materials that more accurately reflect the cultural experiences of Spanish-speaking children living in the United States (Lodge, 97). Such publications include those being produced by Scholastic, Inc. in works such as Lulu Delacre's Latin American folktale collection *De Oro y Esmeralda: Mitos, Leyendas y Cuentos Populares de LatinoAmerica* (1997), the Spanish edition of *Golden Tales: Myths, Legends and Folktales from Latin America* (1996) and Lucia González's Spanish edition of *Señor Cat's Romance and Other Favorite Stories from Latin America* (1997). Also illustrated by Lulu Delacre are excellent examples of efforts by mainstream American publishers to recognize the importance of authenticity in cultural stories from the wealth of stories to be found from Latino authors who live in the United States and who represent the diversity of Spanish-speaking cultures in the United States.

Librarians must also recognize that the Spanish book market in the United States is only one part of an amazing wealth of materials available for children from the Spanish-speaking countries of the world. While materials published in the United States are indeed important, they are not the only source. Children's literature by Spanish-speaking authors from Spanish-speaking countries including Mexico, Central and South America, the Spanish-speaking Caribbean and Spain constitutes a wealth of 'original literature' that must be considered by U.S. librarians if a genuine Spanish children's literature collection is to be achieved.

The Spanish Language Children's Collection Development Policy

The first and most important step in establishing a Spanish children's collection is a commitment on the part of the library system that it will establish and maintain a collection suitable for the needs of the community of Spanish-speaking children and their families. This commitment must translate into a clearly defined policy statement that reflects the nature and scope of the Spanish children's collection.[4] The policy statement formalizes the institutional commitment and establishes a precedent for the continuation of such a collection. Children's librarians must present as evidence the information gathered from a community assessment, including the size and nature of the Spanish-speaking population that the particular library serves. An important measure not to be overlooked is the approximate number of the children enrolled in bilingual/ESL programs in the schools or in the community that a particular library serves. Establishing a clearly written policy mandates that books in Spanish will be collected, and prevents librarians from exercising their own bias against Spanish materials, a problem prevalent among school media center librarians.[5]

Creative Acquisition

Collection development officers and departments who approach the collection of materials for children in Spanish in the same manner with which they approach the collection of the English speaking materials will run into many pitfalls that hinder the Spanish collection development process. The result can be an exercise in futility. By its very nature, the publishing market for Spanish children's books is vastly different from the American market, and the selection tools with which to properly select the materials are notably absent. For successful acquisition, then, a variety of approaches to collection development must be tried, including collecting distributors' catalogs, publishers' catalogs, and attendance at the Spanish book fairs held yearly that showcase the wide array of available material while at the same time allowing librarians an opportunity to examine the books themselves.

Balanced Collections

Content Balanced

A well-balanced Spanish children's collection consists of books purchased in all subject areas and reading formats, including picture books, beginning reading, concept books (ABC/123's), small books, board books, fiction, non-fiction, poetry, history, biography, video, audio, read-alongs, magazines, Big Books and a reference section to support the research needs of elementary school children. The research section must also contain resource materials for teachers and parents and other librarians within the community who need to learn about the vast world of Spanish children's literature. Within this broad range of materials, a well-balanced collection must consist of materials that reflect a wide range of titles from a vari-

ety of publishing areas or zones including books published in Mexico, South and Central America, the Spanish-speaking Caribbean, Spain, and, as well as titles published in the United States. The production of books in Spanish for children is indeed varied if one takes into account the full range of materials published from all of the major Spanish-speaking countries of the world. The purchase of these materials along with the materials published in the United States constitutes the development of a balanced collection that will more genuinely reflect the full range of diversity of Hispanic and Latino cultures of the Spanish-speaking world.

Culturally Balanced Collections

Another important element of a well-balanced collection is that it must include original titles published from the country of origin of the Spanish-speaking countries. Children from El Salvador deserve to read the classic works of authors and poets from their native country. They deserve to have access to the poetry of the well-known Salvadoran poet Claudia Lars as much as they deserve to read, hear and enjoy the works of the well-known Argentine writer for children, María Elena Welsh. Having these materials in the school and public library serves as a bridge for children from these countries who may be having a difficult time adjusting to their new environment. What better way to be comforted than to listen to the language of one's familiar, the soothing sound of the words first heard at birth, words from the mother tongue, words from such classics as Ruben Darío's magically enchanting poem for children "Margarita." All Spanish-speaking children also deserve to be connected to the books and literature of the universal language that is Spanish, as well as to universal classics of Spanish children's literature. Most school textbooks from the Spanish-speaking countries include the universal, classic works, so that children in this country, if they have a schooling history, are familiar with these works of literature.

In addition, children who are learning Spanish can also reap the benefit that an outstanding Spanish children's literature collection can offer. Students such as those in two-way bilingual education programs, or dual language learning programs can also benefit from outstanding literature collections. To present children with literature that reflects their own cultural heritage and background is to nurture their well-being and to develop strong roots from which they can develop into their fullest potential, able to venture out into their own imaginative, creative journey, able to absorb the wealth of knowledge that two broad cultural and linguistic traditions can offer.

Translation Woes

One of the most controversial aspects of books in Spanish for children has been the issue of translations. The issue centers on the quality of the translation. While editorial issues at the publishing level are undeniable they tend to focus on the poor quality of translations. Among librarians the translation debate is evident in the difference of opinions that exist about the merits of quality translation. A less than favorable review of Sandra Cisneros' *Hairs/Pelitos* by noted children's reviewer Hazel Rochman, for example, cites the "occasional" quality of the translations as "poor" yet the translater, Liliana Valen-

zuela , a native of Mexico City and now a long-time resident of Austin, Texas, is a professional translator and the translator of Cisneros' adult title *Woman Hollering Creek and Other Stories*, *El Arroyo de la Llorona y Otros Cuentos*.

Yet seldom heard is the discussion on the decision-making process that determines what books will be translated into Spanish. What makes a book noteworthy of translation? Is it the subject matter? Is it the popularity of the book? Or is it the insurance that the book will sell, and the publishing companies lose nothing by risking nothing. What issues enter the decision-making process to publish, for example, Longfellow's picture book poem *Paul Revere's Ride* (Dutton, 1990) in to Spanish, as opposed to publishing poetry that first originates in Spanish? Are publishers really interested in developing the literacy capacity of Spanish-speaking children? Or, is there an underlying assumption that Spanish-speaking children need to be "Americanized," and that one way to do this is to introduce them to American heroes and American history as early as possible? The dilemma will persist until way into the 21st century until publishers are more honest about their motives, until they understand the importance of native-language learning, and until more Latinos enter the publishing world of children's books and begin to have a say in the decision-making of major children's editorial boards.

Spanish-speaking librarians have long raised the issue of poorly translated books, as have bilingual educators. The latter, on their frequent trips to the Spanish children's section of the local libraries, have expressed their distaste for poor quality translations. But it is also important to remember there are as many opinions about "bad Spanish" as there are about the variety and type of Hispanics in this country. What must be kept in mind, however, is the unique voice behind the telling. If a border school teacher or an inner city barrio person tells their story in their own words and in the language that they grew up hearing, with its own unique brand of vocabulary and style, are we to decry that voice because it is not a 'correct' voice? Is it not just as authentic as Black English is to the flavor of American speech? The issue, then, is the question of which Spanish is the sanctioned, or correct Spanish? What Spanish will be used in producing Spanish books for children? Spanish from Spain, Spanish from Colombia? Barrio Spanish? Lost in the debate is the conversation about "official Spanish" that seeks to establish a canon that most strongly resembles the "political correctness" debate that is prevalent among university scholars in the multicultural discourse. Questions on issues of authorship are prevalent among authors and libraries in the multicultural debate. It is interesting to note that even in a country such as Mexico, language issues prevail. The Nobel Prize winner Octavio Paz declares "The language belongs to everyone and no one" (Taylor, 1997a). Another author, a noted economist and expert on the Mexican book trade states "We are not really countries separated by the same language, but you hear many complaints in Mexico about books translated in Spain" (Taylor, 1997a). Clearly, the issue of translation must take into account the nuances of language that provide the diversity of language use even among Spanish-speaking people within a given country.

The Bilingual Format

Developing a well-balanced collection necessitates that the materials collected will arrive in various formats. One such unique format is the bilingual edition. The bilingual edition poses significant challenges to libraries with multiple needs. While most libraries adhere to the standard cataloging rules that state that the decision to catalog a book is determined by identifying the language of the main title of the book, in many communities it was standard practice to relegate all books "Spanish" to the 460 (languages) or 860 (Spanish literature) Dewey decimal designations. Bilingual books are a popular choice among school librarians, many of who see them as a matter of economics, providing three linguistic sets of children with the same material. Sadly, though, some librarians welcome bilingual books as a way to beef up the Spanish collection. This practice negates the collection of bilingual materials for Hispanic non-Spanish-speakers for whom the book may well have been intended. Such practices may also affect English speaking students who are developing Spanish literacy skills. The result is to segregate or ghettoize the "Spanish" collection by failing to recognize the values of a Spanish collection for dual language as well as monolingual Spanish readers. The dilemma is further exacerbated by obvious neglect of the Spanish collection when it comes to standard collection maintenance practices such as weeding or shelf-reading. AACR2 cataloging rules also pose a challenge to bilingual communities who struggle to provide Spanish-speaking as well as English dominant Hispanic children with materials sufficient for their needs. This practice could well deny English speaking children the opportunity to access stories from cultures and languages different from theirs because of the mistaken assumption that the material is not in English. According to Sanford Berman

(1997), providing access points in the cataloging process, designating bilingual access points is an important cataloging practice not to be overlooked. In addition, he suggests that where the book is shelved should be "strictly a local decision, depending on where it's likely to be best/most used." Children's librarians play an important role in insuring that the collection is given equitable maintenance. Equally important is the role that children's librarian should play in insuring that children come to recognize that the Spanish section of the library is also a treasure trove of literature waiting to be discovered.

Relevancy of Information

The issue of relevancy of information is of particular importance for information books published in the Spanish-speaking countries. This idea of information books for children is a relatively new phenomenon in Spanish book publishing. Most publishers of Spanish-speaking materials are unaware of the importance that American librarians place on dated materials especially in the sciences. In addition to looking at the date of publication of the translated material in question, it is of particular importance to look at the date of the original source. Many of the information books for children in Spanish are translations of previously published books primarily in Great Britain. The politics and intricacies of publishing rights among and between countries, unfortunately, impedes the timely production of information books, the results of which could very well be a dated children's book the minute the material is first made available. The exchange is most evident in the large publishing houses of Mexico and South America who must wait in line for publishing rights after the material is first published in Spain. Original publication dates, then, is information that is crucial in the selection process. Unfortunately, it is not always easily obtainable. Rarely is this type of information available in distributors' or publishers' catalogs. A physical examination of the item in question is the best selection practice in this case. Such a practice is most notably done at the Spanish language book fairs that are held yearly in Mexico, or by special arrangement at the warehouse of the selected distributor. Another suggested practice is to locate the date of publication of the original English text, either through Books in Print or by searching the on-line catalogs of libraries throughout the United States that may own the book.

Perspective

A particular concern should be placed on the point of view, or perspective of the author, especially as it concerns the purchase of history books for children. Who is telling the history that is being collected? The issue becomes crucial in the collection of books from Spain, for example, that may well tell a completely different story of the conquest of Mexico than would a history book from Mexico. The same may be true of historical personages. The Spanish hero Hernan Cortés is such a case in point. Cortés as a historical figure is well-represented in biographies published in Spain. But to Mexicans, Cortés is not their hero. The same would be true of books on Texas history or California history. Mexican heroes such as Juan Cortinas would be labeled villains by the dominant cultures, yet to the countless generations of Mexican Americans, personages such as the *Tejanos* Gregorio Cortéz and Juan Cortinas or the *Californios* Tiburcio Vásquez and Joaquin Murrieta are considered folk heroes for defending the rights of Mexican Americans against oppressive Anglo forces.

The Role of the Children's Librarian in the Selection Process

The selection of materials in Spanish for children mandates that a competent, fluent Spanish-speaking professional librarian be hired for such a role. Such a librarian must be knowledgeable or become knowledgeable about children's books, authors, and illustrators from the Spanish-speaking world. She/he should be knowledgeable about Spanish book publishing companies and trends in Spanish language children's materials. This must be a basic criterion of competency for children's librarian serving Spanish-speaking children. To expect less than competent professionals is to diminish their role of a professional in this critical area of children's librarianship. To expect less undermines the development of a quality Spanish children's collection and deprives Spanish-speaking children of the full range of materials available (Artola Allen, 449).

For children's librarians who are not fluent Spanish-speaking, it is crucial, then, to develop a close, working relationship with a Spanish book distributor who is knowledgeable with the many aspects of Spanish language book publishing for children and who will guide the children's librarian in the Spanish selection process. Developing the Spanish children's collection requires a dedicated person willing to invest his or her time, energy and effort to develop a content-balanced, quality collection that reflects the whole of the distinct Spanish speaking cultures of the world.

Role of Distributors

Distributors of books in Spanish for children play a critical role in developing the Spanish children's collection. They become the book selector in the absence of a librarian well versed in Spanish children's literature. The best of the distributors of children's materials in Spanish have acquired an expertise in Spanish children's literature that renders them competent to select material for a school or public library collection. Such distributors can help to identify the best authors and titles from the Spanish-speaking world of children's literature. For libraries lacking a Spanish competent staff, finding a distributor that is knowledgeable of children's publishing as well as of Spanish children's literature is crucial. Ultimately, it is the distributor who will determine the quality of your collection. Spanish language book distributors scope out the expansive halls of the exhibition center in Guadalajara, Mexico on their yearly pilgrimage to the *Feria Internacional del Libro* scouting for new materials and working with their constituent libraries. In this way, the distributor works to assure that new material is selected, acquired and delivered in a timely fashion.

Increasingly, libraries, like most publicly-funded institutions, must adhere to the criteria for the selection of a vendor based on the lowest bid placed for that service within the city or county's public bidding process. Lamentably, such a one-dimensional approach dismisses the qualitative aspect that a knowledgeable distributor may be able to provide. It is crucial, then, that the criteria for the selection of a Spanish language distributor include a thorough knowledge of Spanish children's literature as well as an ability to identify and select quality materials for the Spanish-speaking child. Some distributors, like Bilingual Publications from New York, for example, offer selection services based on a profile of material requested by a particular institution that is then filled by the distributor based on the criteria requested. Others, such as Lectorum provide approval plans where materials are shipped out, in an effort to allow selectors to view firsthand the material to be considered for purchase.

Review Sources

Among professional review sources, *Booklist* and *School Library Journal* maintain regular columns dedicated to the review of books in Spanish for children. As of this writing, *Horn Book* has discontinued its reviews of books in Spanish for children. The sheer volume of Spanish children's materials currently available, however, demands a broader playing field of professionals that can reflect the diversity of voices and opinions necessary for a vibrant review process. To relegate the review process to a few librarians nationwide is unfair and a disservice to the profession and ultimately to young Spanish readers. Clearly there are not enough reviewers who are presently involved in the Spanish book review process. Professional organizations within the American Library Association: ALSC (Association for Library Service to Children), AASL (American Association of School Librarians), YALSA (Young Adult Library Services Association) and REFORMA the National Association to Promote Library Services to the Spanish-speaking, along with reviewers from the professional journals need to establish long term plans for the development of a cadre of children's librarians who can be trained to review an important aspect of the children's collection—books in Spanish.

Other Selection Tools

Distributors' Catalogs

In the absence of substantial review sources for the selection of Spanish children's books, the distributors' catalogs become crucial tools necessary for a comprehensive development of the Spanish children's collection. The best of them provide annotations for the materials available through their company. In addition, they provide author, title and subject indexes that are crucial to developing an overall, well-balanced collection. They do, however, vary on the types of information necessary for the completion of slip orders. By utilizing a mixture of catalogs, however, a librarian can begin to piece together all the necessary information needed for placing an order for a particular children's book. The meticulous, sometimes grueling process of piecing all the pieces of the acquisition puzzle together is well worth the investment. The result, a quality first-rate Spanish children's collection is well worth the investment, especially when one considers the outcome that it will produce: bringing books and children together, no matter the language.

Libros en Venta

Another selection tool useful in the information gathering process is *Libros en*

Venta, designed by Daniel Melcher, the visionary director of R. R Bowker who also developed the cataloging method for *Books in Print* (Taylor). *Libros en Venta* is a completely separate product from *Books in Print*. But one could safely say that it functions as its Spanish equivalent. Despite its best effort, however, it does not always function as the authoritative source of information for books from the Spanish-speaking world. The listed information is not always the most current, and not all publishers' materials are included. It is, however, the tool that comes closest to *Books in Print*. It is a very useful tool for detecting titles and authors as well as ISBN's when that information is available. It is particularly useful for identifying a specific title that may have been published by various publishing houses concurrently. Its title and author search capacity enables one to detect a newer version of an older title that may have been previously out of print.

Publishers' Catalogs

Publishers' catalogs, when they exist, provide the selector a means of identifying materials that are currently available for purchase. They may contain some of the essential information necessary for the placement of book orders. There is, however, great inconsistency in the type of information to be found in such catalogs. For the most part, the catalogs are not annotated but they are a starting point. A publisher's catalog is an accurate barometer of what a particular publishing house has in inventory, or in stock. Several publishers, including the Mexican publishing houses *Amaquemecan*, CIDCLI (*Centro de Información y Desarrollo de la Comunicación y la Literatura Infantiles*) and *Fondo de Cultura Economica*, as well as the Venezuelan non-profit publishing house, *Edare-Banco de Libro*, have designed colorful and attractive annotated catalogs in a bilingual format. Clearly these publishers recognize the U.S. market as well as the professional needs of librarians in this country. The peso devaluation as well as the high cost of printing in Mexico and in Latin American countries has resulted in limiting frequency of publication to biennium cycles.

Recommended Reading Lists

Three valuable lists compiled by librarians from various public entities in California serve as the basis for a core collection of Spanish books for children from Kindergarten through 6th grade. The First is the "List of Core and Extended Literature," prepared by the staff members of the Office of Bilingual-ESL Instruction. Included in this list of "Extended Literature" are Spanish translations of titles selected for the Los Angeles Unified School District English Core Reading List. "Focus on Books" is another reading list published annually by the Library Services Department of the Los Angeles Unified School District. The list includes 700 titles, of which 450 are given a P1, or the highest rating. The state- recommended "Readings in Spanish Literature" is yet another useful list, this one prepared by the State of California Department of Education. These lists may be obtained by writing to the respective public institutions, but a copy of them appears yearly in the catalog of Bilingual Educational Services, Inc.

New York Public Library List

The New York Public Library's *Libros en Español para los pequeños* (1990, 1993) is an excellent example of a quality selection tool produced by a major public library exercising its professional leadership through the contributions of children's librarians serving Spanish-speaking children. The children's list is exemplary in its selection of titles, targeting children ages 2–5. It is also noteworthy in that it differentiates between translations and original titles written in Spanish. The beauty of the list is that it is ideal for collection development, as well as an ideal selection tool for parents wanting to learn more about the best of Spanish books for their young children. The list is outstanding for its brevity yet clarity in its annotations, as well as for its dual language format. It serves as a core collection model for collection development.

Feria Internacional del Libro

For the last eleven years, beginning on the Friday after the Thanksgiving holiday, one of the world's largest gatherings of Spanish books takes place in Guadalajara, Mexico. Publishers from all the Spanish-speaking countries of the world gather to display the thousands of books that they have carried with them in their attempt to lure readers and buyers into the market. By its sheer vastness, the *Feria Internacional de Libros,* commonly known among American librarians as FIL, has become the most important place for librarians to directly connect with materials from the Spanish-speaking world. At FIL, librarians can see for themselves first-hand the literally thousands of new titles produced by the Spanish speaking countries of the world. Other fairs throughout Mexico include the annual *Feria de Niños,* where children's books are featured at a children's book fair in Mexico City in early December. At yet another fair, the Monterey Book Fair, held in Monterey, Mexico, international professionals from both sides of the border, working through the Texas-Mexico Relations Committee of the Texas Library Association, have organized bus tours from Austin to Monterey, Mexico (Cunningham; Watkins) in an effort to facilitate the foreign book fair experience for professional librarians.

Maintaining a Spanish Children's Collection

Over the years, librarians have bemoaned the paper quality as well as the quality of binding of many of the foreign books being published outside the United States. In recent years, however, librarians have noted an improved quality of both paper and binding (Artola, 1993) as foreign publishers have begun to recognize the United States market as well as the needs of U.S. libraries. Increasingly, hardback books in Spanish are being published outside the United States. Termed *pasta dura,* this particular format does not always conform to the quality of hardback books that U.S. librarians are accustomed to. The cost of book production in Spanish-speaking countries is so high for most publishers, that it makes the book binding process prohibitively expensive. Such costs are normally added on to the cost of a book by distributors and wholesalers. Most distributors offer librarians a choice that includes various options that include binding costs, and may re-bind books for an additional price per book. Libraries who do not normally bind Spanish paperbacks for children need to seriously consider doing this, especially if one consider the short life of a Spanish book at the hands of a young child. Another factor to consider is the short press runs of materials in the foreign market that diminish reprint or in print status of many children's titles. These factors should weigh heavily into the decision to bind or re-bind materials through the distributor or through other sources available through normal book processing mechanisms.

Beyond Picture Books in Spanish

Many libraries that collect books in Spanish for children tend to focus on picture books, the materials for pre-school and early elementary grades, to the detriment of materials in Spanish for good readers, the Spanish Juvenile Fiction collection. The practice corresponds to a commonly held belief that once the child begins to speak and read in English, then the transition to English begins and the purchase of materials beyond the picture books is not necessary. Such cultural assumptions reflect the ideology of a dominant culture that tolerates foreign reading only to the extent required by law. After that, many librarians insist on guiding a child's reading toward the English materials. Unfortunately, graduate training for children's librarians provides no knowledge base for the understanding of second language acquisition. Issues of bilingualism, transition, and the needs of ESL students are blurred. Dominant notions of Anglo and American culture are projected onto Spanish-speaking children in decisions not to purchase juvenile Spanish fiction or Spanish young adult materials. The result can be detrimental to Spanish readers who may not be sufficiently grounded in reading but who fall victims to the librarian's gate keeping approach to culture and reading. If librarians truly believe that reading should be for "plea-

sure" then providing Spanish materials for leisure should not be predicated upon belief systems that dictate that "these children should be reading English." Librarians should not project their own cultural assumptions and act as the 'language police' by limiting the scope of the collection by selected reading levels. Would we provide English-speaking pre-school children with reading materials sufficient to develop their language literacy, but then fail to provide them with continuing reading materials, sufficient to help them firmly establish their foundation in English? To see Spanish-speaking children delight in the joy and pleasure of reading, no matter the language, should delight all librarians who espouse the belief in reading as lifelong learning. Spanish juvenile readers should have the same right to intellectual freedom, uncensored by selection policies or criteria that limit their right to read.

Promoting the Spanish Language Children's Collection

The Spanish children's collection in the library serves an excellent purpose only to the extent to which they are utilized by the community for which they are intended. What good is it to have a collection if it is not promoted or utilized? Library administrators are keen to dismantle collections or do away with services if they feel they are not providing a useful purpose, if the books are just sitting, collecting dust. The lack of circulation of a specific book item also provides fodder for the eager eyes of librarians who wish to censor these materials in the name of good weeding practices. For these reasons, it is important to promote the materials in the collection out in the community, but most especially among the bilingual schools and classrooms where the majority of Spanish-speaking children are most likely to be enrolled.

Spanish books for children, as all books for children, must be valued and appreciated by the audiences for whom the books were intended. But if there is no audience for the materials, then the contrived mythology drives a social construction of reality that reflects an insidious attitude, expressed in the commonly heard phrase "those people don't read." It is unfair to 'blame the victim' for the non-circulating nature of the Spanish children's collection if the community itself is unaware that the material is in the library in the first place. Maintaining a collection of Spanish books demonstrates a good will effort on the part of the library system toward the Spanish-speaking community. It sends a message to the community that the public library as a public institution is committed to serving and providing for the reading needs of their children. But the Spanish children's collection in and of itself is only half the job. The other half lies in the promotion of the materials through programming that include regularly scheduled bilingual story-times and visits to bilingual classrooms. Developing a relationship with the bilingual teachers in the community will also go a long way in insuring that the materials get the most use. Libraries should design special flyers in Spanish that inform the community about the availability of these materials. The flyers can convey the message in Spanish that reading is the single most important activity that parents can do for their young children. Special measures such as these will go a long way in insuring that the Spanish collection remains a vibrant and an important part of the children's section. They can develop partner-

ships with health care providers and the existing network of social services providers in the Spanish-speaking community. They can use such ties to develop family literacy programming, and to launch outreach story-time visits to health care centers and to churches. In the long run, this will also ensure the continuance of libraries.

Implications for Library School Education

Children's services managers must insist on hiring professional bilingual children's librarians who are best qualified to serve the needs and the interests of all Spanish-speaking children included. But the burden of responsibility cannot lie strictly with the children's services manager or as a supportive library system if library schools are not attracting or producing the qualified candidates to their schools. Library schools, especially those in states with expected high Hispanic populations projected by the year 2040 including: New Mexico (55.4 percent); Texas (40.3 percent), California and Colorado (36.5 percent); Arizona (31.7 percent); Nevada (26.1 percent); Florida (21.5 percent); New Jersey (17 percent); New York (15.9 percent); and Illinois (15.7 percent) (Horner, pp. 17, 18) must re-evaluate, re-examine and re-define their commitment to the public good to insure that the term ' public' also includes the Spanish-speaking public, Spanish-speaking youth included. Library schools must develop new and creative ways to attract bilingual candidates who can best serve the needs of the Spanish-speaking youth. As *School Library Journal* so aptly put it in a recent issue: "We need more minority, bilingual and male children's librarians now, not tomorrow." Library schools must work to insure that their graduates are well trained to work with the many ethnic and language groups of American society. Would we ignore the demands of an information society by denying children or adult patrons, for that matter, access to the Internet on the basis that the present staff is not adequately prepared to face the challenges of the information highway? So, too must we insist that library schools produce quality professionals who can provide quality library services *en español*. To expect less is to short-change Spanish-speaking children of equal access to reading materials necessary for their growth and development.

References

Artola Allen, Adela. "The School Library Media Center and the Promotion of Literature for Hispanic Children." *Library Trends*, 41 (1993): 437–61.

Beilke, Patricia and Frank Sciara. 1986. *Selecting Materials for and about Hispanic and East Asian Children and Young People.* Hamden: Library Professional Publications.

Berman, Sanford. E-mail to the author. 21 December 1997.

Books in Print. 1998. New York: R. R. Bowker.

Carlson, Lori Marie. Translation: "A Struggle with Words." *School Library Journal,* vol. 41, no. 6 (1995): 40–41.

Chavez, Linda. 1990. "Collection Development for the Spanish-Speaking." *Latino Librarianship: A Handbook for Professionals,* ed. Salvador Güereña, 68-77. Jefferson, N.C.: McFarland & Company.

Cisneros, Sandra. 1991. *Woman Hollering Creek and Other Stories.* New York: Random House.

_____. 1996. *El Arroyo de la Llorona y Otros Cuentos.* New York: Vintage Espanol-Random House.

_____. 1996. *Pelitos/Hairs.* Ill. by Terry Ybanezs. Translated by Liliana Valenzuela. New York: Knopf.

Cordaso, Julie. "Talking with Pat Mora." 1997. *Book Links: Connecting Books, Libraries, and Classrooms,* vol. 7, no. 1 (September): 25

Cuesta, Yolanda, and Patricia A. Tarín. 1978. "Guidelines for Library Services to the Spanish-Speaking." *Library Journal* 103: 1354–1355.

Cunningham, Nancy. 1997. "Global Reach: An Interview with Mexican Library Association President Elsa Ramirez Leyva." *Texas Library Journal,* 73, no. 3: 108–110.

Dale, Doris Cruger. 1985. *Bilingual Books in Spanish and English for Children.* Littleton, CO: Libraries Unlimited.

Delacre, Lulu, reteller. 1996. *De Oro y Esmeralda: Mitos, Leyendas y Cuentos Populares de Latinoamerica.* Ill. by the re-teller. New York: Scholastic.

_____. 1996. *Golden Tales: Myths, Legends and Folktales from Latin America.* New York: Scholastic.

Delgado, María Isabel. 1996. *Chaves' Memories/Las Memorias de Chaves.* Houston: Piñata Books.

Duran, D. F. 1979. *Latino Materials: A Multimedia Guide for Children and Young Adults.* Santa Barbara: American Bibliographic Center with Neal-Schuman Publishers.

González, Lucía, reteller. 1997. *Señor Cat's Romance and Other Favorite Stories from Latin America.* Ill. by Lulu Delacre. New York: Scholastic.

Horner, Louise L. 1997. Table 1. Resident Population by State. Projections for 2020. *Hispanic Americans: A Statistical Sourcebook.* Palo Alto: Information Publications.

Johnson, Mary Frances. 1978. "A Guide to Spanish Language Books for Children." *Wilson Library Bulletin,* 53, no. 3: 244–248.

Libros en Venta. 1998. Baltimore, MD: National Information Services Corporation NISC USA CD Rom.

Lodge, Sally. 1995. "Speaking Their Language: Publishers discuss the challenges and rewards of Spanish-language books for kids." *Publishers Weekly,* vol. 242 (August 28): 86-89.

_____. 1997. "Spanish-language publishing for kids in the U.S. picks up speed." *Books Across the Border.* Special supplement of *Publishers Weekly,* 244, no. 35.

Schon, Isabel, et al. 1987. "Books in Spanish for Young Readers in School and Public Libraries: A Survey of Practices and Attitudes." *Library and Information Science Research,* 9, no. 1: 21–28.

School Library Journal editors. 1997. "Diversity: Still a Dream." *School Library Journal,* 43, no. 7: p 31.

Taylor, Sally. 1997. "A brave new world of books." *Books Across the Border.* Special issue of *Publishers Weekly,* 244, no. 35: S 3.

_____. "In search of the Spanish market." *Books Across the Border.* Special supplement of *Publishers Weekly,* 244, no. 35: S 3.

Watkins, Christine. 1997. "Chapter Report: Exchanging Information." *American Libraries,* 28, no. 9: 11.

Notes

1. For a complete listing of Schon's work see the web site of the Center for the Study of Books in Spanish for Children. Http://coyote.csusm.edu/campus_centers/csb/english/

2. See the 1997 edition of *Hispanic Americans: A Statitistical Sourcebook,* edited by Louise L. Horner (Palo Alto: Information Publications), for projections of Hispanic population for 2020 and 2040.

3. An adapted children's edition, beautifully illustrated by Antonio Franconi was published bilingually by Clarion Books in 1994.

4. See Wei Chi Poon's excellent article "Collection Development Principles, Guidelines and Policies" in *Developing Library Collections for California's Emerging Majority,* T. A. Scarborough, ed. (BAYLIS, September 1990) p. 22–25, for a guide to planning for ethnic collection development.

5. See Schon et al. (1987) for a study of the practices and attitudes of librarians in school and public libraries.

Appendix A: Library Terms/ Types of Materials for a Spanish Children's Collection

Fiction	Ficción
Easy	Facil
Non-fiction	No-Ficción
Information Books	Libros de Información
Big Books	Libros Grandes
ABC / I23	ABC / 123
Biography	Biografía (or)
Biographies	Biografías
Reference	Referencia or Consulta
Video	Video
Read alongs-	Libros en Cassette
CD Rom-	CD Rom

Appendix B: Recommended Distributors
of Spanish Language Children's Materials

El Almacen de Libros de Nana
(Nana's Book Warehouse)
848 Heber Ave.
Calexico, CA 92231
1-800-737-NANA
(619) 357-4271

Bilingual Publications
270 Lafayette Suite 705
New York, NY 10012
(212) 431-3500
(212) 431-3567 (fax)
Books on Wings

Donars
P. O. Box 808
Lafayette, CO 80026
1-800-552-3316
(970) 663-2124
(970) 667-5337 (fax)

Hispanic Books Distributors
1665 W. Grant Rd.
Tucson, AZ 85745
1-800-632124

Lectorum
111 8th St.
New York, NY 10011-5201
1-800-345-5946
(212) 929-2833

Libros Sin Fronteras
P. O. Box 2085 Olympia, WA 98507-2085
1-800-454-2767
206-357-4332 (FAX)
libros@wln.com

Mariuccia Iaconi Book Imports
970 Tennessee St.
San Francisco, CA 94107
1-800-955-9577
(415) 821-1596
(415) 821-1596 (fax)

CHAPTER EIGHT

Considerations for the Development of Spanish Language Collections in School Libraries

Hector Marino

The education of children whose native or dominant language is other than English has become an area of major concern to educators in the United States. The failure of these students in the traditional "English only" curriculum has been documented in numerous reports, among them the Coleman study of 1966 and various compilations of the U. S Commission on Civil Rights (1971, 1973, 1975). Court cases such as Lau v. Nichols 1974 and Serna v. Portales 1974 have further served to focus attention on the unique educational needs of many linguistic and cultural minorities and upon their legal right to obtain appropriate instruction.

In the near future, one out of every four American public school children will come from a minority ethnic group. Of today's K–12 public student population, 5 million cannot fully understand or fluently speak and read English. Most of them are new immigrants who speak Spanish at home and entered school in the last decade. The percentage of students whose native language is Spanish continues to grow (it is now more than 25 percent in California, nearly 50 percent in Los Angeles), with many from poor or single parent families.

Despite this significant change in the composition of American classrooms and studies such as the recent one from The National Research Council which found that students who used books in their native language are more likely to develop high levels of English proficiency, school libraries have been slow to respond. One major problem frequently cited in serving bilingual and limited English proficiency (LEP) students is the lack of native language materials and the unavailability of bilingual library staff. (Krashen, Pucci, Allen). However, this new multicultural student body, reflecting the country's pluralistic society, dictates that immediate attention be paid to the educational resources needed by these students.

As stated in the 1988 *Information Power*, the first national school library media guidelines since 1976, one of the missions and challenges of today's school libraries is to: "provide resources and learning activities that represent a diversity of experiences, opinions, and social and cultural perspectives, supporting the concept that intellectual freedom and access to information are prerequisite to effective and responsible citizenship and to democracy."

To meet these guidelines and to respond to these demographic changes, school library media centers (SLMC) must reexamine their standards and decisions regarding information access. Students with non–English language proficiency do not have equal access if the only information available to them is in a language they cannot read. School districts need to be aware that failure to remedy this situation could result in a legal action against the school district.

The major focus of this chapter concerns the school library and its ability to effectively serve LEP students, primarily Spanish-speaking children, with increased holdings and appropriate collections. This article will provide basic recommendations for collection development in order to meet the needs of the new school children.

Also given here is a sample Spanish language collection development policy formulated in a large public school district.

Strategies for the Selection and Acquisition of Spanish Language Materials

One of the most important responsibilities of any school library media specialist is to purchase appropriate materials for those individuals who will use the collection. The importance of selecting materials that will satisfy the needs, interests, and abilities of all students in the school is paramount.

To be truly inclusive, school library media centers with a population of linguistically and culturally diverse students have an obligation to provide books and materials that specifically meet the needs and interests of these students. For this reason, and to promote multicultural awareness among the school's English-dominant students, the school library collection must contain works in both the students' native language and English about students' native countries and books by and about authors from these countries (Dame).

Specific Strategies

The following are a few of the most important strategies that school library media specialists should consider as they assume their role in serving Spanish-language students:

1. Formulate a written collection development policy with the help of interested and knowledgeable teachers, administrators, community members and librarians.

This policy is a powerful document

for decision making and action. Once approved by the school board, it fosters not only continuity and stability but also serves to educate decision makers on the purpose and future direction of the school library program.

2. Collect information about the local community, the school, its students and its faculty through demographic data on ethnicity, socioeconomic levels, general educational level, drop-out rate, age distribution, and other factors.

Keep in mind that while Latinos are united by a common Spanish language, they are divided by geography, country of origin, cultural heritage, class, and the time and circumstances of their arrival. Each subgroup is distinct and best understood individually (Cuesta).

3. Explore funding sources, including the instructional budget, federal and state grants and formal cooperation among media centers, public, special, and other libraries.

Adequate financial support is crucial to any program of development. Cultural diversity in the collection is far too important to depend solely on special and temporary funding. It must be integrated into every area of the collection and be part of the regular SLMC budget.

4. Determine which materials are needed to support the school/district curriculum.

5. Create a selection committee composed of native language teachers to judge the Spanish-language material to be purchased. The following questions should be considered:

- Does the book reflect the culture of origin or has it been altered so that it seems to be an American version?
- Does the book reflect specifics within the culture without distorting or stereotyping those elements?

- If the book is translated, is it true to the spirit of the original and are the illustrations still appropriate?
- Are various ethnic groups' contributions to American history and contemporary life shown?
- If the book is historical fiction, does it present the pre–Columbian cultures from a Mexican or Latin American perspective or from an old-colonial Spanish perspective?
- Is the Spanish-language spelled correctly and used appropriately? Are accents in their proper places?
- Who appears to be the primary audience for this material?
- Are authors/publishers of various countries represented?

Origin of Book

The school media specialist should be aware of the different variations of the Spanish language. Although Spanish is spoken around the world by millions, the grammar and vocabulary of each country varies. While Spanish language material is more readily available from publishers in Spain, this material, because of these language variations, is often inappropriate. Students will be confused by unfamiliar grammar structure and vocabulary. Whenever possible, it is preferable to purchase books written by authors from the country of origin of the students.

The origin of the book can be ascertained through its International Standard Book Number (ISBN), a unique number for each title, edition of a book, or monographic publication published or produced by a specific publisher or producer. Each ISBN consists of ten digits separated into the following parts: Group identifier (country), publisher or producer identifier, title identifier, check digit.

The ISBN for some Spanish-language countries are coded in the first two or three digits. For example the ISBN 950-08-0366-6 includes the following information:

950 = Argentina
08 = Publisher
0366 = Title identifier
6 = Check digit

Major Spanish-language countries and their codes are the following:

Mexico   (968 and 970)
Spain   (84)
Argentina (950)
Venezuela (980)
Colombia (958)

Acquisitions

In the absence of a qualified selection process, many school libraries use vendor catalogs with a preponderance of translations of popular English-language classics, core collections put together by distributors, and visits to local bookstores. Often jobbers submit approval plans that list surplus titles that publishers hope to sell and not necessarily the most appropriate material. In other words, the task is turned over to vendors.

This haphazard method of selection does not result in the most appropriate collection for students. It is important that selection be based on the needs of the students. Only after comprehensive lists of recommended material for elementary and secondary students have been developed, and after hands-on access to representative publisher material to ascertain quality by your selection committee should

books be ordered. Sometimes publishers and distributors offer samples or preview material that can facilitate the selection.

After selection, a reliable vendor can easily integrate the purchase from several sources to reduce the cost and delivery of the material.

Conclusion and Recommendations

The population of Spanish-language readers in the public schools will continue to grow in coming years and school libraries must address the special needs of this group. Through a combined effort of community and school representatives, material which enhances the learning of students can systematically be added to the library collection.

Building school collections of Spanish-language materials takes long-term commitment, sensitivity, and hard work. Ideally, every school district with a significant number of Spanish speakers should have a staff member specifically assigned to the acquisition of these materials. Library staff who work in this field must become competent in recognizing the literature, the publishers and distributors.

Once significant development of the collection has begun, the librarian should promote its use among the school staff and parents. These groups should be encouraged to explore the acquired titles so that they may recommend their use to students. Upon reviewing the collection, teachers will be able to suggest additional material to be added. To increase use, librarians should also develop programming related to the collection. For example, they might host a party to celebrate a holiday or other special day celebrated in a particular country.

There is little doubt that school libraries play an important role in our increasingly multicultural society and that a well-planned and representative collection can add to the educational experience of every student.

The following is an example of a Spanish Language Collection Development Policy developed by a school district in a major metropolitan area with a large Latino population in the public schools. As the majority of that population is Mexican, the policy specifically addresses acquiring material for that population. This policy was formulated over 1995–1997 by a committee composed of school administrators, teachers, and librarians.

Spanish Language Collection Development Policy

Mission Statement

The _____ Public Schools Library Media Centers (SLMCs), through their Spanish language collections value and reflect the diversity and changing needs of the Spanish speaking students and community. School librarians strive to improve the quality of education in our schools through excellence in library services and collections that support the curriculum and the recreational needs of the students. We seek to provide materials that will encourage each student to achieve to the best of his/her ability; enhance lifelong learning through the promotion of information literacy, and provide the instructional resources students need to pursue educational goals.

Students and teachers should have ready access to a wide range of print and non-print resources. The collection should include current, representative, and relevant resources and information in amounts which satisfy instructional needs and match individual and learning styles. Library Media Centers promote literacy and the enjoyment of reading, viewing, and listening for young people of all ages and stages of development.

Goals

1. The Spanish language collections of the _____ Public Schools' SLMC's will manifest, acknowledge and validate the diverse cultural heritage and experiences of the Spanish-speaking community.

2. The _____ Public School's SLMC's will have a district-wide collection that will support the educational , informational, cultural, and recreational needs of all ages and reading levels within the Spanish-speaking student population of _____ Public Schools.

3. The _____ Public Schools' SLMC's will be responsive to demographics and the changing needs of the Spanish-speaking population of _____.

4. The _____ Public Schools will have library staff in each school who are informed, trained, capable and motivated to meet the special requirements of service

to the Spanish-speaking community. Learning basic Spanish skills will become part of in-service training for librarians and support staff in bilingual schools.

5. The _____ Public Schools' SLMC's will provide appropriate access to the Spanish language collections in each school.

6. The _____ Public Schools' SLMC will be responsive to the needs of the school/district's Spanish-speaking students, acknowledging their linguistic and cultural characteristics.

7. The _____ Public Schools' SLMC's subscribe to the Library Bill of Rights, and will help to inform and educate the Spanish-speaking population on issues of intellectual freedom.

Objectives

1. Determine and identify the levels and ranges of need for Spanish language materials in each school.

2. Determine the percentage of the SLMC budget to be spent for Spanish language materials to reflect the linguistic needs of the student population. (Budget).

3. Define and establish, district wide, a complete Spanish language collection ranging from core to reference collections. (See Standards....).

4. Solicit and encourage the participation of the Spanish-speaking community in the planning and acquisition of the district's Spanish language collections.

5. Devise and implement a district-wide staff development plan for library staff responsible for delivery of service to Spanish speaking users.

6. Provide and purchase materials from different sources that reflect the diversity of cultures of the users of the Spanish language collections.

7. Select materials representing a variety of point of views; develop Spanish language collections on an inclusive rather than an exclusive basis.

8. Provide relevant, up-to-date print and electronic materials of high quality, and follow procedures for maintaining currency of information.

9. Catalog and process all Spanish language materials in a timely fashion. Cataloging will include full level of cataloging with an accurate Dewey classification number, Spanish/English titles, and subject headings in Spanish and in English. The statement of responsibility should always include the name of the translator which should also be traced in an added entry. Notes or annotations and the summary of the work should be added.

10. Develop clear and consistent signs for all locations where Spanish language materials and related services are available. This includes Spanish/English library forms, notices, signs and informational/instructional publications.

11. Establish and maintain systems of contact with other institutions, such as public and university libraries; utilize and expand existing networks to share information pertaining to Spanish language materials.

Review and evaluate annually all of the above points, and revise or redirect them as necessary.

Budget

1. The budget plan should begin with an analysis of the goals and objectives of the SLMC to identify the expenditures needed to operate the programs as planned. Individual school district budgeting procedures differ considerably. Therefore these suggestions must be adapted to each district's budget requirements.

2. Because the library media specialist may be competing for funds with other departments in the school, budgets must be carefully thought out in close cooperation with the building principal.

3. Negotiate the budget in such a way that the library media specialist does not have to confront staff members with whom s/he must work. District guidelines can reduce the adversarial role and preserve equity across the district.

4. Sources of funding

Funding sources for Spanish language materials in the school/district include, but are not limited to:

- Regular LMC budget from the Administration/Staff Development/ Libraries line item.

- State Department allocation of $_____ per pupil for instructional materials, which may include library materials.

- Federal funding (i.e., titles I and VII)

- Private grants.

- School-wide fund raisers/PTA funds.

- Gifts.

Selection

General Criteria

Each site librarian will form a collection development committee in his or her own building. This committee will advise and help in the preview and selection of appropriate Spanish language materials based on the criteria described below. The committee will include at least one fluent Spanish speaker who can adequately judge the quality of the language and/or translation.

As with English language collections, quality is the highest priority for Spanish language materials. This includes not only the caliber of writing, but also the accuracy of reference data and translation where applicable, as well as the quality of illustration and overall production/packing quality.

Production values vary from publisher to publisher. The selector should base his decisions on first-hand examination whenever possible. Hardcovers and library bindings, when available, are preferable over paperbacks. Poor quality bindings can be re-bound at a cost of approximately $ 5.00 prior to circulation, if necessary. Durability increases cost-effectiveness. Since the majority of users of the school/district's Spanish language collections are of Mexican origin, materials originating in Mexico by Mexican authors or Mexican-American authors are most appropriate when available. Careful consideration should be given to vocabulary and grammatical variations when materials originate in Spain or other Spanish-speaking countries.

Translations of books from English are not always of equal relevance or reading levels for students. Translated works should be carefully evaluated for quality of translation, keeping in mind that works done originally in Spanish are preferable to translations. In children's materials, an additional concern should be the appropriateness of illustrations. It is important to avoid cultural stereotypes and to include literate role models. Selectors of materials for young adults should be wary of extremes of literalness or generality that can render a translated work useless.

Use of dual language material, that is material with the same content in two languages side by side, is not recommended. Use of such material often leads to greater confusion for all the native speakers who are learning English. A related concern to selectors of Spanish language materials is currency of information in non-fiction items. Errors and misrepresentations can slip past publishers just as easily as inaccurate translations; this is another factor in favor of personal examination of materials.

Selection tools for Spanish language materials differ from those for English language materials in one crucial factor: there are fewer conventional sources. Librarians must be particularly alert not only for review sources, but also for selection tools appearing in the library literature, publishers trade publications, reference resources, workshops, conferences, and book fairs. Resources also appear with increasing regularity via the Internet. The expertise of colleagues is also a valid source.

Some review sources include *Booklist, School Library Journal, The Reading Teacher, Multicultural Review, Journal of Reading, Nexos, Azteca, Boletín International, Uno Mas Uno,* and *La Opinión*. It is recommended that schools consider subscribing to one or more of the above, as well as to any other review publication relating to Spanish language materials.

High quality and cultural relevance in Spanish language collections will foster repeated use and exploration of other collection areas.

Standards for a Spanish Language Library Collection

1. The Spanish-language library collection should support the major content areas of _____ school/district's curriculum and represent a balanced range of student interest and needs, including the appreciation of literature.

2. The collection should be consistent with the general criteria for selection established in the *Spanish Language Collection Development Policy*.

3. The collection shall include reference and browsing materials that will support the educational, informational, cultural and recreational needs of all ages and reading levels within the Spanish-speaking student population.

4. The size of the collection should be dependent upon the total of Spanish-speaking students served.

> a) The Spanish-language collection for a school of 200 or more students should be based on the following formula: *10 titles × number of monolingual students*
>
>> EXAMPLE: This "extensive" option should include:
>> | | |
>> |---|---|
>> | print and nonprint materials | 2,000 titles |
>> | magazines | 10 |
>> | newspapers | 2 |
>> | film, videos, etc. | from the Bilingual Central Library |
>
>> NOTE: 1. The above represents an average collection for 200 or more Spanish-speaking students regardless of the type of school (elementary or secondary).
>>
>> 2. The browsing collection should include 10 titles per student with multiple copies as needed. This collection shall include 2 or 3 items in non-print format such as kits, videotapes, audiocassettes and CD-ROMs.
>
> b) The Spanish-language collection for a school of 199 or less students should be based on the following formula: *5 titles × number of monolingual students* .
>
>> EXAMPLE: This "basic" option should include:
>> | | |
>> |---|---|
>> | print and nonprint materials | 500 titles |
>> | magazines | 5 |
>> | newspapers | 2 |
>> | film, videos, etc. | from the Bilingual Central Library |
>
>> NOTE: 1. The above represents an average basic collection for 100 Spanish-speaking students regardless of the type of school (elementary or secondary)
>>
>> 2. The browsing collection should include 5 titles per student with multiple copies needed. This collection shall include 2 or 3 items in non-print format such as kits, videotapes, audiocassettes and CD-ROMs.

5. The reference collection should include at least one current set of encyclopedia and the following *reference* material:

> Atlases
> Dictionary (Spanish only)
> Dictionary (English/Spanish–Spanish/English)
> Thesaurus
> Fact books
> World almanac

6. The *browsing* collection for secondary schools should reflect the diversity of Spanish speakers, including the diversity of educational backgrounds which commonly exist among Spanish-speaking populations. Materials should be provided at all levels of complexity, for a full range of interests, with emphasis on works originally written in Spanish. Items to be selected should include works from Latin America and classics from Spain, with emphasis on works from Mexico. Also deserving of particular representation is the Hispanic/Latino tradition in the U.S., which has been given voice in fiction, non-fiction and poetry.

a) Fiction:

> • Classics of young adult literature should emphasize authors who write originally in Spanish, for example, Pablo Neruda, Octavio Paz, Carlos Fuentes, Isabel Allende, Gabriel García Márquez, Jorge Luis Borges, Julio Cortazar, Mario Vargas Llosa, and Miguel de Cervantes.

> • Folk tales
> • Short stories
> • Novels
> • Poetry

b) Non-Fiction: (major topics of the school district standards for each subject area)

> Spanish language non-fiction collections are curriculum specific, and in this sense differ little from non-fiction collections in English. Topics include: environmental issues, science, history, economics, politics, geography, math, folklore, cultural festivities, sports, the arts, all aspects of the U.S./Latino experience, psychology, self-help, teen-age health problems, and drugs.

c) Biographies: (at least 6 titles)

> The Spanish language biography collection should provide positive role models for Spanish-speaking youth. People represented should come from a variety of socio cultural and economic backgrounds. The following are examples of significant Latino figures:

> • Cesar Chavez
> • Benito Juarez
> • Emiliano Zapata

      • Pancho Villa
      • Frida Kahlo
      • Joan Baez
      • Gloria Estefan
      • Pablo Picasso
      • Diego Rivera
      • Isabel Allende

d) ESL Materials

e) Periodicals:
Printed format:
      • Magazines:(i.e., *Geomundo, Hispanic, Tú, Americas, Mecanica Popular*)
      • Foto-novelas
      • Local newspapers:
Non-Printed format:
      • Electric Library
      • Ebsco with configured help screens in Spanish
      • SIRS Research
      • Discover

f) Non-print formats:
      • CD-ROMS
      • Videos
      • Kits

7. The *browsing* collection for elementary schools should include:

Wordless books, picture books, pattern books, emergent readers, and folk tales (including indigenous mythology, Spanish language nursery rhymes, songs, riddles, tongue twisters, etc.) are appropriate for all elementary grades.

a) Fiction:

Selections should include easy chapter books, children's novels, series, and classics. The classics of children's literature should emphasize authors who write originally in Spanish.

      • Folk tales
      • Indigenous mythology
      • Songs
      • Short stories
      • Traditions
      • Holidays
      • Poetry

b) Non-Fiction:

A basic Spanish language non-fiction collection should fill the informational and recreational needs of children at all reading levels. Spanish language non-fiction for juveniles will be collected in the same areas as English with emphasis on curriculum-related and recreational topics popular with children:

- Science
- History
- Economics
- Geography
- Math

c) Biographies: (at least 6 titles)

Biographies which feature both historic and current Hispanic personalities are becoming increasingly available and should be an important part of the non-fiction collection. Works selected should provide positive role models for Spanish-speaking children. People represented should come from a variety of socioeconomic and cultural backgrounds. The following are examples of people elementary school students would be interested in reading about:

- Cesar Chavez
- Benito Juarez
- Emiliano Zapata
- Pancho Villa
- Frida Kahlo
- Joan Baez
- Gloria Estefan
- Cervantes
- Pablo Casals
- Pablo Picasso
- Diego Rivera

d) ESL Materials (High interest, low vocabulary)

e) Periodicals:
   Printed format:
   - Magazines: (i.e., *Scholastic-en-Español, Billiken, Highlights*)
   - Local newspapers:
   Non-Printed format:
   - Electric Library
   - Ebsco with configured help screens in Spanish
   - Discover

f) Non-print formats:
   - CD-ROMS
   - Videos
   - Kits (Tape, book, and teacher's guide).
   - Computer applications (i.e., "Kid's catalog")

References

Allen, Adela Artola. 1987. *Library Services for Hispanic Children: A Guide for Public and School Librarians.* Phoenix: Oryx Press.

American Association of School Librarians. 1988. *Information Power: Guidelines for School Library Media Programs.* Chicago: American Library Association.

Cuesta, Yolanda J. From Survival to Sophistication: Hispanics Needs—Library Needs. *Library Journal* 115 (May 15, 1990): 26–28.

Dame, Melvina Azar. 1993. *Serving Linguistically and Culturally Diverse Students.* New York: Neal-Schuman.

Güereña, Salvador, ed. 1990. *Latino Librarianship: A Handbook for Professionals.* Jefferson, N.C : McFarland.

Krashen, Stephen. 1997. *Why Bilingual Education?* ERIC Clearinghouse on Rural Education and Small Schools.

National Research Council. 1997. *Improving Schooling for Language-Minority Children: A Research Agenda.* Washington, D.C.: National Academy Press.

Pucci, S. L. Supporting Spanish-language Literacy: Latino Children and Free Reading Resources in Schools. *Bilingual Research Journal* 18, no. 1–2 (1994)): 67–68.

Schon, I., Hopkins, K. D., & Davis, W. A.. The Effects of Books in Spanish and Free Reading Time on Hispanic Students: reading abilities and attitudes. *The Journal of the National Association for Bilingual Education* 7 (1982): 13–20.

Tarín, Patricia A.. Books for the Spanish-Speaking Si Se Puede. *Library Journal* 112 (July 1987): 25–28.

Valencia, R. R. 1996. Latinos and Education: An Overview of Socio-demographic and Schooling Conditions. Paper presented at the 1996 Educational Test Service Invitational Conference on Latino Issues. Princeton, N.J.: ETS.

White, Howard D. 1990. School Library Collections and Services. *School Library Media Quarterly,* Fall 13–20.

Publishers

This listing includes publishers of Spanish language educational materials.

A. M. Data Systems [www.libertynet.com] produces educational software on CD-ROM and diskettes for IBM and Macintosh computers. Ethnic groups include African, Asian, European, Hispanic and Native Americans.

Addison-Wesley Longman [www.aw.com] provides language arts K–4, and Math 8–12.

The Agora Language Marketplace [www.agoralang.com/] an on-line index of companies offering language related publications, products, and services and an information source for the foreign language professional.

Altus (MEXICO) produces excellent multimedia in Spanish.

Amaquemecan (MEXICO) excellent picture books, folk tales and short stories. Some books on or about children with disabilities.

America's Stirfry [www.americas-stirfry .com] offers a broad variety of educational books and videos in English, and Spanish.

Anaya (SPAIN) [www.anaya.es] the largest conglomerate in the Spanish publishing world. Publications includes children's books, Dorling Kindersley and fiction translations, and major encyclopedias, also produces CD-ROM's multimedia.

Andres Bello (CHILE) children's books from Chile.

Annick Press, Ltd. (CANADA) easy children's literature.

Arte Publico Press [www.bookwire.com/book.info] fiction and children books in both English and Spanish. Language arts (Literature) K–12.

Aspectos culturales produces social sciences K–12.

Atlantida (ARGENTINA) original fiction, DK and extensive collection of U.S. fiction in translations, young adult titles and the popular series "Choose your adventure"

Avante (MEXICO) excellent variety of educational books.

Barron's Educational Series, Inc. [www.agoralang.com] site presents the Foreign Service Institute Language Series training program which includes French, Hebrew, Korean, German, Italian, Portuguese, Greek, Japanese and Spanish.

BilinguaTec books, magazines and software in both English and Spanish.

Binet Bilingual Software offers language arts (literature), science K–6, software and tapes.

Broderbund Software [www.broder.com] excellent source for international software.

Cal y arena (MEXICO) authentic fiction and children's literature.

Cambridge University Press [www.cup.org] printing and publishing house of the University of Cambridge with academic and educational books, journals, ESL and Spanish language materials.

Cascadilla Press Home Page [http://www1.shore.net/~cascadil/linguistics.html] site provides information on linguistics books and software.

Castillo (MEXICO) excellent and inexpensive K–12 textbooks, some fiction by local authors.

Charlesbridge Publishing [www.charlesbridge.com] fiction and non-fiction in both English and Spanish mostly translations. Language arts, science K–6 and Math 2–3.

Chelsea House Publishers [www.chelseahouse.com] produces biographies.

Children of the Sun: [www.brightmoments.com/blackhistory] Multicultural Resources focuses on culturally conscious multicultural literature, audio books, and information on and about children with varying degrees of social and cultural traditions.

Children's Book Press excellent awarded bilingual books. Language arts (literature) K–6.

Children's Press presents translations appropriate for language arts (literature) and science K–2.

CIDCLI (MEXICO) [www.cidcli.com.mx] excellent original children's literature from Mexico.

Citem (MEXICO) limited production of pop-up children's books.

Colihue (ARGENTINA) excellent children's books by local authors.

Conafe (MEXICO) offers superior children's books produced by small local publishers. Publishes popular series "Educacion ambiental" Language. Language arts (literature) K–8.

Corunda (MEXICO) limited original collection of children's works. Includes works by author Silvia Molina and the excellent series "La tortuga veloz."

Crabtree Publishing [www.crabtree-pub.com] children's books and K–9 curriculum material.

Curbstone Press [www.connix.com/~curbston] about by Latino authors, few in Spanish.

Curriculum Associates [www.ultranet.com/cainfo] offers educational books, multimedia software and videos for elementary and secondary school, special education, workplace and adult education.

Dawn Publications [www.dawnpub.com] has interesting translated children's books on environmental protection. Science K–6.

De la Flor (ARGENTINA) serious literature by Argentine writers and works in translation; humor, especially well-known "Mafalda" and other Argentine humorists; children's books.

Diana (MEXICO) popular literature, technical books, general non-fiction, ESL, translations and Dorling Kindersley books in Spanish.

Dominie Press, Inc. [www.dominie.com] produces popular series "Libros carrusel."

Editer fiction books focuses on local Hispanic authors. In Spanish.

Educal, S.A (MEXICO) mostly local literature and few children books.

Ekare (VENEZUELA) superb contemporary children's literature based on Venezuela and translations of oustanding children's literature by world-wide base of children's authors.

El Ateneo (ARGENTINA) publishes K–12 textbooks and non-fiction material.

Emece (ARGENTINA) [www.emece.com.ar] original fiction by Argentine and Latin American writers; tremendous selection of U.S bestsellers in translations.

Entre Mundos Publications publishes books by Latino and Latina authors on the Latinos experience in the United States.

Esfinge (MEXICO) publishes educational K–12 textbooks and some classical works in Spanish.

Estrada (ARGENTINA) [www.el-libro.com] specializes in K–12 textbooks.

Eurolibros (COLOMBIA) superb children's books, though limited, for science and language arts areas.

Exceller Software [www.exceller.com] ESL and foreign language reference and instructional software programs for Windows and Macintosh.

Everest (SPAIN) leader publisher for children's books, eyewitness books and encyclopedias.

Fernandez (MEXICO) [www.fesa.com.mx] publishes K–12 textbooks, educational material, children's literature classics and translations. Language arts (workbooks—writing), science, math and social science.

Fondo de Cultura Economica (MEXICO) [fceusa.com] publishes popular series "A la orilla del viento," picture books from Mexico, children's literature in translation and social sciences.

Gessler Educational Software [www.gessler.com] a exciting variety of educational software.

Glencoe/McGraw-Hill [www.glencoe.com] publisher for Grades 6–12: print and electronic materials for literacy, ESL, foreign languages, language arts, and other subject areas.

Globe Fearon Educational offers excellent social studies books for middle and high schools.

Grolier lists excellent encyclopedias produced in Mexico.

Hachette Latinoamerica, S.A publishes excellent reference materials.

Hands-on English contains teaching materials for teachers and tutors of adult ESL students.

Hampton-Brown Books publishes excellent material by Alma Flor Ada and selected children's books.

Harcourt Brace School Publishers [www.hbschool.com] learning site that includes educational activities for children, teaching and learning resources, parent and staff development and technology training.

HarpersCollins exciting translated reading series.

Heinemann [www.macmillan.com.mx] publisher of professional materials and provider of professional training for teachers K–College.

Heinle & Heinle Publishers [www.heinle.com] publishes original texts, software, and multimedia products for students and educators in foreign languages and ESL/EFL programs.

Houghton-Mifflin [www.hmco.com] publisher of textbooks, instructional technology, assessments and other educational materials for K–College.

Laredo Publishing superb collection of picture books by Alma Flor Ada and Vivi Escriva.

Larousse (MEXICO) leading publisher of reference books, especially dictionaries. subject-arranged encyclopedias, ESL and audiocassettes. Children's books introduced by Hemma.

Lectorum [www.lectorum.com] publishes beautiful children books.

Lee & Low Books (www.leeandlow.com) multicultural literature for children.

Limusa/Noriega (MEXICO) children's literature, atlas, and technical books especially translated works on technology.

Los Andes Publishing, Inc. [www.losandes.com] focuses on K–12 Spanish literature, textbooks, software, content materials, and computer books.

Macmillan/McGraw-Hill School Division [www.mmhschool.com] contains K–8 educational materials, multimedia software, videodiscs, and videotapes. Areas covered are Reading/Language Arts, Mathematics, Social Studies, Music, and Bilingual programs.

Many Cultures Publishing [www.studycenter.org/mcp.html] develops, produces, markets and distributes educational materials, multicultural curriculum units bilingual storybooks with audio cassettes and teacher's guides.

Marin Publications publishes U.S history and 8–12 social studies materials.

McGrawHill-Mexico site is in Spanish and provides books and information in Spanish for professionals in the fields of education, and business.

MECC (Minnesota Educational Computer Consortium) foreign language material.

Milliken Publishing Company [www.millikenpub.com] produces K–12 supplementary, educational products, resource guides, cross-curricular theme units and software.

Mimosa Publications translated educational material. Math K–3.

Monteavila (VENEZUELA) [www.monteavila.com] serious literature by local and Latin American authors, and children books.

Multicultural Publishing and Education Council [www.mpec.org] national networking and support organization of African, Arab, Asian, Hispanic, Jewish, Latino, Pacific Islander, Native, and European-American publishers of authentic multicultural materials.

Multilingual Bookstore [www.esl.net] source of books in over 100 languages, ESL teaching materials, and general language teaching and learning materials.

Network of Educators on the Americas (NECA) multicultural publications that go beyond "heroes and holidays." NECA publications help integrate the experiences of the peoples who have been left in the margins of the curriculum: African Americans, Latinos, Asians, women, and working class people of all races.

Norma (Colombia) the largest publisher in Colombia, part of the Carbajal Group, publishes children's books by local and international authors, adult non-fiction and multimedia encyclopedia "Domine" CD-ROM.

North-South Books publisher of children's books by European authors.

One World: Multicultural Titles (Ballantine) includes books written by and focused on African Americans, Native Americans, Asian Americans, and Latino Americans

Optical Data School Media [www.opticaldata.com] produces science and math programs and curriculums, videodisc-based problem-solving and science programs and supplemental science programs for minorities in science.

Oxford University Press USA [www.oup-usa.org] publishes works in all academic disciplines, children's books, materials for teaching ESL, dictionaries and reference books.

Pangea (MEXICO) publishes children's books by local authors and excellent biographies.

Patria (MEXICO) publishes K–12 textbooks, fiction, non-fiction and bestseller series "Piñata."

Pioneer Living in the USA practical publications in simple English for ESL teachers, immigrants, refugees, and all foreign born Americans.

Pleasant Company [www.redcrane.com] publishes excellent series "Josefina, an American girl."

Prentice-Hall (MEXICO) K–12 educational material and U.S translations especially works on technology.

Prentice-Hall Regents [www.phregents. com] a leading publisher of K–12, Adult and Academic ESL, EFL, VESL and ESOL books, and multimedia materials.

Quirquincho (ARGENTINA) [www.quir quincho.com.ar] excellent chapter books by creative local authors.

Red Crane Books [www.redcrame.com] books on all aspects of the Southwest.

Rourke Publishing Group translated books for language arts, social studies and science K–8.

Rigby [www.rigby.com] offers translated educational material for language arts K–6.

Santillana (SPAIN) [www.santillana.com.ar/] K–12 textbooks, fiction and non-fiction children's books.

Scholastic, Inc. [www.scholastic.com] children books on language Arts, mathematics, science, multilingual and multicultural education.

ScottForesman [aw.com/sf] educational publisher in curriculum areas, and distributor of interactive multimedia products for modern languages.

Selector (MEXICO) produces non-fiction, inexpensive format. Some original fiction from Mexico.

Shen's Books and Supplies [www.shens. com] publishes books on peoples of Asia, Australia, Europe and Latin America, distributes books in Spanish and Asian languages and provides professional materials for teachers.

Sigmar (ARGENTINA) excellent children's books especially early-childhood. Translations of Dorling-Kindersley books.

Silver Burdett Ginn [www.sbgschool.com]

reading and language arts 3–6 and math K–6.

Sitesa (MEXICO) children's books, including some translations of American classics, and science for children.

SM (SPAIN) leading publisher located in Madrid, especialized in children's, young adult books and textbooks especially produced for Puerto Rico schools. Published popular series "Mundo maravilloso" and chapter books "El barco de vapor."

SpanPress Inc. excellent Spanish language materials. Featuring author Cecilia Avalos. Language arts K–6.

Sudamericana (ARGENTINA) original fiction by local and Latin American writers; excellent of U.S non-fiction in translation; exciting original works for children by noted Argentine children's authors and illustrators.

Sundance bilingual material. Language arts K–4.

Tecolote (MEXICO) very exciting, though limited, collection of children's books on the culture and history of Mexico. Publisher of the popular series "Ya veras."

Televisa (MEXICO) [www.televisa.com] publishes World Almanac in Spanish and specializes in Spanish magazines.

Time/Life [www.timelifeedu.com] has an Illustrated Science Encyclopedia and A Child First Library of Learning in Spanish.

TIYM Publishing Company [www.tiym. com] products include the Anuario Hispano-Hispanic Yearbook, resource directories, and a scholarship database for minorities.

Trillas (MEXICO) excellent, inexpensive, extensive collection of books in all fields, primarily educational. Original children's books and translations of U.S classics.

Vergara (ARGENTINA) general non-fiction and bestsellers galore.

Video On Line Services Internet based online service in thirty-eight languages; Spanish, Arabic, Chinese, French, Greek, etc.

World of Reading Foreign Language and ESL [www.wor.com] software, books, tapes, and videos.

Book Distributors

AFB [www.afb-adlers.com] specializes in Spanish novels, anthologies and dictionaries. 8220 Christina Ave. Skokie, IL 60079 (800) 235-3771, (708) 676-9944 fax (708) 676-9909

Aims International extensive list of material from Latin America and Spain. 7709 Hamilton Ave. Cincinnati, OH 45231 (800) 733-2067, (513) 521-5590 fax (513) 521-5592

Astran exciting collection of Spanish language books mostly from Spain. 591 SW 8th St. Miami, FL 33130 (305) 858-4300 fax (305) 858-0405

Bilingual Books For Kids [www.bilingual books.com] distributes books, musical and language-learning tapes, and games for the bilingual kids.

Bilingual Educational Services offers bound books. 2514 S Grand Ave Los Angeles, CA 90007 (800) 448-6032, (213) 749-6213 fax (213) 749-1820

Books on Wings good collection of material for libraries.

Chulainn well organized selection of Spanish language titles. 28625 Kennedy Gulch Rd. Conifer, CO 80433 9303) 838-4375 fax (303) 838-4791

Continental Book Co. books, dictionaries and encyclopedias from Spain and Latin America 80-00 Cooper Ave, Bldg.#29 Glendale, NY 11385 (718) 326-0560 fax (718) 326-4276

D.D.L. Books Inc. selective list of educational material including books from Spain. 6521 NW 87 Ave Miami, FL 33178 (800) 635-4276, (305) 592-5929 fax (305) 477-5632

Delta Systems Home Page [www.delta-systems.com] distributes ESL/EFL and foreign language materials in Spanish and other languages.

Donars Spanish Books distributes Spanish language materials. 653 Cressa Dr. Loveland, CO 80537 (800) 552-3316

Econo-Clad [www.econoclad.com] extensive list of translations. Services includes bindery and cataloging.

El Almacen de Libros de Nana selective list of excellent books. 848 Heber Ave. Calexico, CA 92231 (800) 737-6262 fax (619) 357-4271

Giron Spanish Book Distributors unique list of books, primarily from Mexico.

Hispanic Books Distributors complete list of bilingual and Spanish titles. 1665 W Grant Rd. Tucson, AZ 85745 (520) 882-9484 fax (520) 882-7696

Lectorum Publications, Inc. [www.lectorum.com] the largest book distributor of Spanish language materials. 137 W 14th St. New York, NY 10011 (800) 345-5946 (212) 929-2833 fax 727-3035

Libros Sin Fronteras [www.wln.com/libros] excellent list of titles from the Americas. P.O Box 2085 Olympia, WA 98507-2085 (206) 357-4332 (voice/fax). (800) 454-2767 (orders)

Madera Videos unique list of videos in English and Spanish.

Mariuccia Iaconi Book Imports [www.mibibook.com] distributes Spanish books for children, literature kits and reference books. 970 Tennessee St. San Francisco, CA 94107 (800) 955-9577 (415) 821-1216 fax (415) 821-1596

Niños offers an selective list of materials for libraries and schools.

Permabound [www.perma-bound.com] extensive list of titles with special bindings.

Pro Lingua Associates [www.prolingua associates.com/]distributes ESL/EFL, foreign language (Spanish, French, Japanese), cultural orientation and teacher resources and training materials.

Spanish Book Distributors [www.sbd books.com] specializes in Spanish books, CD-ROMs, reference materials, translations and literature.

ACADEMIC LIBRARIES

CHAPTER NINE

Serving the Hispanic Student in the Community College Library

John Ayala, Luis Chaparro,
Ana María Cobos, and *Ron Rodríguez*

Introduction

This chapter is made up of four segments. The first part, by Luis Chaparro of El Paso Community College Library, is a demographic profile of Latino/Hispanic students in the U.S. Chaparro gives a current and future overview of the impact of Latino demographics on community colleges and their libraries. The second part is by Ron Rodríguez, a librarian from Rio Hondo Community College Library in Whittier, California. His part, titled "Community College Libraries at the Crossroads" illuminates the impact of the library in serving the changing demographics of community college at the local level. The third part is authored by Ana María Cobos of Saddleback College Library in Mission Viejo,

California. Here, she discusses her various roles in teaching, in collection development, and in outreach to Latino students and the broader campus community. The fourth and last part is authored by the organizer of this chapter, John L. Ayala, who, in addition to being Dean of the Library, is an administrator for Fullerton College in Fullerton, California. The author explains and offers methods of service, giving his insights into personnel, services, and materials from an administrative perspective.

Demographic Profile

by Luis Chaparro

One of the most daunting challenges facing the United States in the next millennium is the changing demographic landscape. The major ethnic groups— African American, Asian Americans, Native Americans, and Latinos are key players in the transformation of our diverse American landscape. These minority groups are growing at an accelerated pace while the current majority group— Anglo American—is showing a steady decrease. By the end of the century, the non–Latino White proportion of the U.S. population is projected to decrease to less than 72 percent with the above-mentioned groups making up the rest as follows; 13 percent African American, 11 percent Latino origin, 4 percent Asian American and less than 1 percent Native American. However, by the middle of the next century the percentages are projected to change radically; 53 percent for Whites; 16 percent African Americans, 10 percent Asian American and 23 percent Latino (Day, p.9). Within the next two years, the Latino population is projected to reach 31 million people. By the year 2010, it will increase to 39 million (Exter, p. 59). It is projected to increase to almost 90 million people by the year 2050 (Cardenas, p. 26).

This spectacular growth is also reflected in the enrollment of Latino students in colleges and universities. Between 1982 and 1992, the increase of Latino students in institutions of higher education was ten times the increase of Whites. It is projected by the year 2005, almost 16 percent (approximately 12 million students) of the total student population enrolled in U.S. colleges and universities will be Latino (Outtz, p. 66).

The community college, the two-year educational institution, that offers primarily the associate degree is a unique American invention. Since their creation around the turn of the century, community colleges have played a crucial role in

expanding educational opportunities to a great segment of the American population. Currently there are eleven hundred community colleges throughout the United States with California and Texas having the greatest numbers. In 1994, this nationwide network of community colleges enrolled almost 11 million students in credit and non-credit courses (Phillippe, p. 4). In 1992 more than half a million Latino students attended community colleges comprising 36 percent of the minority group representation (Phillippe, p. 24). Enrollment of Latino students in community colleges has doubled in the past decade and in 1994 a majority of Latino students (56.2 percent) were enrolled in two year colleges (Carter & Wilson, p. 15).

This brief demographic profile of Latino students in the American college system serves to frame the following section that discusses the key roles that community college libraries play in the education of the growing Latino student body.

Community College Libraries at the Crossroads

by Ron Rodríguez

In the late 1990s the community colleges are undergoing some of the most critical changes ever. The changes are producing dramatic effects that will certainly mark the end of a liberal era and the beginning of a new one marked by conservatism and a harsher attitude towards the "have-nots" in California. Latinos are playing an ever more prominent role in the future of California's community colleges. Additionally, the impact of welfare reform has yet to fully develop but seems likely to force even more change upon California's community colleges and their libraries.

The implications of students whose lives are being radically altered will find community college libraries which are generally known for offering intensive one-to-one library assistance, even more driven to provide this personalized and intensive assistance despite a lack of librarians and increasing expectations from all students on the services offered. In a time when larger classes are encouraged and orientations (bibliographic instruction) seem only to get larger, how should community colleges and their libraries respond to large demographic shifts, students who have little to no high school library experience to draw from and the challenges of welfare reform that will affect significant numbers from campus to campus.

The California Community College system consists of 71 districts with 106 colleges throughout the state of California. During the fall of 1996, over 1,396,400 students were enrolled throughout the state of California. Of that population, 333,544 students were Hispanic which represented 23.9 percent of the total student population and the number is rising. To give further perspective, in 1990, the Hispanic student population was 244,777 or 16.2 percent of the total student population. [1]

Along with Hispanic students, the Asian Pacific student population is also rising. Across, the nation, the Hispanic population is climbing. According to the U.S. Census, the Hispanic population comprises 28 million or over 10 percent of the total U.S. population. The Hispanic population in the U.S. has witnessed tremendous growth over the last thirty years, moving from roughly six percent of the population in 1960 to about ten percent in 1995. [2] By the year 2000, the U.S. Census estimates there will be 31 million Hispanics in the U.S. and by 2005 there will be over 36 million. [3]

Your situation may be different and varied, but for the California and southwestern states, the relationship between the Hispanic student and the community college library service is one that should be written about and explored to determine what works best to help insure student success. At Rio Hondo College, the library has an acute awareness of the student's informational and curricular needs, but takes measures to purchase books and other materials that Hispanic students will find useful and interesting. Students are very interested in knowing more about themselves, their history and their communities. Students have taken extreme interest in the Internet and set up free commercial e-mail accounts to chat with one another. There are many Internet resources like CLNET that have given students a new energy, understanding, enthusiasm and self-confidence. At the same time, it is reality that very few of our students have a computer at home. Indeed, across the nation, many Hispanics do not even have a telephone in their home. The current rate of those who do not have a telephone is a little more than 13.5 percent [4]

The young age of the Hispanic community and its relative inaccessibility to computers at home make it extremely important for Hispanics to have access to computers and advanced telecommunication devices at school. If the current trend continues, the U.S. economy could be faced with its largest cultural group under-educated, under-trained and ill-prepared to qualify for the thousands of new jobs in the knowledge services arena. [5] The foregoing makes it abundantly clear that community colleges have a pivotal role in states and the U.S. as a whole in regard to economic stability and growth.

Rio Hondo Community College, like many other schools that have a significant

Hispanic population, has problems with student retention. Hispanic students are often in need of intervention programs designed like the "Early Warning" program at Rio Hondo. This program is activated for every student who falls below a designated performance standard within the first three weeks of class. The Library also participates in the "Early Warning" process by offering intensive library skills research orientations as needed. In my experience, for every student that finds success in his or her research, there is another that gets so demoralized due to their lack of information literacy, they abandon their homework and consider dropping the class and sometimes do. Information literate people are those who have learned how to learn. They know how to learn because they know how knowledge is organized, how to find information, and how to use information in such a way that others can learn from them. Information literacy should be a goal for every community college.

The academic career of the Hispanic student is many times already burdened by part-time or full-time work demands, child-care issues, an insufficient high school education and other factors. Just when it seems that life cannot get more complex, it does. This new variable in students' lives is the federal welfare reform bill of 1996, H.R. 3734. Under this law, welfare recipients will be required to be in a work activity after receiving aid for two years, and will be subject to a lifetime limit of five years of aid. There are specific requirements for the states such as the expectation that the state is to have at least 25 percent of the adult participants receiving aid working at least 20 hours per week. This rate increases to 50 percent in the year 2002 when welfare recipients must be working 30 hours a week.

At the present time, there are over 139,000 welfare recipients in the community colleges in California. These individuals will need to have education and training leading up to a family supporting job. Community colleges will likely respond with short-term, intensive, open entry /open exit classes; job preparation classes; more work study opportunities on campus, expanded job development and job placement. This partial list of probable responses will be put the library in a position of being reactive or being proactive in dealing with individuals needing upgraded support services. Libraries may consider the purchase of circulating laptop computers for students to access full-text databases; short-term intensive courses on information literacy, on-site child care, electronic reference and advisement service and peer mentoring as ways to meet the challenge. Libraries will also find their book budget taxed by the need to purchase more publications designed to inform about all kinds of jobs, careers, resume writing and even software programs to help do the same. Librarians may decide to work more closely with other faculty and counselors and find ways to integrate what each does in some way, large or small. There are many strategies that can meet the challenge. Librarians may find that imagination and teamwork will go farther than the extra funding, if any, that will trickle to California's community college libraries to meet the demands of welfare reform.

Community college libraries will be strained to provide high quality service in light of changes such as welfare reform and dealing with the ever increasing demands for new and better library services. Meeting the challenges in the best way possible calls for community college librarians and administrators to communicate now.

Reaching Out to Latino Community College Students

by Ana María Cobos

In this section I outline my efforts to reach out to Latino students at Saddleback College. My basic philosophy is to integrate all my activities and reach out beyond the library's four walls to be more effective in my efforts. In addition, I strongly believe in sharing my skills and knowledge freely with colleagues or friends and ask others for help and/or suggestions whenever necessary.

Teaching Chicano Literature

I have been teaching Chicano Literature in the fall semester during the last three years. In this course I integrate my librarian training and skills as much as possible with the course material. I emphasize good research skills throughout the semester and needless to say I conduct an in-depth library orientation for the students early in the semester. In addition, I always bring to the classroom relevant newspaper articles, postings from listservs, information about campus events, readings in local bookstores, art exhibits, plays, and films, and I encourage student participation in these activities by offering extra credit points.

I also take advantage of local expertise to enrich my class. For example, I invite a campus colleague who is an expert on Chicano theater to lecture on this topic; a colleague from Los Angeles Harbor College presents a lecture on Sandra Cisneros. As a result of these contacts my students benefit not only in the classroom but also beyond. One example is that my students received free tickets to see *I Don't Have to Show You No Stinking Badges* by Luis Valdez which was directed by the instructor who was guest lecturer in my class. Yet another example is that to encourage attendance I had a role in promoting this play among the local Latino community. Finally, through this same contact I organized a large group (including many current and past students) to attend a production of *Zoot Suit* by the San Diego Repertory.

Library Research Skills and Bibliographic Instruction

I was the first librarian to teach an advanced course in library research skills in our division. Because I also teach the Chicano Literature course a handful of Latino students have followed me into this library class. I encourage students to become volunteers to assist others in this class once they have completed the course. Two Latino students have done so and have helped to recruit new students (often Latinos) among their classmates. Assignments for this course often include Latino or other emerging-majority examples.

At Saddleback College we have a librarian whose primary job is bibliographic instruction. However, because I know most of the Latino instructors at the college I have become their "de facto" liaison to the library. When they request orientations for their classes they ask for me. My orientations focus on search strategies and terminology (Chicano, Latinos, Mexican Americans, etc.) as well as the inconsistent and inadequate treatment in LCSH and periodical indexes of research topics in Chicano/Latino studies. I also introduce library materials not easily found with the standard tools. Students in these classes often request me when working on their assignments.

In the Library

COLLECTION DEVELOPMENT

At Saddleback College Library each librarian has selection assignments according to expertise and need. We are very fortunate to have one librarian who is responsible for Women's Studies and Multicultural Resources. I am responsible for selecting materials in the Health and Human Services division but I am constantly making recommendations to my library colleagues for books written by Latinos or about Latino topics.

I take several steps to keep abreast of current publications in Chicano/Latino Studies. First, I receive Margo Gutiérrez's "Selective List of Acquisitions" published by the University of Texas at Austin Libraries. Second, I subscribe and participate in several listservs (CHICLE, REFORMANET, LALA-L) where I often glean information about new publications. In addition, I peruse several library publications.

Because our book budget is inadequate, at best, for our needs, I am often looking for grant funding opportunities. I have been at Saddleback College since 1992 and I have been quite successful in securing small grants to develop our multicultural holdings. The Saddleback College Foundation, the Friends of the Library and the Associated Student Government have all supported my efforts through matching funds. In spring 1997 I applied for and received a small grant from the Latina Leadership Network of the California Community Colleges. With these funds I purchased forty new Chicana/Latina literature titles from one of our local Latino-owned bookstores where I received a discount. These new books were exhibited in the library during Hispanic Heritage Month.

LANGUAGE PROFICIENCIES

My colleagues in the library know that I speak Spanish, French, German and Portuguese. Because I speak Spanish, many Latino students whose English is not very strong come to me for assistance with their reference and information needs.

Other Activities

In 1994 Saddleback College initiated a program in cross-cultural studies and I have been involved as an advisor since its inception. We developed the mission of the program, worked on curriculum development, and program promotion. The Cross-Cultural Center has a small library which I have helped to develop through the years. Faculty and students benefit from this focused collection.

I am faculty advisor to the Multicultural Friendship Club whose membership is largely Latino. I have helped the students to organize activities to commemorate Hispanic Heritage Month (I offer extra credit to my Chicano Literature students to attend programs), *Cinco de Mayo*, Multicultural Week, among other celebrations. Together we have made field trips to local museums, attended films and musical events. This club is by far one of the strongest on campus in terms of its activities and membership.

I am the faculty liaison to the Friends of the Library. The main activity of this support group is their booksales and in the spring we hold one very large booksale for an entire week. I have been successful in recruiting student helpers (set up, sort, put away) both from my classes and from the Multicultural Friendship Club. Some of these helpers have become members of the FOL.

I often serve as a campus resource because of my contacts outside of the college.

In fall 1996 when the college was preparing for its spring KinderCaminata, I was asked to provide some community contacts. I contacted Ruben Martínez of Martinez Books & Art from Santa Ana who not only participated as a program speaker but also helped to secure a large donation of children's books for the "goody bags" the children received that day.

I volunteer at my son's elementary school and my role is to participate in the school district's Bilingual Advisory Committee. Through my involvement with this group I have managed to start an after-school tutoring program for children who are developing their English language skills. Most of these children come from Spanish-speaking households. In the meetings of this committee I take the opportunity to instruct the parents about the many opportunities available to them through Saddleback College. I often give out my business card and receive calls from parents requesting assistance for their college level children and I am able to refer them to the appropriate staff on campus. I also participate in school programs such as Career Day where I talk about librarianship. Furthermore, I have involved two of my own children as volunteers in the after-school tutoring program.

To summarize, I am successful in my work because I love what I do! I accomplish a great deal because I am able to integrate many different activities at the same time; I do not hesitate to turn to friends and/or colleagues for assistance and I share my knowledge and expertise widely with students and colleagues.

An Administrator's Perspectives

by John L. Ayala

The theme of this essay is to illuminate the need for quality library service to Hispanic community college students. I will attempt to give an administrative perspective and demonstrate services to Hispanic students which we have provided at Fullerton College to help in reaching this population and making service to Hispanic students more effective.

The most important aspect of library service to any group of students anywhere is the personnel in the library who serve the students. Sensitive and responsive public service personnel who have been trained in serving culturally diverse populations are an asset to any library organization. Friendly and professional personnel who respect differences of culture and language can make the library a positive and productive experience for a Hispanic student or any student whether from the diverse population or from the majority population. The professional attitude of the library staff which I have managed for close to a decade has always been a positive one in attempting to serve diverse library populations. Their willingness to train and educate themselves in serving the changing population of the library has been exemplary and of great assistance to our students, staff, instructors and administration in their information seeking behavior.

Whenever a workshop, seminar or special class came up on serving diverse populations I could always count on a significant number of my staff, a diverse group in themselves, asking for permission to attend the event. Why, you ask, were/are they doing this? The answer is clear. When I arrived in 1990 the population of my college was approximately 70 percent majority population and 30 percent minority. The gap between the two was rapidly closing. My staff and I realized this was happening. I encouraged the staff to take advantage of any resource to facilitate their understanding of this change. As of now the population of our institution is approximately 60 percent majority and 40 percent minority and continues to rapidly change.

The approximate breakdown of Hispanic students is 25 percent and they take 30 percent of the classes offered at Fullerton College in Orange County, California just south of Los Angeles. We, at Fullerton College, are members of HACU (Hispanic Association of Colleges and Universities) and by federal government definition a Hispanic Serving Institution which makes us eligible for Title III HSI grants. 25 percent or more of our enrolled students are Hispanics (approximately 4500 students) which qualifies us as an HSI. I will illuminate this fact and how it relates to what we are doing in the library.

Familiar and friendly faces break down barriers. My librarian staff is small and getting smaller. This makes it difficult to hire a diverse librarian staff. The answer to this puzzle is that you hire a diverse part time librarian staff for both day and evening positions. These are people that the college community can identify with and feel comfortable when seeking information or assistance. The turnover in clerical staff is more frequent and gives more of an opportunity to employ a diverse and representative group to serve the students an the community. The student staff affords another chance to hire a representative diversity of the college and greater community. Why do you need to employ a representative staff? There are many answers, and here is mine.

When I became Dean of the Library at Fullerton College, the staff complained that the students and its newspaper characterized the library as a racist institution. After surveying the staff I didn't believe that characterization. Isolating the problem and encouraging solutions in terms of training and sensitivity brought a change to the estimation of the library by the greater college community. There are other answers to the cultural sensitivity question and I will address these later in this essay.

Money is always a problem when attempting to give service to any group of students. The library made a decision to devote a percentage of the materials budget to buy diversity materials books, periodicals, etc. We also bought display material to honor diversity. We applied for Funds for Instructional Improvement money to pay for materials and translators to translate help sheets, and instructional material for bibliographic instruction into Spanish and Vietnamese.

We are currently working on a CD-ROM program for bibliographic instruction that is being developed by Golden West College. GWC is a sister in our on-line consortium. A Fund for Instruction Grant from the State of California and a Hispanic Serving Institution Title III federal grant have been combined to fund this effort. The CD-ROM will instruct the students on how to utilize our on-line catalog resources. Both grants were for larger purposes. The libraries involved in both projects attached their concepts to the larger concepts and were able to obtain funding to assist students in the library. When we are finished in the English language version we will attempt to convert the CD into a Spanish translation and eventually into Vietnamese. We made a very explicit commitment to purchase diversity and multicultural materials in both monograph and serial form. We used state Instructional Equipment funds, special funding from community college diversity programs and donations from various sources to buy these materials to represent our diverse college community and curriculum. We also bought display material from a variety of proprietary companies and ALA to honor the diversity of our community. We celebrate Hispanic Heritage Month, Cinco de Mayo (Mexico's defeat of the French at Puebla in 1862), Women's History Month, Black History Month, Native American Month, Asian/Pacific American Month, etc.

We display posters of famous ethnic Americans and others during those months and also display cultural artifacts and art works. We currently have a genealogy display from the Society of Hispanic Historical & Ancestral Research on the Ordoñez family of Chihuahua, Mexico and New Mexico, USA.

These displays raise the comfortability quotient for diverse peoples using the library and make the environment familiar, inviting and warm. The library has received many compliments on displaying these types of materials and no complaints that I personally have heard. When Octavio Paz won the Nobel Prize for literature in the early nineties we displayed a banner in the library congratulating him and displayed some of his books. This makes a positive impression on literate Latinos and garners praise from many quarters.

After our first Black History Month Display went up in 1991 a delegation of African American staff members came by to thank the library for its thoughtfulness. This type of effort is worthwhile and makes friends and supporters for the library. I also believe that this is a statement in itself that in 1990 we were a racist institution and in 1991 we were receiving compliments for our sensitivity and recognition of multiculturalism. Our "Friends" group has had Hispanic authors and poets come in and make presentations at "Friends" events. These types of presentations draw in Hispanic students and the general public.

My personal involvement as an advisor to a Hispanic student group MEChA (*Movimiento Estudiantil Chicano de Aztlan*) has given the library visibility with the students and the student activity program at our college. This shows interest, involvement and commitment to student priorities and brings students into the library where we can expose them to our services and resources. We also orient new faculty to our services and explain our multicultural resources. I believe that the library needs to exhibit a user-friendly attitude to everyone and emphasize a multicultural sensitivity and openness. Treating all patrons professionally and appropriately with respect to their differences and backgrounds only brings positive feedback and spreads the message to all patrons that the library is a helpful resource for quality academic enrichment.

Conclusion

The authors hope that this chapter has been informative concerning the challenges in serving Hispanic/Latino students in the community college library. We have elucidated some methods and we have discussed what we believe are some cogent aspects of service to our students.

References (Chaparro)

Cardenas, F. 1994. It's full speed ahead. *Hispanic Business*, April, 26.

Carter, D. J., & R. Wilson. 1996. *Minorities in Higher Education*. Washington, DC: American Council on Education.

Day, J. C. 1995. *National population*

projections (U.S. Bureau of the Census. Current Population Reports, Series P. 23–189). Washington, D.C: U.S. Government Printing Office.

Exter, T. G. 1993. The largest minority. *Demographic Forecasts*, February, 59.

Outtz, J. H. 1995. Higher Education and the New Demographic Reality. *Educational Record* 76, n. 2, 3: 65–69.

Phillippe, K. A. (ed.) 1995. *National Profile of Community Colleges: Trends and Statistics 1995–1996*. Washington, DC: American Association of Community Colleges.

References (Rodríguez)

1. Wisely, Chuck. "CA Community College Statewide Enrollments." *California Community Colleges Management Information Services Statistical Library*. 5 May 1999. California Community Colleges Chancellor's Office. 11 November 1999. <http://misweb.cccco.edu/mis/statlib/stw/studF96.htm>

2. Rodriguez, Santiago. "Hispanics in the United States: An Insight Into Group Characteristics." *Department of Health and Human Services*. July 1995. <http://www.hhs.gov/about/heo/hgen.html>

3. "U.S. Hispanic Population Growth Projections (1995–2025)." 11 November 1999. <http://www.state.mn.us/ebranch/ssac/english/usproj.htm>

4. "FCC to Probe Telecommunications Gap in America." *AFNET*. [1998] 5 August 1998. 11 November 1999. <http://www.afamnet.com/NationalPage/frontpage/080598_fcc.htm>

5. "Information Literacy at Washington and Lee: What Our Students Need to Know." *American Library Association, 1989*. 11 November 1999. <http://www.wlu.edu/~joverhol/newchalk/nov98/define.html>

CHAPTER TEN

Libraries in the New Millennium— and What About the Students?

Susan Hinojosa

As we enter the 21st century facing challenges such as Propositions 187 and 209, efforts to retain and graduate all students are an essential part of our responsibility.... For many of us who either attend or work at U.C. Berkeley, it is inspiring to see a diverse community of staff, faculty, and administrators who make students feel welcome and affirm the fact we, too, belong here.
—Rights of Passage: Reader (ES 98 and AAS 98)

Libraries have typically supported students through carefully developed and maintained collections, reference services and bibliographic instruction programs. Bibliographic instruction has long been an established service in our libraries and has been one of the primary methods that we have used to interact with students, but only on library resources. Methods might differ and levels of instruction might also fluctuate depending on library budgets and personnel, but for the most part everyone agrees that instruction of some sort needs to be provided by the library. This is especially true in academic libraries. In California, incoming university students have not had the experience of being able to use fully functional libraries—either public or school. For the most part these have disappeared (schools) or are functioning at very reduced hours and level of staffing (public)and collections have also suffered from many years of budget deficits. Working at the Library at the University of California at Berkeley, I have seen first hand the initial shock and bewilderment that students exhibit when they first arrive, try to navigate the campus and then are first required to use the Library to do research. All of a sudden, with no in-between steps these students go from experience with a much smaller school system to trying to understand and use a full fledged research university with many academic departments, complicated policies, that also includes a library system with all its new technological innovations, huge collections and far flung library units and services. Seeing this, I have often felt frustrated by the inability to help students navigate the university.

Most libraries provide some form of library instruction usually in the form of public workshops, research guides as handouts, individual appointments with users, class sessions, or self-guided materials to the use of on-line catalogs, tours of the buildings, or help screens on computers. All these methods and more are useful depending on the library, the user, the circumstances, and type of information needed. However, all of these library instruction methods have one particular similarity—the contact between the librarian and the student is usually one time and brief. We meet students at an appointed time, one class session, one tour, one brief talk over the reference desk, one workshop. Rarely do we have the opportunity or the time to see the student as a whole person—academics and personal. Those of us working with minority students have been critically aware of the need to provide a more inclusive and supportive network on our campuses. From a variety of perspectives (Admissions, Counseling, Library, Health Services, Housing, Financial Aid, etc.) we have noticed the gap.

The Ethnic Studies Department at the University of California, Berkeley, has been able to create and develop a course that attempts with great success to mesh the student needs with the academic needs and to provide the campus staff support. I am privileged to be a part of this course, Chicano Studies 98, "An Introduction to University Life from the Chicano/Latino Perspective." As a librarian I have seen the advantages of representing the library as an equal to other campus student services and a very important part of the student's higher education life and academic experience.

The opportunity to work closely with a wide range of campus programs responsible for critical student services has been personally rewarding but also very helpful to my library work.

Chicano Studies 98—
Brief Background

At the University of California, Berkeley, a few instructors recognized the need for a more inclusive and supportive structure for incoming Chicano/Latino students (transfers or freshmen). The class was developed during the momentum of the Third World Strike that resulted in the creation of the three present programs—Asian American Studies, Chicano Studies and Native American Studies. Now a part of the Ethnic Studies Department, Chicano Studies 98 strives to meet the needs of students new to the campus, and new to higher education. Its founder, Prof. Larry Trujillo was a leader in the Third World Student Movement. He recognized the need for a more inclusive, supportive class, a network, that would bring students and Chicano/Latino faculty and especially staff together to explore the university and at the same time offer a familiar and comfortable zone for students. Through the weekly class sessions, readers, frequent guest speakers, and campus tours, the class acquaints students quickly with the relevant university and student services. Taught primarily by volunteer campus staff, the class offers the clear advantage of addressing students needs by having the information presented by the very people responsible for the work. Chicano/Latino students now have a network on campus that can quickly and efficiently refer them to the right person and office for help on financial aid, work-study, research, health questions, counseling, tutoring services, and more.

Chicano Studies 98 is strongly recommended to students in the Fall Semester when up to 10 sections may be available. Students are new to the university in the Fall and this is when the class is most useful. New Chicano/Latino students are encouraged by counselors, faculty and peers to take the class. It is recommended that it be taken for one unit, although two units is possible with instructor approval on a Pass/Not Pass basis. Taught by staff (counselors, admissions officers, psychologists, librarians, academic coordinators, etc.) from throughout the university, Chicano Studies 98 has been able to bring together for the benefit of students a unique combination of university and higher education expertise and experience. Since the classes are "team-taught" this has also been a very useful method for Chicano/Latino staff to meet and know each other. The development of what is now a large group of experienced CS 98 instructors has also meant that students needing special help or advice, i.e. financial aid, housing, grades, can be put in touch with someone who is directly in charge of that program or information resources.

The CS98 experience has indicated that our Chicano/Latino students frequently are the the the first generation of their families born in the United States, and are the first in their families to attend a university. They need our support to ensure their success and retention in universities and colleges. Classes like Chicano Studies 98 have helped these students belong at places like the University of California.

Instructors

With class enrollments ranging from 8 to 9 students per section up to 20 students (usually the maximum allowed and only by instructor approval), Chicano/Latino staff with minimal teaching experience have felt encouraged to teach the class with other more experienced staff. The small classes meeting one hour per week have persuaded many staff to try the experience, and the personal contact with the students has made the experience very worthwhile. These relationships with students frequently last the entire time that the students are at the university. For many of us, this is a very satisfying stage of our work on the recruitment, retention and successful graduation of minority students at a very competitive university.

CS 98 class preparation is shared with other instructors and usually requires up to 2-3 hours of preparation a week at the most. Departments have been very generous in approving staff leave and staff have appreciated both the contact with students, each other and the opportunity to learn new skills. If work conflicts arise, another instructor is usually available. As the class is co-taught, it is up to the instructors how often they are both in the classroom, but the pattern is that both are present during class times. The practice of teaming experienced teachers with less experienced ones has assured new instructors for future classes and also made the commitment easier for staff.

The above mentioned staffing method has only been possible because of the strong support and work from the Academic Coordinator in the Chicano/Latino Student Development Office, and the work of the corps of experienced CS 98 teachers. The Coordinator position assures the correct handling of student records, student grades, and formal communication with the Ethnic Studies Department and Registrar. This office also publicizes the program and ensures that campus counselors and advisors recommend the class to incoming students. This office has also cast a wide net for instructors with recruitment from: Admissions, Health Center, Personnel Office, the Library, Student Learning Center, Law School, College of Letters & Science—any interested staff member can teach who is interested in working with Chicano/Latino students and has the support of their department.

Objectives and Syllabus

> *To introduce new undergraduate and graduate students to campus life at Cal; To examine the structure, function and academic mission of the University; To survey the wide range of academic support services on campus; To explore the various extracurricular activities at Cal and in the community* (from Fall Semester '97 course syllabus)

U.C. Berkeley operates on a semester system—15-16 weeks of instruction. The CS 98 course syllabus is regularly revised to incorporate new subject areas or new schedules. Instructor flexibility is built in and only those events, such as tours need

to be covered within a certain period of time. Below is a listing of topics from the course syllabus, CS 98 Course Objectives (Fall Semester 1997):

Time Management
The Information Superhighway
Study Skills
Stress Management
Academic and Advising Support Services
Socio-Political Climate on Campus
University Health Services
Extra-Curricular Activities
Academic and Career Planning
Social Choices
Interviewing Techniques
Reconocimiento

As instructors wish, midterms, and exams or a final exam may be scheduled. In addition, a final paper, or several shorter papers may be required during the semester. One popular option is to require the students to keep journal entries throughout the semester focusing on their experiences on campus. One future goal is to make better use of these journals to evaluate the class, improve campus services, and to make these available to future students in some format.

Typical class sessions and assignments require that students keep a calendar of all activities for a week and discuss this in class (time management). The Library is a focus throughout—as a place to do research, find information for class assignments and as an excellent place to get quiet time and study. The goal is to help students develop those skills (time management, study and research skills) necessary to succeed at highly competitive U.C. Berkeley. This is balanced with the need to meet other students and experience new activities (extra-curricular activities); to know about and receive those services needed to keep healthy (University Health

Services; discussion on alcohol, drug use, sex, and stress management (social choices); and also taking advantage of the campus support services (the Library, Academic and Advising Support Services, and Academic and Career Planning). Added to this mix are class sessions that aspire to be frank and open discussions on current social and political issues that might affect the students, such as affirmative action, and culture & race. *Reconocimiento* is a term in Spanish that means recognizing, knowing of yourself. Students are asked to discuss identify themselves. How do they identify—Chicano, Latino, Mexican, Mexican American, *Cubano*? What do these terms and identities mean to them? Typically, most of the students have not had to probe the question until their arrival at U.C. Berkeley and can be very unprepared for the questions.

The Library

Over the last five years, the Library has been very successfully incorporated into Chicano Studies 98. It has been gratifying to see all instructors immediately ask for the Library tour and the accompanying library assignment.

When leading students through the Main Library, and the Ethnic Studies Library, I have a few goals in mind. I want students to know me and that I am available to help them. I want students to feel comfortable in the Library and to know that all the collections and services are there for them. On the tour and especially through the library assignment (copy attached), students are also trained in some basic skills: use of the two on-line catalogs (Gladis & CDL Melvyl) to do simple searches by author, title and subject; use of electronic magazine databases;

they are introduced to the unique Chicano Database; the use of a CD-ROM Database (lately the 1990 U.S. Census for home town lookup); and Internet searches. All of the sections and questions on the library assignment are designed to acquaint students with basic research techniques and the use of a variety of library resources regardless of format. The examples used in the assignment are also carefully chosen to show students the research possibilities in Chicano Studies—the subject headings, the databases, the books, the authors (campus Chicano faculty) should all be of personal interest.

The tour of the Ethnic Studies Library has always been an important part of the library assignment. Students are asked to visit the Ethnic Studies Library, browse the collections and to identify an item of interest. Few students have experienced this type of collection and most find this exercise very rewarding.

Future Plans and Goals

Chicano Studies 98 is an evolving class. As instructors and students perceive or express particular needs the class will be adapted to address those subjects. As one example, computer skills were identified as an area where Chicano/Latino students needed assistance and training. This area was identified and studied as part of a Spring Semester 1997 survey conducted by the academic coordinators in the African American and Chicano/Latino Student Development Offices. As expected, the survey verified the lower availability of computers and fewer computer skills of our incoming minority students.

CS 98 now requires the regular use of email for class work and class communication. Student questionnaires try to elicit information on computer availability and campus computer training information is given to students. The library assignment requires students to use on-line catalogs, email results, search the Internet and to search and download from CD-ROM databases. Training in the development of web pages has been considered, as has more advanced training on the use of popular software to assist students in writing papers.

CS 98 has provided the much needed central place for the development of campus services that support Chicano/Latino students. Through the continual development of the CS 98 class, the training and identification of campus staff that can help students succeed academically and personally, and the recognition of the need for new student skills such as computer skills, CS 98 is likely to remain a critical resource for students and staff. Given the future demographics of California and states such as Texas, Florida, New York, and Illinois, libraries need to look outside their doors and become part of vital programs such as CS 98. Librarians and libraries can only profit by supporting these classes and becoming an integral part of their design.

Appendix

Chicano Studies 98   NAME _____
Fall Semester 1999

An Introduction to the Library

Welcome to the UC Berkeley Libraries!
This short library assignment will take you through the basic commands of the UC Berkeley on-line catalogs: **GLADIS, MELVYL, the CD-ROM Databases, and the World Wide Web (WWW).** As you follow the instructions in this assignment you will learn some basic search techniques—how to find books by author, title, and subject, how to use on-line databases to find magazines articles and how to search the internet.

The entire assignment can be completed using the on-line PC terminals in any of the campus libraries. It is recommended that you use the on-line catalogs in Main or the Ethnic Studies Library.

ON-LINE CATALOGS—GLADIS & MELVYL

Gladis is the UCB Library's catalog—on-line. It contains a listing for books, magazines, maps, video materials and much more. For more information on Gladis check the leaflet "Gladis: The UC Berkeley Online Catalog" that is in your packet.

GETTING STARTED
Go to a library PC terminal. To start, select the appropriate icon from the PC screen.

Select **Gladis**. A welcome screen will appear.

Gladis (UCB Catalog)
UCB Library Pathfinder
Melvyl Online System
Melvyl System (via Web)
CD-ROM Databases by Subject
World Wide Web

FINDING NEWS AND INFORMATION ON GLADIS

Before having you look for books in the catalog, it is useful to know about some of the other information that is available through a Gladis terminal.

In Gladis at the --> type **news** <enter> to retrieve a list of several NEWS items available on Gladis.

(Note: whenever you see the message "continued on next screen" at the bottom of the screen, press the <enter> key to see more.)

type **news fall** <enter>. What are the hours for the Moffitt Library Study Areas Monday through Thursdays?

Type **news jobs** <enter>. Where are the listings for student library jobs posted?

FINDING BOOKS ON GLADIS

BY TITLE: Type the command f (for find) to begin any search, then add the search code **ti** (for title) followed by the title of the book. Your search should look like this (f ti ....)

Find a book called *Dia de los Muertos: a celebration...*

type: **f ti dia de los muertos** <enter>

Gladis will display several records. Select the record for this book.

Which libraries have copies of this book?

_____

What is the call number for the book in the Ethnic Studies Library?

_____

BY AUTHOR:

Gladis lets you find books under an author's **personal name** by using the **pn** code.

Find a book by our Vice Chancellor, Genaro Padilla.

type: **f pn padilla, genaro** <enter>

You will get a listing with two names. Choose the first entry on the list by typing 1 <enter>. Another list will be displayed showing titles of books by or about the author. Scan the list until you find the 1993 book *My history, not yours: the formation of Mexican American autobiography.*

(type number <enter> to display the record.)

Which libraries have copies of this book?

What is the call number for the Main Library copy?

Where is this book shelved in the Main Stacks? (check the call number listings at the entrance to the Main Stacks or the maps on each of the Main Stack Floors.

Shelved on Level _____

BY SUBJECT

You can find books on a particular subject by typing in the correct subject headings (code **su**). For example, if you are looking for books on the subject of Mexican Americans you would type: **f su mexican americans** <enter>

How many subject entries did you retrieve? _____

Select the first heading by typing **1** <enter>. Select any title that interests you.

Give author, title and library location of a book found (at the --> type the number <enter> this will give you the complete record)

FINDING MAGAZINES IN GLADIS

To find where magazines are located, search the catalog the same way you would to find books. Look up the magazine *Hispanic Business*

f ti hispanic business <enter>

Which libraries have subscriptions to this magazine?

EXIT GLADIS AND RETURN TO THE MAIN MENU. At the --> type bye and you will go back to the main menu.

Select C. Melvyl Online System

FINDING MAGAZINE ARTICLES ON MELVYL

By hitting the enter key reach the second full screen of Melvyl with the title **Databases and Systems** on top of the screen. At the bottom of the screen you will see a list of six databases by general subject field. These subject areas are: **Biomedical, Business, Government/Legal, Humanities, Science/Engineering, and Social Sciences.**

At the --> type **social** <enter>

You now have a listing of 10 social sciences databases plus 2 listings for the Melvyl catalog (TEN and CAT)

at the --> type **mags** <enter>

Mags is the Melvyl Magazine & Journal Articles Database covering over 1500 magazines since 1988.

At the MAGS --> type **f su Hispanic Americans - political activity** <enter>

From the approximately 140 magazine citations retrieved by your search, select one (type **d #**) with full text. Give author, title, title of magazine, volume, and dates (month/day/year).

Send this information to your email account. Type: **mail**, record number, text **to** (your email address).

See library leaflet (in your packet)*Save and Mail Commands on MELVYL* for more information on saving and mailing records.

By displaying your citation (d # of citation) and then adding **loc ucb** the location of the magazine on campus is given.
    type: **d # loc ucb** <enter>

Where is your magazine located on campus?

The **Chicano Database** is another one of the Social Sciences Databases. To enter, this database, type **chicano** at the Melvyl prompt.
    At the Chicano--> type **f su college students**

Select an article of interest and give the citation (author, title, journal title, vol., dates) below.

Where is this magazine located? Exit the Chicano Database (type bye at the prompt) and search Melvyl. Use the **pe** code (for periodicals).
    type: --> f pe (title of magazine)

EXIT MELVYL & RETURN TO THE MAIN MENU (remember how to get back to the main menu: type **bye**)

Select CD-ROM Databases by Subject

CD-ROM Databases by Subject

Now click on **Government Information** and choose the **1990 US Census, STF3A (CA Bay Area Detail).**

—under **State** choose **Place**

—select a city (choose your home town):

Name city: _____

under city choose "General Profiles" and choose from Social Characteristics, Labor Force & Community, Income & Poverty, and Housing Characteristics

Give one of the statistics (category and number):

What else can you find out about the city selected? Give a few examples.

Find out anything interesting about your home town?

Exit the CD-ROM Databases and go back to the main menu.

Select World Wide Web

Make sure that you are at the University of California Libraries at Berkeley homepage (http://www.lib.berkeley.edu/).

On the lower right side of the web page, under "Reference Resources" select Encyclopedias & Gateway Sites. Click the "go to" button and following the instructions select the *Encyclopædia Britannica.* Do a search on a subject of interest.

Name of subject: _____

Describe the subject coverage briefly:

Exit Britannica.

Type in the LOCATION box this address:
    http://clnet.ucr.edu

Click on the Diversity box and browse. List another web site of interest. Address:
http://_____

Briefly describe:

ETHNIC STUDIES LIBRARY (30 Stephens Hall)

Visit the Ethnic Studies Library. Take a look at the library, its collections (Asian American, Chicano, Native American and Comparative Ethnic Studies) and browse the reference section.

Select *The Latino Encyclopedia* (Ref HN51 L285 1996 v1-6). Cite an article of interest.

Need help? Send me a note at: shinojos@library.berkeley.edu)

Susana Hinojosa
GSSI
223 Doe Library

LIBRARY SERVICE TO IMMIGRANTS

CHAPTER ELEVEN

Queens Library's New Americans Program: 23 Years of Services to Immigrants

Mônica Scheliga Carnesí and María A. Fiol

Traditionally a borough of immigrants, Queens is the largest of the five counties of New York City, New York. It is also one of the most racially and ethnically diverse counties in the United States. According to the 1990 U.S. Census, Queens' total population is just under two million people, of which 36 percent were born in a different country and 44 percent speak a language other than English at home.[1] A recent study conducted by the New York City Department of City Planning examining the flow of legal immigration between 1990 and 1994 revealed similar findings: 30 percent of New York's recent immigrants have chosen Queens as their new home.[2] Such is the diversity of ethnic and immigrant communities living and working in Queens that a seven-mile sub-way line connecting Times Square and Flushing has been nicknamed "The International Express." Each stop on this elevated line introduces passengers to a variety of ethnic communities, with different neighborhoods reflecting a multitude of nations from around the world. Overall, more than 120 countries and 100 languages are represented, making Queens the most ethnically diverse borough of New York City.

Queens residents are served by the Queens Borough Public Library (QBPL). The Queens Library, which celebrated its Centennial in 1996, is the largest public library system in the country in terms of circulation, and the second largest in terms of holdings, with a central library in Jamaica and sixty-two branches.[3] Each branch serves a distinct neighborhood with a unique, and in most cases, diverse international community make-up. The Corona Branch, for instance, serves a predominantly Spanish-speaking area, where over 70 percent of the population is of Hispanic origin. In the Elmhurst Branch neighborhood, nearly 82 percent of the area residents speak a language other than English at home, including Spanish, Chinese, Korean, and a number of South Asian languages, among many others.[4]

In order to better serve its growing international population, the Queens Library formed the New Americans Project, or NAP, in 1977. Initially with a staff of only one and funded by a Library Services and Construction Act grant, NAP continued to grow throughout the years because of the library administration's commitment to provide Queens' immigrants with library services tailored to their needs. In 1981, attesting to its success and in keeping with the library's tradition of social responsibility, the administration chose to fund NAP from the library budget. In 1993, in recognition of the permanent role NAP had come to play, the library changed the name from the New Americans Project to its current name, New Americans Program, an agency within the Programs and Services Department. Today NAP has an office staff of eight professionals, a full-time secretary, and a part-time clerk, who altogether share considerable language expertise—ten different languages are spoken, including Spanish, French, Portuguese, Tagalog, Lithuanian, Bengali and Mandarin Chinese. Finally, NAP also counts among its numbers a field staff of twenty-three English as a Second Language teachers.[5]

NAP's goals have been to extend library services to Queens residents whose primary language is not English and to facilitate immigrants' initial period of adjustment. Programs and services were developed to introduce new immigrants to the library and to assist them in adapting to their new country. When NAP was first developed, services were targeted to the three largest immigrant groups in Queens: Latinos, Chinese and Koreans. Today Latinos are still considered the largest immigrant group in the borough—nearly four hundred thousand—making up nearly 20 percent of the population.[6] The five countries with the largest representation are Colombia, Dominican Republic, Ecuador, Mexico and Peru.[7] However, Queens is also home to immigrants from practically all other Central and South American countries, as well as from Spain. Together, they represent an impressive portion of the total population served by the Queens Library, customers for whom special services were created in response to their own special needs. The projection for the year 2000 is that Latinos will become the largest minority group in the New York City, representing 29 percent of the total population.[8]

The idea of creating special services geared exclusively to the needs of immigrants originated from the understanding that public libraries—as we know them in the United States—are quite unique to this country. Immigrants for the most part come from countries where libraries are perceived as being for the use of scholars alone, where books may not be allowed to circulate, where community information referral services are all but nonexistent. It is unrealistic, therefore, to expect immigrants to seek out libraries by themselves. Public libraries should be the ones working to make themselves visible to immigrants, developing community outreach services to welcome newcomers to their branches, and introducing them to their free resources and services.

As NAP has continued to grow, new and varied services were created to meet the needs of the constant influx of new immigrants. Today NAP has six components: English as a Second Language classes, Demographic and Information Services, a Mail-a-Book program, Cultural Arts programs, Coping Skills programs, and Collection Development.

English as a Second Language

English as a Second Language (ESL) is the largest NAP component; it is also among the largest free ESL programs for adults in the borough. We offer eighty-eight courses a year at the Central Library and twenty-five branches at the Beginning and Intermediate levels, as well as two Advanced classes per semester.

The classes are managed and carefully monitored by the ESL Coordinator. Each year, nearly three thousand students are enrolled, representing more than seventy countries and speaking over forty different languages. In the Spring '99 term, 39 percent of the students were Spanish speakers coming from a variety of Spanish speaking countries, and 16 percent were Chinese speakers from Taiwan, Hong Kong and Mainland China. We have had students from places as far away as Togo and Nepal. Within a single classroom, a teacher may encounter speakers of as many as fifteen different languages, including Dari from Afghanistan, Telugu and Malayalam from Southern India, and Amharic from Ethiopia.

There are two terms a year, one in the Spring, the other in the Fall. Each class runs for about fifteen weeks, two sessions a week of 2½ hours each, amounting to twenty-eight sessions. A one-day registration on a first-come, first-served basis is held at each branch where classes meet. At the registration, students are screened by the teacher for level of proficiency. Thirty students are registered and a waiting list is kept in case students drop out. In some branches with heavy demand we are forced to turn away as many people as we register. To ensure themselves a place, students may begin lining up outside the library at 5:00 or 6:00 A.M.—in rain, snow or sleet—for a 10:00 A.M. registration. An alternative to this problem is currently being implemented: selected branches conduct a mail-in registration where students mail in application forms to be entered in a computer drawing. Those selected are later informed of the date, time and location of the class registration.

The task of turning students away has been made a little easier by the creation of a referral list. Produced three times a year through a telephone survey, it lists free and/or low-cost ESL programs available throughout Queens. The programs are listed by neighborhood along with the agency name, telephone number, address and availability of class levels. Students who are not able to register with us can use the list to find other nearby ESL programs.

In our classrooms, vocabulary and grammar are conveyed through lessons about everyday situations, such as going to the doctor or the supermarket, or renting an apartment. We teach the four language skills—reading, writing, speaking, listening—but emphasis is placed on learning how to speak and understand. All students receive a full introduction to the library and are taken on a tour of the library where the classes take place. They are given library cards and encouraged to return and to take advantage of all of our services.

Recently we have begun offering computer training to students enrolled in the ESL Advanced class to teach them how to use InfoLinQ, the library's OPAC system, and to search the Internet through InfoLinQ Web. The Queens Library web page is known for its innovative use of technology and for bringing multilingual Internet services to library customers. WorldLinQ, a multilingual electronic information system being developed in partnership with AT&T connects users to news sources, web sites and other Internet services throughout the world in their native languages. Currently WorldLinQ is available in three languages: Spanish, Chinese and Korean.

NAP also offers ESL Literacy classes. These are classes designed to meet the needs of non-English speakers who have less than four years of schooling in their own languages. These students would have difficulty entering the standard Beginning Level ESL class because of their lack of basic literacy skills. By the end of this course, students are able to write simple sentences. They gain the fundamental skills necessary to succeed academically in the standard series of ESL courses.

Demographic and Information Services

Demographic and Information services help us determine where the various ethnic groups are located in the borough, so that library services can be tailored to specific communities wherever they reside. Using the 1990 U.S. Census as the principal source of information, NAP staff have been able to develop a number of valuable

reports and studies such as: *QBPL Service Areas: An Ethnic and Language Profile*, and *International Migrants to Queens: A Profile of Demographic and Social Characteristics*, among others. The first study has helped us determine the nationality of our Spanish-speaking customers, and tailor the collections and all other programs accordingly. The information for the profile was taken from the 1990 U.S. Census Summary Tape File 3 (STF3). The STF3 is published on CD-ROM as a number of different products. STF3-A contains statistics at various geographic levels, down to the census tract and block group. STF3-B shows the data categories for Zip Code areas.[9] Since the Spanish-speaking communities of Queens come from every country in Latin America, this profile has been invaluable in letting us know where the various nationalities reside and has helped us place Spanish language and other materials collections of interest to individual national groups at their closest branches. Information services has also compiled and published the Third Edition of the *Queens Directory of Immigrant Serving Agencies*, a detailed listing of over 150 organizations providing services in over fifty languages.

Books-by-Mail in Other Languages

The Mail-a-Book program was one of NAP's first services and a predecessor to our specialized Collection Development initiative. Available in seven languages (Spanish, French, Italian, Greek, Russian, Chinese and Korean), Mail-a-Book provides annotated, descriptive lists of over one hundred titles (fiction and non-fiction) per language. This is the only service provided by NAP that is limited to

Queens residents, due to financial considerations. Through Mail-a-Book, Queens residents can request up to four books at a time—per list—to be sent to their home completely free-of-charge. The books are sent in a reusable bag that contains a postage paid return label. Additional titles can be requested with each mailing. Mail-a-Book is the first contact many immigrants have with the library, and while its circulation is modest compared to our current branch language collections, it is still maintained as a superb public relations tool for introducing new immigrants to the library. The Spanish language Mail-a-Book list has one of the highest circulations of all of the lists—second only to Russian in the past three years—as new immigrants from the former Soviet Union relocate to Queens in great numbers. The booklists have a finite number of items, and sooner or later customers reach the point where they have to come to the library if they want to read more. It is believed that the voracious reading appetite of many immigrants is partly responsible for the Queens Library having the largest circulation of any urban library in the country—over fifteen million items for fiscal year 1997.

Cultural Arts Programs

Cultural programs highlight and celebrate the arts of the many ethnic groups living in Queens. Programs include music and dance performances, festivals, poetry readings, bilingual storytelling, author talks and craft demonstrations. Although immigrants appreciate all our services, it is the Cultural Arts programs that elicit their warmest responses. These programs boast an impressive yearly attendance of over five thousand people, attracting an audience made up not only of the immigrants from the culture being presented but also a large number of other Queens residents, immigrants themselves or not, who enjoy having the opportunity to learn and appreciate the arts of different countries. Great care is taken in selecting individual artists and groups to perform, and every year new programs are organized and presented at different branches throughout the system. Benefiting from New York City's great pool of international artists and Queens' own talented local residents, NAP has been able to present cultural arts performers representing almost every country in Latin America, as well as from Spain. In the past few years one of our most popular events has been our all-day Latino festivals, organized in celebration of Hispanic Heritage Month. These festivals are responsible for our highest attendance numbers, presenting crafts and musical performances throughout the day. Past festivals have included Andean, Colombian, Ecuadorian, and Venezuelan music, Peruvian and Honduran dances, crafts from Mexico, Puerto Rico, Nicaragua and the Dominican Republic, among many others. Individual programs are also organized and presented throughout the year, their popularity a clear sign of Queens residents' interest in multicultural programming. NAP presents over fifty cultural programs a year, of which 23 percent focus on the arts and culture of the Latino communities living in Queens.

Coping Skills Programs

The Coping Skills component of NAP is one of its most unique services. Funded in 1986 by a New York State Library grant for one year, it was re-funded without change the following year and then permanently integrated into NAP's budget in 1988. Basically speaking, coping skills programs consist of lectures and workshops presented in selected languages designed to help immigrants adjust to life in the United States. Information is presented in an informal yet professional manner on topics such as immigration law, parenting, education, career options, health and family relationships, among others. To present these programs we hire lawyers, psychologists, teachers, social workers and other professionals, all of whom are fluent in the language of their presentation.

The purpose of these workshops is to provide newly arrived immigrants with practical, useful information to help them cope with the difficulties and stresses associated with moving to a new country. Workshops last from about one hour and a half to two hours and are presented entirely in languages other than English. Use of simultaneous translation is avoided; besides the time involved in speaking in English and then in the immigrant language, with simultaneous translation audiences are less likely to be responsive and attentive to the presentation. Programs are presented at selected branches or at the Central Library, mostly weeknights and Saturday afternoons, according to branch space, time availability, community makeup, and topic chosen. Workshops are usually offered as one-time events, but from time to time series have been organized in which 2- or 3-part programs are offered weekly, covering a single overall theme in more detail. Interaction between the presenter and the audience is encouraged, and all programs include a question-and-answer period. Information is presented informally, in plain language, but in an organized, professional manner.

Several factors determine the choice of topics. Two of the most important considerations are the particular needs of each community and the availability of speakers in that field. However, some topics are universal and of common concern to most immigrant groups. These include immigration law, tenant's rights, parenting skills, education, health and community resources. The majority of Coping Skills programs planned in a year are presented in Spanish, representing 35 percent or more of its total programming. Recent programs presented in Spanish have focused on topics including communicating with your child, dealing with attention deficit disorder, practical information on how to become a home health aide and how to start a child-care business at home, health information on breast and ovarian cancer, recent changes in the immigration and welfare laws, recognizing and dealing with depression, and information for new and/or expectant mothers, among many others.

Both Coping Skills and Cultural Arts programs are promoted using appealing bilingual flyers, targeted mailings to cultural and immigrant-oriented service agencies, and press releases published by the ethnic media. Flyers are double-sided; on one side the information is printed in English, the other side in the language of the presentation. This is done in order not to alienate our English-speaking customers. This way everyone, including other library staff members, is made aware of the upcoming program, the date and time of the presentation, and consequently of the library's efforts to serve all people in the community.

Collection Development in Other Languages

Collection development focuses on building branch collections of varying sizes in selected languages. NAP has special collection development programs in Spanish, Chinese, Korean, South Asian languages, and most recently in Russian. Our collection development efforts also include the purchase of materials in other languages on a smaller scale where need has been identified, and includes languages such as Greek, Haitian Creole, French, Portuguese, Polish and Italian.

The Say Sí Collection

Let us describe how this service to the Spanish-speaking population developed: in 1985 the Library conducted a Gallup poll which found that, compared to other groups, the large Hispanic community of Queens was not well aware of the library and was not using its services. The library's response was to start a collection development and public relations campaign called *"Diga Sí a Su Biblioteca,"* or "Say Sí to Your Library," which came to be known by most library staff as the "Say Sí Project." During the first year of Say Sí, comprehensive book collections were placed in seven branches and the Central Library. Since then the number of branches has expanded to twenty plus the Central Library; additionally, music, video cassettes and audio books have been added to the collections. At the same time that the collections were being placed in the branches, a public relations campaign was implemented to ensure that the Latino community knew what was being made available. The campaign included the development of Spanish language brochures, bookmarks and library card applications, as well as a bilingual manual to be used by non-Spanish speaking staff when serving Spanish-speaking customers. Translated press releases were sent to the Spanish-language media, and soon the community started to look for the Say Sí collections.

The Say Sí campaign more than achieved its goal of increasing awareness and use of the Library by Latinos. A follow-up poll conducted by the library two years later showed that the percentage of Latinos who held library cards had risen from 32 percent to 47 percent. In terms of percentage, this meant that Latinos were using the library as much as the rest of the Queens population.

The fact that we are located in New York City, where one can find a number of excellent distributors has greatly facilitated our purchasing of Spanish language materials. According to Susan Freiband, former chair of the Committee on Library Services to the Spanish Speaking (of the American Library Association's Reference and Adult Services Division) "there is no substitute for direct, hands-on experience with new materials, and for face-to-face communication with publishers, distributors, or booksellers."[10] Throughout the years, we have also developed good relationships with distributors in other parts of the country, since sometimes we find titles we want which are carried only by one or two specific distributors.

Another method that has helped us develop good, balanced collections is attendance at the Guadalajara Book Fair every year. The large number of materials displayed at the Fair give us a much bigger picture of what is being published, not only in Mexico but in other countries of Latin America, and Spain as well. It is important to keep in mind that when selecting from local distributors' stock, one has access only to their selection. At the book fair we see materials that may never come to the U.S. We work closely with our distributors, through which we order all new titles selected in Guadalajara. Since the Spanish-speaking residents of Queens come from all Latin American countries, it is important to have materials from and about all of these countries.

The Say Sí collection is among the country's largest Spanish collections for general readers. There are over ninety-six thousand items at the Central Library and the twenty Say Sí branches. We carry a large selection of non-fiction titles, from cooking to politics, from history to parenting, from the mysteries of the occult to the newest computer programming books. In fiction, we order both classics and popular fiction, from books by established authors such as Neruda, García Márquez, Sor Juana Inés de la Cruz and Vargas Llosa, to translations of English language popular fiction. We also carry books by the many Latino authors living and writing in the U.S., as well as books by emerging new authors from Latin America and Spain. Some branches have translations of books by such classic authors as Kafka, Kundera and Gogol, and works by these authors also circulate very well. All Say Sí Collections are maintained by NAP staff through frequent visits to the various branches. Collections are weeded and updated, and there is constant communication with the branch managers as to what the Spanish-speaking community wants.

Collection Development in Other Languages

Following the success of the Say Sí collections, additional collection development programs were initiated to serve other large immigrant groups settling in Queens. In 1988, in order to satisfy a growing demand for Chinese language materials, the library launched the Ni Hao program, named for the universal Chinese phrase for "hello." Since then, NAP has built a well-rounded collection totaling over eighty eight thousand items in the Central Library and twenty eight branches, with emphasis on publications of modern literature by best selling authors from the 1920s to the present. The Ni Hao collection is also balanced in terms of types of materials and places of publication (Taiwan, China and Hong Kong), and is sensitive to the needs of Mandarin and Cantonese speakers.

Koreans are Queens' third largest immigrant community. In 1991 NAP received a federal Library Services and Construction Act (LSCA) grant to establish Korean collections in two branches. Since 1993, using the library's own materials budget, supplemented by small grants and donations, the Hannara collection— which means "one nation"—has grown to include fourteen branches. Just as with the other special collection development programs, materials are available in a variety of formats, reading levels and subject matters.

Our third collection, initiated in 1994, is the Namaste-Adaab ("Greetings" in Hindi and Urdu) program, which provides materials in the languages of India, Pakistan and Bangladesh. It has made available over seventeen thousand items in six South Asian languages (Bengali, Gujarati, Hindi, Malayalam, Punjabi and Urdu) housed in six branches. A committee of librarians, each with their own language abilities, is in charge of selecting and monitoring usage of the collections.

NAP's newest collection development program is called Privyét ("Greetings"). For years NAP had purchased titles in Russian for a select number of branches, but a marked increase in the number of immigrants from the former Soviet Republics and a growing demand for new materials has led us to establish this formalized collection. Using NAP's materials budget, over twenty-four thousand items were purchased, including children's and adult books, audio cassettes and CDs to be placed in eight branches with the largest concentration of Russian speakers.[11]

Conclusion

Throughout the years the New Americans Program has striven to keep all of its components interrelated. Customers served by any of NAP's components are regularly informed about the others. For example, ESL students are aware they can request Mail-a-Book lists and are informed of all Cultural Arts and Coping Skills programs as they become available. Customers who attend our programs hear an introduction in their language provided by one of NAP's or other library staff describing the many services we provide. Special book displays arranged during program presentations promote our special collections and encourage use. In this way all components work together to extend services to immigrants at every point of their contact with the library.

After twenty years, NAP's services are no longer considered to be in the special services category, but are seen as an integral part of the library. This change in attitude happened by degrees. The first step took place when the program was integrated into the library budget. Long term plans could then be made without the uncertainty of the grants process. The most significant step came when branch managers started to view our services as a necessity rather than a frill. Whereas in the early days we had to persuade them to accept our programs, today they call us requesting one more ESL class, or one more program, or two more shelves of books. Throughout the Queens Library system immigrant services are considered to be essential and important.

Serving immigrants is not easy, but it is extremely rewarding. Observing the courage of a non-English-speaking man or woman sacrificing dignity to express themselves in imperfect English; seeing the joy in people's faces when you hand them a book in their native language, or the gratefulness in their eyes when they receive a piece of information that will help them deal with their landlord, or their child's teacher, or the immigration officer—this is the reward of our work. If we do it well, our newest Americans and their children will see public libraries as an institution that offers as much enrichment to them as to other groups in the community.

References

1. "Queens Borough Public Libraries Service Areas: An Ethnic and Language Profile based on the 1990 US Census," New Americans Program, Program and Services Department, Spring 1995.

2. New York City Department of City Planning, *The Newest New Yorkers 1990–1994* (New York: Department of City Planning, 1996), 52.

3. "Queens Library Facts", Jamaica, N.Y., Queens Borough Public Library, Public Relations Dept., 1997.

4. "Queens Borough Public Libraries Service Areas: An Ethnic and Language Profile based on the 1990 US Census," New Americans Program, Programs and Services Department, Spring 1995.

5. Adriana Acauan Tandler, Head, QBPL New Americans Program, interviewed by authors, Jamaica, N.Y., 3 October 1997.

6. "Queens Borough Public Libraries Service Areas: An Ethnic and Language Profile based on the 1990 US Census," New Americans Program, Programs and Services Department, Spring 1995.

7. "International Migrants to Queens: A Profile of Demographic and Social Characteristics Extracted from the 1990 U.S. Census," New Americans Program, Program and Services Department, Fall 1995.

8. New York City Department of City Planning, *The Newest New Yorkers 1990–1994* (New York: Department of City Planning, 1996), 4.

9. Derek Coursen, Data Coordinator, QBPL, interviewed by authors, Jamaica, N.Y., 7 October 1997.

10. Susan J. Freiband, "Developing Collections for the Spanish Speaking," *RQ* 35, no. 3 (Spring 1996) : 331.

11. "Annual Report, 1996–1997," New Americans Program, Queens Borough Public Library, Jamaica, N.Y.

CHAPTER TWELVE

Library Service to Hispanic Immigrants of Forsyth County, North Carolina: A Community Collaboration

Jon Sundell

Over the past decade North Carolina has become home to a rapidly increasing number of Hispanic immigrants. During this time the Hispanic population of Winston-Salem and Forsyth County has grown 1000 percent from about 2,000 to about 20,000 residents. Whereas formerly most working class immigrants were seasonal migrant workers living outside of Winston-Salem, these are now vastly outnumbered by full time residents living within the city. Like most government agencies, Forsyth County Public Library had few resources to directly address the needs and interests of this population. We owned barely any books in Spanish, although we borrowed about two hundred

from the State Library for three month periods, along with literature in other foreign languages. We conducted no form of promotion to inform the Spanish speaking population per se about library services.

In the fall of 1996 Forsyth County Public Library applied for a Library Services and Construction Act grant through the North Carolina State Library to begin serving the Hispanic population. With the $41,000 received from that grant it began a program of service to Spanish speaking people the following winter, setting up multimedia collections in seven library locations and energetically promoting services through an emerging network of services addressing the new population. After three years this program is seeing a slow but steady increase in library use by the Hispanic population. This article presents an account of our program, discussing its failures as well as successes, and projecting plans for new services. It is hoped that it will shed some light on how to best serve new Hispanic immigrant populations and how to network with other organizations sharing that mission.

The Immigrant Population

Over the last two decades the United States has seen a tremendous influx of Hispanic immigrants attributed to a variety of social, political, and economic factors. During the 1980s the violence of civil wars and military repression in El Salvador, Guatemala, and Nicaragua caused many people to flee for their lives, carrying horrific memories of family members tortured, killed, or "disappeared." Others have sought relief from economic deprivation, sometimes fleeing poverty so harsh it was as fatal as war. The 1990s have brought a dramatic increase in the number of these economic refugees due to hardships caused by disastrous weather, harvests, and circumstances of the economy and trade practices. Hispanic immigrants in Forsyth County, North Carolina are primarily of the economic type, three-fourths of them coming from Mexico, particularly from the rural southern state of Guerrero, whose principal city is Acapulco, although there are also a few hundred from Central America, especially Guatemala, who probably came here in part to flee the violence at home. For whatever reasons, these Hispanic immigrants have come to our county and state

in search of a better life, following news from family members and friends of good job prospects here and a fairly welcoming community.

In 1996 a special Hispanic census was conducted in Forsyth County. It revealed a number of factors of interest to the library in providing and promoting services.

- A significant portion of our Hispanic population (40 percent) were relatively new immigrants, who had been in the United States less than three years. Most of them (71 percent) had been in Forsyth County for less than this time. As a result, the public library is a fairly unfamiliar concept, especially since it is rare in Latin American countries.
- Nearly half of Hispanic households had at least one child. Total enrollment in the public school system was about 1200 children aged 5 to 16 years old.
- Educational level of adults was relatively low. Nearly one-third (34.7 percent) of those surveyed had grade school education or less, and another 27 percent did not complete high school. In my discussions with teachers of English as a Second Language and other community resource people, the picture of literacy is even lower than this, the functional literacy of the average grade school education being about second grade level by U.S. standards. Nevertheless, it can also be said that there are many people here who are fully literate. Also on the positive side, almost three-fourths of adults surveyed indicated an interest in further education, although the number to realize this interest will obviously be much smaller.
- Nearly 89 percent of Hispanic adults were gainfully employed, compared to 79 percent of our general county popu-

lation. This included 96 percent of adult males and 76 percent of adult females. Nearly 94 percent of those employed worked at least full time, and close to 29 percent worked more than 45 hours per week. The majority of these jobs were blue color wage jobs in construction, manufacturing, and packing. It is a very common, if not prevalent, characteristic of Hispanic immigrants to have their time and energy almost totally consumed by work, leaving little time for unfamiliar diversions. Frequently in households with children one adult works a first shift job, ending around 3 or 4 P.M., and the spouse works second shift. However, since there is usually just one car, the person at home is unable to come to the library during his or her time off.

- About 59 percent of the adult Hispanic population said they had a from fair to good knowledge of the English language. Another 23 percent had some or little knowledge, while 17 percent did not know any English. These figures for English ability seem considerably higher than the reality. My impression in speaking to the average group of Hispanics is that only about a third are fairly competent in this area. Forsyth Technical Community College has seen a steady increase in the number and size of its classes, which have quadrupled in the last three years to a current roster of 28 classes and an average attendance of 20 students per class.
- The most commonly reported free time activity reported was going to church (65 percent), followed by watching television (55 percent), and resting at home (52 percent).
- The two main formal sources of information were television and newspaper, with church leaders and friends reported as most important informal sources.
- The ranking of most frequently expressed need for service was as follows: English classes (57.9 percent), Spanish television, immigration, health, Spanish radio, and employment. The library, being a relatively unknown concept, was practically lost in a 2.9 percent category of "other" services.

Several aspects of these statistics point to barriers in library usage by Hispanic immigrants: they tend to be unfamiliar with the public library, as well as our language and culture generally, and have little confidence in using it because of a low education and literacy level. Since many are undocumented and also because they are accustomed to widespread government corruption in their home countries, there is also a mistrust of government agencies. A heavy work load which absorbs most available energy and difficulties with transportation make visiting the library a more demanding undertaking.

On the other hand the survey indicates there are some important points of access to reach the Hispanic immigrant community, the greatest one being the churches that so many attend. It also indicates there is a strong interest in learning English and furthering their education, roles in which the library can play a part. Obviously, the ready availability of basic level reading material should have a high appeal, although one would not want to ignore the substantial number of more literate potential users. In reaching this population it also makes sense to keep in mind certain cultural tendencies of Hispanics that factor in more prominently in an immigrant population new to influences of mainstream United States culture. Foremost among these would be the great importance given to personal relationships and face to face contact.

The Library Collection

When our grant was written by Bill Roberts, director of Forsyth County Public Library, he proposed a Hispanic collection in our branch at Kernersville, a town to the east of Forsyth County which had been the oldest area of Hispanic settlement, and in Belview Mini-library, a one room mini-library operated three afternoons a week by the library's Children's Outreach Department on the southside of Winston-Salem, the area with currently the greatest Hispanic population. When I, as the new program director, looked at the distribution of Hispanic households, I found that they were dispersed into several different areas of the city and county, although in each area Hispanic residents tended to cluster together. In fact, the northside population had doubled its school population within one year. I therefore decided to place collections in the Main Library, four traditional branches of East Winston, Kernersville (east end of Forsyth County), Reynolda Manor (northwest), and Southside, as well as the Belview Mini-library on the southside and our Children's Outreach bookmobile, which would make a semi-weekly stop at Lakeside Apartments, a complex that is heavily populated with Hispanics. When a new branch was constructed at Carver School Road to the northeast of East Winston, I placed a Hispanic collection there, and more recently collections have been added at Clemmons and Rural Hall branches to accommodate Hispanic population expansion in the extreme western and northern portions of Forsyth County.

After consulting with several Hispanic librarians, particularly Oralia Garza de Cortés, I decided to centralize all the adult and children's materials in the branches in one area, so that patrons could find materials easily, including both Spanish language materials and English as a Second Language materials directed toward Spanish speakers. In most locations we have used multi-purpose shelving units that combine straight shelving with E book divider shelving, periodicals shelving, and AV divider shelving. In the Main Library, we have separated the collection partially, placing all adult books in the Humanities Room, which houses the other foreign language books; children's materials in the Children's Room; periodicals in the Periodicals Room; and videos, cassettes, and CDs in the adult AV area. Almost all locations at Main and the Branches are marked by a large red sign with white letters reading "Materiales Para la Gente que Habla Español," resembling "Español" spine stickers which we purchase from the Highsmith Company.

At the outset of the program I drew up a questionnaire inquiring what type of materials Hispanic patrons would like to see. A librarian who was fluent in Spanish used this to personally interview people receiving tax assistance on Saturdays at a local high school. I paid close attention to the survey results in placing orders, and also sought advice from several of the area ministers. Periodicals was an interest frequently expressed, so we began subscriptions to about a dozen magazines. I invested about 15 percent of our first year's budget (an amount that would make up about 25 percent of subsequent years' smaller budgets) in this area, feeling that it would be a major draw to the adult population, presenting familiarity, attractive photographs, and bite-size articles on current, high interest topics. We ordered for all locations: *Buen Hogar, Deporte Internacional, Geomundo, Mecánica Popular, Muy Interesante, Ser Padres, Selecciones, Tú, TV y Novelas,* and *Vanidades*. In addition, I ordered *Eres, Furia Mundial, Newsweek en Español,* and *Proceso* for the Main Library. I would have liked to have ordered them for all branches, but because of financial limitations I limited those titles—*Eres* because it seemed to overlap with *TV y Novelas* and *Vanidades; Furia Mundial* because it was somewhat specialized; *Newsweek* and *Proceso* because they appealed to a more educated audience.

The magazines proved to be worth the investment, becoming the most heavily used among adults of any print material. Initially all locations also received a newspaper—either *Excelsior* or *Nuevo Día* from Mexico or *Prenza Libre* from Guatemala. However, since these received less usage and since all of these and many other newspapers can be instantly accessed via the internet, most of their subscriptions were sacrificed in order to add magazines to the three new locations. With similar motivation, I ordered a starter collection of Latin music, mostly in cassettes, since that is what the questionnaires indicated, but also in CDs. I followed the recommendations of Nelson and Hilda Zuleta, leaders of the Miami based band, El Grupo Cañaveral because they have an excellent eclectic grasp of Latin music. I came to know the Zuletas when they came to give some performances in our first months. I ordered a variety of *ranchero, norteño, salsa, merengue, cumbia, tejano,* and a little *classical*. I later ordered more of the current Mexican stars like Los Tigres del Norte and Los Broncos. On the whole the music recordings have circulated well.

Another AV item of interest has been cassette and book collections for learning

English as a Second Language (ESL). Because so many local people take ESL classes at Forsyth Technical Community College I ordered materials that would complement, rather than duplicate, what they were offering—thus the use of cassettes. I initially ordered a large number of the *Ingles Para Todos* series, but felt when they arrived that the small print and lack of pictures made the books a little intimidating for most of our users. A couple of ESL teachers at Forsyth Tech concurred with my opinion. More recently we have ordered *El Inglés Práctico Para Personas de Habla Española* by Educational Services, which is very clear, simple and accessible, and Barron's *Aprenda Inglés Facil y Rápido,* which is more comprehensive but attractive and appealing.

By far the biggest AV attraction, however, has been our video collection. I initially ordered a wide assortment of educational, artistic, and children's and adult feature films from several educational sources; the following year I ordered a large number of feature films from Madera Cinevideo and Million Dollar Video. The focus so far has been on popular, familiar Mexican films with stars like Cantinflas, Antonio Aguilar, Vicente Fernández, and Pedro Infante, although we are starting to also build a collection of U.S. feature films with dubbing and subtitles. The videos have been extremely popular, bringing at least a dozen Hispanic patrons into the Main Library every day.

Among the books in our collection, the most important have been children's picture books. These have generally had an instant appeal to children, a factor that not only brings them pleasure but helps to illustrate the joy of reading to parents and draws them into the library. It has been impressive on many occasions when speaking to family groups to pull out the picture books and see the children swarm over them. These books are attractive to adults also as they are simple, colorful, fun, and at a comfortable reading level for most parents. Additionally, concern among the immigrant families for their children having a better life motivates many of them to provide books for their children. There has so far been a scarcity of good toddler titles in Spanish, but these are increasing. I buy board books wherever I can find them, including the Guadalajara Book Fair, and these circulate well. Our elementary age Hispanic children, as well as toddlers and preschoolers, seem fascinated with this format, and the parents like it as well because they are often worried about their younger children damaging books and having to pay for them. (A number of children come on our bookmobile wanting to check out books, but their parents will not let them because of this fear.) Consequently some of the new board books aimed at 3-6 year olds are quite popular.

Probably the most attractive Spanish language picture books we've bought have been translations of English language story time favorites—books like La Oruga Muy Hambrienta, Vamos a Cazar un Oso, or La Viellecita Que No le Tenia Miedo a Nada. These were easy to select because I was familiar with the English versions. The availability of the English language version also attracts readers who are interested in learning English. In many cases I have actually bought an English language copy to be shelved with the Spanish version in the Hispanic section, marking the English language copy with a small purple dot on the spine to identify it as a companion book. For the same reason, bilingual books have also been very popular. Many of these are also boldly illustrated, and they have the advantage of presenting Hispanic characters and culture. Most of them tend to be at an upper elementary reading level, making them too difficult for some children and adults—but more attractive to others. The spines of our bilingual books are marked with the usual "Español" sticker plus a purple dot. It is important to provide a substantial number of books of Hispanic origin and not just books in the Spanish language. I have found many of these, while having literary value, to be a little bland in their artwork and overall format, and thus not as able to attract and hold the interest of children unaccustomed to reading. I therefore recommend previewing these whenever possible before buying them.

We have bought a number of juvenile fiction titles in Spanish, but have found them getting less use than the "easy reading" books because the children old enough to read them are most often reading in English, and preferring to read in that language. However, if and when I can find the time to do book talking in the middle and high school classes, I think there will be an increased interest in these books. Although the non-fiction titles also get less use than the easy readers, I think the greater necessity of these books for those children with weak English skills will hopefully increase their use in time.

Among adult books, we have bought a representative sampling of serious Hispanic fiction and poetry for each branch location, with two or three titles, for example, by Gabriel García Márquez, Isabel Allende, Pablo Neruda, and others. In the Main Library we are acquiring a broader range of authors and titles. Equally important, however, is a sampling of light fiction—Corinne Tellado romances, silhouette romances, Western *bolsilibros*, and other easy books, either Hispanic in origin or translations. I have just ordered a series of the new "Encanto" bilingual romances, which I expect to circulate well. One of the big quandaries has been whether to carry adult comic books, or what are often referred to as *fotonovelas*. This format is very popular with working class Mexicans. The subject matter, often sentimental and more often blatantly sexual and violent in nature, is also popular with many Mexicans, but is found offensive by others. In seeking advice over the Reformanet electronic list as to whether or not to carry these, I received considerable counsel in both directions. I have so far only selected a few titles as acceptable, especially given the fact that we are shelving our adult and children's materials together.

Our surveys expressed considerable interest in a number of non-fiction topics, particularly biography, parenting, self-actualization, history, humor, and do-it-yourself books. We are steadily building a collection in these subject areas, previewing books whenever possible to see that their language is simple and interesting, and their format inviting , preferably with fairly large print and some illustrations. *Selector*, which I was able to preview at the Guadalajara Book Fair, has proved a very suitable, as well as economical, publisher in this regard, and, to some extent, *Panorama* and *Grupo Norma*, although some Panorama titles seem a little dull to me, and some of *Grupo Norma*'s are too sophisticated.

I have recently ordered display racks to hold free pamphlets and information available on many of these subjects. Quite a bit of useful, accessible, and sometimes attractive information is now published in Spanish by governmental and non-profit organizations who are eager to give it away free. In North Carolina, for example, the Smart Start Forsyth Early Childhood

Partnership and the Healthy Start Foundation produce many useful pamphlets, calendars, and charts to assist parents of young children. The North Carolina Bar Association publishes pamphlets on legal subjects such as "Family Violence" and "Landlords and Tenants." Of course the federal government has numerous booklets available in Spanish on a wide variety of topics. Along with these pamphlets we will display flyers on local activities and services as well as the three free North Carolina periodicals, *Que Pasa*, *El Bilingüe*, and *La Voz de Carolina*. These special displays will help communicate the concept of the public library as a free source of useful information to our Hispanic residents.

Promotional Tools

Library Brochure

One of my first undertakings was to create an attractive bilingual brochure introducing the library's services to our Hispanic population. Having heard the Mexican folk song "De Colores" sung in a number of local churches, I decided to use this as a hook, titling the brochure *La Biblioteca—Un Lugar de Muchos Colores* and writing out the lyrics of the first verse on the cover. I arranged for lots of Hispanic people I knew to come in to the library and pose for various pictures, including the cover, where a multicultural cast of friendly children and adults stands in front of the Main Library. There are sections describing the library's collection, getting a library card, the different kinds of computers, sharing books with children, and programs for children and adults. It is written in a very simple style, printed in 14 point type, each two page spread containing one or two photos of faces familiar to many people in the community. Although carefully orchestrated, the pictures look warm and natural. Many people have said they find the brochure accessible and appealing, and that it presents the library as a friendly face. Although quite a few copies were set out at stores and restaurants when we started the program, most of them have been given out personally when introducing the library to groups of people, a method which is probably much more effective.

Bilingual Assistants

After an initial programming effort with outside professional performers failed to attract many Hispanics to the library, I decided to invest $5,000 of the grant money allocated for resource people in bilingual residents who could do story times and provide other services for Hispanic patrons. The idea evolved of providing bilingual assistants in our Hispanic branches during certain target periods, people who could help prospective patrons fill out forms for library cards, find materials they needed, learn to use the computers, and do whatever they wanted to accomplish in the library. They would also present a story time when children came.

We decided on Saturday from 10 A.M. to noon as a time we thought would be convenient for both patrons and workers. By having two or three people rotate at each of our branches, I felt that this would minimize the obligation of weekend time by our assistants and provide more links with the community that I hoped would bring people into the library. We made up lots of flyers and sent them out to the churches to be handed out and announced. The bilingual assistants made announcements personally in their own churches or work

places and invited individuals to come to the library. A graphic artist volunteer who helps with our publicity made up some very attractive posters to go in the branches themselves at the check-out desks and on the walls. The response was minimal, often with no one coming to most of the branches during this time. After hearing some complaints about the time being too early, we changed the time to 1 to 3 P.M., but saw little change. When the Hispanic immigrants receive extensive personal help, they seem grateful and often delighted with the assistance, but few have been willing to commit or organize their time to intentionally take advantage of it. Consequently when the money ran out, there seemed no reason to continue the service on a voluntary basis. However, the connection I established with this group of twelve bilingual resource people has been helpful in other endeavors. Many of them have assisted with library booths, outreach story times, and visits to Forsyth Technical Community College classes.

One of our bilingual assistants, Ana Navas, also worked at our Belview Mini-library on Tuesday afternoons assisting patrons. Although this is situated within the heavily Hispanic southside neighborhood, not too many of the immediate houses have Hispanic residents. Ana, who is well known in town as the secretary at a large packing company that employs mostly Hispanics, managed to invite in a few children and adults, so that usually a handful of people came to use the small facility for an hour or two. Since the mini-library is set in a recreation center, groups of Hispanics come there at certain times of year to play soccer or basketball. Being very outgoing, Ana invited the children into the mini-library, where they could read, be read to, use the computer, or receive some assistance with their homework.

After the grant money ran out, Ana volunteered for a couple of months more, but then had to stop because of changes and increasing demands in her schedule. I had difficulty finding a bilingual replacement, and when I took over personally on Tuesday afternoons I found that most of the people who had attended had moved to another neighborhood and it was difficult to find new ones who wanted to attend. I spoke a couple of times to the large group of male soccer players who met during the warmer weather in the recreation center field, but they showed little interest in taking advantage of the mini-library before or after their soccer game. It did not seem worthwhile to make a major effort to recruit patrons for this small location, which, like our offering of bilingual assistance at our branches, was available only at short specific times. After a couple of months I stopped offering this service. For the time being some of the books remain in the mini-library so that they can be used on Monday, Wednesday, and Friday afternoons when the English speaking Children's Outreach staff member is there. However, since the mini-library serves a small, targeted group of juvenile patrons, the Spanish language materials have gotten little use.

Gift Books

After about the first year and a half we began offering gift books to Hispanic patrons as an incentive for obtaining and using their library cards. The patrons can select their book when they have received their card through the mail and go into the library to use it, thus requiring at least one trip to the library. There is an assortment of about 12 titles to choose from, ranging from board books to adult books, most in Spanish, but some bilingual or in English. Most of them I order from the Bookmen, Inc. at their 40 percent paperback discount. Of these the most popular is *Webster's Worldwide Dictionary English/ Spanish, Spanish/English*. Published now by Promotional Sales Books and copyrighted by Minerva Books, Ltd. this book is available through Bookmen at the bargain price of under $1.00. Also very popular with adults is *El Inglés Necesario para Vivir y Trabajar en los Estados Unidos*, a pocket reference book for everyday situations which is ordered directly from BFS Publications in Los Angeles. These are both very handy reference books for this new immigrant population, most of whom are struggling to learn enough English to get along in their new home. *Margaret and Margarita, Margarita y Margaret*, by Lynn Reiser is very popular with preschool and primary age girls. Other bilingual books, *Con Mi Hermano/With My Brother*, by Eileen Roe *and Arroz Con Leche: Popular Songs and Rhymes from Latin America*, by Lulu Delacre have also done very well. On the whole I would say that the gift books have been one of our most effective promotions for the library, giving patrons a useful and handy gift that many would be otherwise unsure how to obtain.

Networking

As the Hispanic immigrant population has grown over the past decade a number of institutions have adapted or been created to serve it. In the last two or three years the number of services has mushroomed. One of our principal strategies has been to network with these groups in order to promote and deliver our services. This not only enhances the delivery of library services but results in better delivery of overall services to the Hispanic population.

Hispanic Services Coalition

About a year and a half ago, just as our program was beginning, the "Neighbors in Ministry" project of a local Episcopal church invited all organizations to come together to share information and experiences. Calling itself the "Hispanic Services Coalition" this open ended group has continued to meet on a monthly basis, keeping each other updated on their activities, and occasionally presenting special programs on particular subjects such as immigration law or health services. This has made it fairly easy for organizations to forward clients' attention to other groups that can help them. It has also provided an opportunity for organizations to collaborate on different activities. On many occasions I have visited programs being held by other organizations, presenting an introductory talk and/or a story time, providing flyers and brochures about our services, and signing up people for library cards with our Spanish language registration forms.

A number of organizations, particularly the Hispanic churches, Casa Guadalupe immigration assistance center, and the Association for the Benefit of Child Development Best Start Center have each received a sampler deposit collection of 25-30 books, mainly children's picture books and high interest non-fiction in paperback format, and magazines. It is set in a tiered face-out display case with a sign on top explaining that the materials are donated by the public library, and that many more books, magazines, cassettes, CDs, and videos are available to be checked out at the library using a card that can be applied for with the registration form available in the adjoining map display. The map display case contains maps, registration forms, our brochure, and program flyers. It is up to the churches how they use the books—whether they check them out or keep them in the church. Most choose the latter. Quite a few books have nevertheless disappeared, leading me to create signs and stickers instructing the users: *"Por favor no se lleve este libro. Dejalo para que otras personas puedan disfrutarlo."*

A couple of years into its existence, the Hispanic Services Coalition was approached by the Winston-Salem Foundation, one of the larger foundations in the city, to develop an overall plan for meeting the needs of the Hispanic community. The Foundation had recently received about five proposals that overlapped considerably, giving the impression that organizations making the proposals might be duplicating each other. The Foundation asked the Coalition to come up with a way of coordinating these efforts. As a result the Hispanic Services Coalition applied for and received a planning grant to survey the full range of needs of Forsyth County's Hispanic population. They survey was to determine what was currently being done to meet those needs, as well as to put together a plan for providing or improving service in those areas of greatest need.

Thirteen major areas were identified: Education, Language and Literacy, Family and Early Childhood, Health Care, Immigration and Documentation, Cultural Issues, Transportation, Employment and Business Development, Housing, Recreation, Communication, Spiritual Concerns, and Advocacy and Leadership Development. A project director was hired for the six-month grant period and committees were formed for each area. I agreed to chair the education committee and to serve on the overall steering committee of what we called the *Forsyth Hispanic Community Planning Project.*

The education committee, which had already been discussing a means of enhancing homework assistance programs in the county, was one of the committees putting together a proposal for future services. It would serve as an umbrella organization to support and enhance the work of four existing homework assistance programs serving Hispanics and add several new ones in locations not covered. Of the current programs two take place in churches as part of *Kids Cafes,* a collaborative project with the local Northwest Food Bank, which provides free food and a cook's salary if other organizations will provide space, support staff, and programming. A third one takes place in Hall Woodward Elementary School and is funded by the ecumenical Downtown Church Center. The fourth is run by the Salvation Army Boys and Girls Club in a donated apartment in Motor Road Apartments, a Hispanic apartment complex.

Among his or her duties, a full time project director would recruit and train volunteers for these existing sites, hire and train paid leaders for new sites, pursue funding for future years and future programs, and ensure the establishment of reading and literacy development as an essential ingredient of the program. This would include group story sharing, individual reading time, and reading instruction and support in both English and Spanish. I already make occasional visits to these homework centers to do story sharing with the children. Through this program I would not only do this personally, but train staff and volunteers to do this on a more regular basis. In addition, the homework assistance project would supply materials to the centers including homework reference materials selected with the help of Winston-Salem/Forsyth County Schools and leisure reading materials selected with the help of the public library. Sites would also receive either full size permanent computers or laptops to run homework support programs and internet connections. The 4-H program of the Cooperative Extension Agency would coordinate enrichment activities for the children.

An important part of the program would be communication and work with parents, both in terms of keeping them informed of their children's progress and training them in how to support their children. Working with the Language and Literacy Committee of the Community Services Planning Project, the homework project director and education committee would provide adult literacy training at homework assistance sites, most likely as an adjunct of a program being developed by Forsyth Technical Community College with the Mexican Embassy.

The Hispanic League of the Piedmont Triad

The Hispanic League of the Piedmont Triad was founded by the Sara Lee Corporation in the early 1990s when the Hispanic population was starting to grow but there was not yet much community response to the need. While its mission and objectives are very broad, its strongest accomplishments have been in the area of promoting cultural awareness, providing educational motivation, and assisting the Hispanic population in its integration into the greater community. The Hispanic League is best known for a large annual fiesta it organizes which puts Hispanic culture in the spotlight for a day, providing an opportunity for local Hispanics to celebrate their commonalities and differences, and for other community members to share that experience with them. *Fiesta* presents a variety of exciting entertainment, including live music from ranchero to salsa, folk dance performances and a *merengue* dance contest. Lots of raffles, food, and assorted booths add to the fun and the atmosphere.

The first few years the children's activities were limited to busting a piñata and doing a few crafts, so when our Hispanic library program started I proposed presenting Spanish language stories and music as a children's activity. The idea was eagerly accepted by the organizers, who were happy to receive additional input and assistance. The first year of the "children's stage," (It was down on the ground right in front of the kids but used a sound system.) when we were close to the main stage and had problems with power failure in our sound system, there were a number of frustrating times when it was difficult to be heard. The next two years the children's area moved to a new, more tranquil location, which worked much better. We generally have had an audience of 20-30 children and adults for the two or three sets I do with another storyteller or local musician. The last two years I also asked some local bilingual assistants to lead Hispanic children's games, and this past year I hired *Solazo*, one of the main stage groups who also do some children's music, to do a children's set. While I'd like to see a little larger and steadier audience, I think the children's stage has made an important contribution by adding Hispanic stories, songs, and singing games to the overall fiesta. It gives a fuller picture of Hispanic culture for the Hispanic children, who are often unaware of these aspects, as well as for the English speaking participants. And it, of course, adds to

the visibility of the library. As coordinator of the children's stage, I have also joined the general planning team of *Fiesta*, making my voice heard in several other regards, particularly the importance of providing encouragement and cheap space to non-profit organization.

As well as running the children's stage, the library has maintained a booth at this event, displaying a large sample of our materials for Spanish speakers and registering people for library cards. I get bilingual assistants and library personnel to manage the booth in four shifts, since most of my time is tied up with the children's stage. Registration has diminished each year—from 110 to 70 to 35—due to a variety of factors, such as placement and the ability to announce our presence from the stage. I think the greatest factor may simply be that increasing numbers of the Hispanic attendees already know about the library and have cards.

After the first year participating in the Hispanic Fiesta, I asked the League if they would like to be a co-sponsor of Lanterns of Hope, a multicultural program that is described later in the article. The League was eager to help out with the event and also donated money to help with expenses. In addition, they donated money for a Guatemala Festival, which my church had put on for the past ten years, helping to pay for a Guatemalan speaker to talk about the movements for social change in his country. After a couple of years of collaboration, the Hispanic League asked if I would serve on their executive board. Although this presents yet another demand on my time, I felt that the collaboration would be advantageous to the library, as well as enabling me to help lead the Hispanic League in constructive new directions. As head of new programs I helped establish a radio program on health issues to be broadcast on *La Movidita*, the most popular Spanish language radio program. Through my networking experiences in the Hispanic Services Coalition I was able to redirect what was originally to be a one-person show into a group effort drawing on a broad range of health providers serving the Hispanic community.

First Line—Spanish Line

During early meetings of the Hispanic Services Coalition there was considerable discussion about having a Spanish language information service that could answer questions about various services available. Since Forsyth County Public Library already had an English language Information and Referral Service and one staff member who spoke fairly good Spanish on board, the library volunteered to create a separate Spanish language line. We printed up some simple red and white refrigerator magnets and pocket cards giving the phone number and began distributing these through the coalition meetings and other locations. Frequently, people who received them wanted to know what we meant by "organizations and services" in the community, so we printed up a half page Spanish language information sheet giving examples of a dozen organizations and services covered by First Line. As well as being a useful service to the Hispanic community, First Line's Spanish Line has helped to raise the visibility of the library with other organizations.

Churches

In Forsyth County there are currently eight Hispanic churches or churches that have a Spanish language service for Hispanics. In the 1996 Hispanic census the most commonly reported leisure time activity (indicated by 65 percent of respondents) was going to church, and the church strongly represents the most trusted institution in the Hispanic community. From the outset of our program I have spent considerable time getting to know the pastors and acquainting them with our services. Early on I invited them for a meeting at the Main Library, giving them a tour of our emerging collection. I also arranged for several of them to pose for photographs in our brochure, *La Biblioteca—Un Lugar de Muchos Colores*, in order to make it a more familiar and friendly document.

I had originally envisioned pastors as the best people to introduce library service to their congregations, since they had the confidence of their parishioners and spoke much better Spanish than I do. However, while some of them gave out brochures to their congregations, the response was very limited. I think that the image of the library remained very remote to those listening, since they associated their pastor with the church and not the library. The degree of knowledge and enthusiasm they brought to the task may also have been limited. Consequently, once I felt our collections were substantially set up, I began arranging general visits to all the churches to personally promote the library service. After discussing the procedure in detail with the ministers, I would arrive on Sunday about a half hour before the service with collated piles of our information—four or five flyers describing our different services plus Spanish language adult and children's registration forms tucked into our twelve page general brochure. The ushers would pass these out to the congregation as they came in. At the end of the service, during announcement time, the minister, outreach director, or other appropriate person would introduce me warmly to the congregation with general comments about the great opportunities the library has to offer Hispanic people.

I would speak for about ten minutes, beginning with a general introduction to library service, and then ask the parishioners to refer to selected pages of their brochure or the enclosed flyers as I discussed those aspects of our program: a sample list of the types of materials we provide in Spanish or bilingual format; the importance of reading to children; description of programs like bilingual assistance, story times, literacy class, or our film festival; procedure for obtaining a library card and checking out materials. I would invite the congregation to fill out registration forms at the end of service and give them to me or to assigned assistants from the church, for which purpose the ushers passed out pencils to those who needed them. As people brought us their registration forms, we would give them a map to the Main Library (for videos) and whichever was their local library, reminding them that they would receive their card in the mail in about two weeks.

This has been fairly successful to get a start on registrations, garnering about eight to ten registrations from small congregations to between thirty and fifty from the large ones. Although it is hard to tell exactly how many of these people are using their cards, my impression is the majority of them use them at least initially but that about half of them do not continue. On a couple of occasions with smaller congregations, I have brought a display of materials and allowed people to check out one item apiece against their library application. This seems to work pretty well, the main drawback being that it is already a considerable

wait for applicants to have their registration form inspected for readability and completeness. In the future I would like to enhance the presentations with a short skit and perhaps a story board, two techniques that are commonly used in "popular education" campaigns in Latin American countries. I think these would be very helpful in communicating the value and excitement of the library. However, it would have to be kept short in order to fit into the format of a 10-minute announcement time. I would also need the assistance of several volunteers to carry out the skit.

Occasionally, I have come to visit the churches on their Wednesday evening meeting or at a special event such as a summer picnic or an annual bilingual mass joining their two congregations. On such occasions I usually do a story time with the children, and if possible with parents, as well as the short informational presentation to the adults. A couple of assistants have recommended promoting the library by means of a Book Fair. At such an activity the church would plan a kind of festival, either outside or inside, with refreshments, music (either live or taped), and possibly other entertainment to attract its members. The library would present a story time and provide a substantial display of its materials, inviting people to sign up for a library card and check out one or two items.

Establishing a solid relationship with a church pastor or director of Hispanic outreach has been a necessary and worthwhile investment of time. It is also highly beneficial to cultivate one or two people who are both prominent in the church, especially through work with children, and willing to focus energy on library services. They would be more willing and able to give full attention to encouraging people in use of the library and its services and to develop outreach programs within their own facilities, some of the possibilities of which will be discussed later. Identification of such people has so far evolved with several churches, but has not officially been arranged with all of them. I hope soon to form a Hispanic library board, that will serve such a purpose, as well as generally helping direct the course of library service.

Catholic Social Services— "Casa Guadalupe"

Casa Guadalupe is a special Hispanic project of Catholic Social Services that provides personal assistance to Hispanic residents with immigration problems, income taxes, and a variety of other needs. Individuals or families come into the office on a walk-in or appointment basis for interviews. We have provided the office with a deposit collection and information display like those in the churches. Children make eager use of these materials, pulling out the books and poring through them as soon as they get to the office. *Casa Guadalupe* also has some other projects, including some family literacy classes they experimented with and home visits they now do to assist parents of young children. At the request of the director of Catholic Social Services we purchased about 70 paperback books for the literacy classes. The teacher, Melinda Hohn, who is now doing the home visits, has returned the favor by taking along a small pile of books on her visits, explaining their use to the mothers, and signing them up for library cards using our Spanish registration forms. She then sends the registration forms on to me to be entered on the computer.

Sister Joan's Door-to-Door Ministry

One of the local Catholic churches, Saint Leo's, provides a Hispanic outreach person instead of a mass on site. During the school year, Sister Joan Pearson visits Catholic families, particularly on the north side of town, instructing the children in catechism or, more recently, directing local lay leaders of religious formation in that effort. During the beginning stages of her ministry she took along with her a pile of library books, flyers, and registration forms which she distributed to families. A few families probably took these into the local library to sign up, but since Sister Joan did not take the time to actually register people for cards and send me the forms, the impact has been less than with Melinda Hohn of *Casa Guadalupe*. However, by traveling around with Sister Joan and meeting personally with some of the families, I have been able to make a greater impression. If and when there are paid assistants in the Hispanic Services department, accompanying Sister Joan will probably be part of their duties for the first year.

As well as being an excellent connection with individual families, Sister Joan has proved to be an ideal contact for identifying grass roots leaders in the different community settings. She noticed early on in her work that a grass roots leadership network had evolved in the different apartment complexes to organize their local religious celebrations such as the commemoration of Our Lady of Guadalupe and the Christmas *posadas*. That same structure helped her establish directors of religious formation in each of the complexes. Sister Joan pointed out at several meetings of the Hispanic Services Coalition, especially as we began applying for and implementing the planning grant, that grass roots leadership we spoke of in a theoretical sense already existed in this religious context (and probably for other local functions as well.) The task at hand would be to engage those leaders in assisting with a broader range of efforts assisting their neighbors.

During the summertime, Sister Joan coordinates a summer camp for about 100 Hispanic children, staffing it mainly with teenage Hispanic volunteers as counselors. The library provides a large selection of books—about 100—that are used for read-aloud sessions and silent reading by the children themselves. I have also ordered Summer Reading Program materials for Camp Saint Leo, including thematic stickers, bookmarks, reading certificates, activity sheets, and booklets where children mark down the books they read. When she can, Sister Joan attends our librarians' statewide meeting for the Summer Reading Program where she gets some ideas and inspiration by seeing some of the activities that librarians have planned along with the summer theme. Many of the children take home library registration forms and have them signed by their parents, thereby obtaining library cards. The first year they also came for a tour of the library.

In the third year of the summer camp, as the education committee was beginning to discuss the idea of introducing first language literacy in homework assistance centers, I suggested the idea of trying out this process with some of the campers. Margaret Scruggs, a retired reading teacher, worked up a simple program that she presented with a bilingual assistant Miriam Hernandez once a week for the six weeks of the season. While it was not sufficient time for the youngest children, it was quite successful with second

through fifth graders, who got a lot of satisfaction out of learning to read some simple Spanish readers.

Health Care Providers

A number of different organizations that counsel parents in the rearing of young children use our materials to introduce parents and kids to books and the library. ABCD, the Association for the Benefit of Child Development, has a program entitled "Best Start" with an office in the Reynolds Health Clinic, where most Hispanics and other low-income people go for health care. The Best Start office counsels parents in various aspects of child rearing, utilizing our books as part of their resources. They have recently begun to provide 8-week courses introducing parents to various community resources. They come to the library as part of this program, where I provide a tour and a program introducing how and why to share books with their children and help them check out some materials.

Forsyth Hospital has a program that counsels mothers of newborn babies. A Hispanic counselor, Carla Pereira, has been very active in sharing a small collection of books with the mothers and signing them up for library cards. She reports that a number of mothers have given excited reports about their forays into the library. Parent Line is an organization at Bowman Gray School of Medicine that counsels parents over the phone with various problems. Bilingual staff member Margaret Bocanegra (wife of one of the Hispanic pastors) frequently advises parents to read to their children, mailing them registration forms and directing them to the library to check out books.

Triad Hispanic Ministries, a community service organization formed out of *La*

Iglesia Bautista on the southeast edge of Winston-Salem, runs a monthly medical clinic at Beck's Baptist Church on the second Saturday of each month and at *La Iglesia Bautista* the third Saturday from 9 A.M. to noon. Both these churches have deposit collections from the library, and either I, or a bilingual assistant, usually come out to do a program with the children and parents. While the parents and children are in the long process of waiting for service, children and parents are invited to the front of the room for a story time session; those parents who do not come forward generally observe with interest from their seats. We then go around and personally ask each adult if they have a library card and, if not, help them fill out a registration form if they are interested. I discovered early on that although the majority will not request a registration form when addressed as a group, they are usually interested in filling one out when asked individually. For a few months I made an arrangement with Eunice Alcantaris, a talented young congregation member who was already assisting at the third Sunday clinic, to do the story times with the children. Creative and artistic and accustomed to conducting Sunday school with the children at church, Eunice was a perfect choice – except that her first commitment was to the church and she always found herself too busy helping the patients with translation and other needs to get to the story time. I have had better luck since using assistants who come in from outside the church. About a year into our collaborative efforts Triad Hispanic Ministries asked me to serve on their board of directors, which I agreed to. Not much time is involved, and this participation helps us to build a stronger relationship that benefits the library as well as the THM's efforts and the general welfare of the Hispanic community.

Forsyth Technical Community College— English as a Second Language Classes

Forsyth Tech, our local community college, has developed an excellent series of programs serving the Hispanic population, chief among them their classes in English as a Second Language. In the last three years they have grown from a handful of students to nearly thirty classes at six levels of course difficulty from literacy to advanced. A map display case with library information and materials is prominently displayed in their hallway outside the refreshment room. About a year into the ESL program I negotiated with basic skills coordinator Jim Weiss, the director of basic skills with whom I had already done some networking. He distributed fact sheets and sample information to the teachers and encouraged them to contact me for a visit to their classes or for a class tour of the library. However, after six months, when nothing came of it, I convinced him to simply schedule me for a visit to the classes. While the teachers had not taken the initiative to contact me, they were in fact very supportive of these visits, and the students have been very receptive. I come around at the beginning of each semester, before class size drops off, to visit all the classes. The first time I set up a display in the hallway, which was nice but time consuming since the process takes several days, so now I simply go to the classes with the brochures, forms, and a handful of books to explain our services and register them on site. The Forsyth Tech connection has so far proved our largest source of library patrons, since the students are well motivated. However, because most of them work all day and go to classes four nights a week, they do not have a lot of time to read!

One complication of visiting ESL classes at the community college or the public schools is that there are frequently a few non–Hispanic members of the classes. I therefore have to say everything in English even if I am also explaining it in Spanish for basic level students. I also have to generally be careful that the content and tone of my talk does not seem to slight them. Since gift books are one aspect of the library presentation that get the students' attention, we recently added a couple of titles for non–Hispanics and are using coupons to help them be identified by library personnel giving out the books.

Public Schools

The public schools appear to be an excellent access point to the Hispanic population, since so many families have a child in school. I have found many English as a Second Language Teachers, as well as school social workers, eager to have me visit their classes to share stories and tell their students about the library's services. The children have generally responded very enthusiastically, and this serves as a good introduction to reading. Unfortunately, it seems difficult to make an impression on many parents without talking to them directly, and without the parents' involvement, we cannot get the children into the library. An average of about 5 percent of children visited have gotten their parents to fill out an application form and returned it to the teacher for a library card. In those cases where I have simply sent materials to classes without a personal visit on my own, there has been

almost no visible response. Nevertheless, where visits to the schools are made, I think the image the children take home with them is important, and it will gradually lead to more enthusiastic use of library materials when these are available, either in the library, in their church, or in school.

More recently I have been visiting parents in the schools during PTA meetings and other special events, particularly Multicultural Festivals, an approach which has proved much more successful. While I may speak to only ten or fifteen parents, almost all of them register for library cards. I am currently working with Joy McLauglin, the lead ESL teacher who serves unofficially as an ESL coordinator, to develop a series of parent orientation sessions at the ESL schools, in which the library would provide one or more sessions on sharing books with their children. If we can bring this to pass, it should be an excellent link to involving families in the library. Judith Rodríguez, the director of New York City's *Connecting Libraries and Schools Project (CLASP)*, has done numerous workshops of this kind in the New York public schools and feels they are very effective in introducing parents to the importance of reading to, and with, their children. She has been able to persuade many principals to make parents' attendance at these sessions a requirement. Among other formats, she often pairs off parents and has them read to each other, then report to the group on what they have shared.

An effective way I have been able to reach middle school students is through a collaborative effort of the Hispanic League and the RJ Reynolds Tobacco Company. Jason Underwood, an RJR employee, came up with the idea of offering prizes to middle school ESL students to motivate them to work harder in their studies. In the fall of the year, a group of volunteers from the Hispanic League goes with Jason to visit the schools and introduce the program. Jason explains the criteria for winning: students are judged mostly on the effort they put forth and the progress they make in their studies, rather than the ending point they attain. Other visitors, most of whom are Hispanic, tell the students about their careers, thus serving as role models, and encourage them to also reach for professional accomplishments. I talk about the library and the valuable role that developing reading skills and habits plays in their academic and lifetime success. I leave the school public library information and registration forms, which the contact teacher distributes and sends back to me. Visiting the students in this way helps to put the role of reading in a larger context of improving their overall development. In effect, the impact of the other visitors helps to validate the importance of the library and reading.

I have visited the high school ESL classes on my own, as well as at a parents' night sponsored by the Hispanic League, and found the high school students to be quite receptive to the library's services. Most of the students who have managed to continue school to this point are fairly motivated and are looking for tools to help them succeed. At the time of writing this article, I had just discussed with the high school ESL teachers a reading and writing project in which the upper level students will read library books from a multicultural book list and write book reviews, short stories, poems, interviews, essays, and informational articles relating to their own cultural background. The writings will be published in bilingual form in an annual or semi-annual collection by the library.

The Sawtooth Center for Visual Art

The Sawtooth Center conducts many workshops on traditional crafts and creative arts and craft activities in its home location and at various outreach locations. Outreach director Kathy Gauldin has attended meetings of Hispanic Services Coalition on a fairly frequent basis, and has looked for ways to include the Hispanic community in her work. In the *Photovoice Project* Hispanic participants took and developed photographs reflecting their personal and community lives, then wrote a description in Spanish and English which was included in the frame below the picture. Kathy approached me to display the work in library locations, to which the Main library and Reynolda branch agreed. When Kathy was looking for a Hispanic Outreach staff member, I checked with several of my bilingual assistants, and Luli Beckles applied for and obtained the position. I arranged for them to do a quick mural at the Lanterns for Hope program and Hispanic fiesta in 1999. We have subsequently discussed collaboration on story times, including a plan to have Luli work with children in an apartment complex while I shared parent training sessions with Rocio Sedo, a Cooperative Extension outreach nutritionist. That particular project failed to enlist sufficient participants and got sidetracked, but I feel the model is a good one, and we should be able to implement it before long.

Spanish Language Media

Perhaps because the world of Hispanic immigrants in our area is still fairly small and new, the Spanish language media in and near Forsyth County have been very cooperative in publicizing library services.

We have four radio stations broadcasting in Spanish in our area. All were receptive to doing an interview on the air, and when I went to visit the radio stations, I took along a sample of our materials so that the announcers and program directors could see first hand the kind of materials we provide. The stations have invited me to interview before special events, and they appear willing to read public service announcements and sometimes talk about the events informally. However, I am not overly confident how often PSA's are read, and probably ongoing announcements of library service are not used beyond about a month's time.

One of the Spanish language newspapers in the arca, *Que Pasa*, has also been very receptive to coverage of library events. However, two months after Julio Pando, Jr., the editor, visited me at the library he had only printed a photograph (one which I gave him from our brochure) and no article. Sensing that he was interested but overwhelmed with work, I offered to write the article itself, which he printed on a full page of the next edition. When we started our Hispanic Film Festival, Julio printed our actual poster, artwork and all, which looked rather like a paid advertisement. We have now started running a column called *Querida Biblioteca* about library materials and activities, written by our bilingual library assistants. It appears that if we are willing to do the work ourselves, *Que Pasa* is more than happy to publish it. This is the kind of attention one might receive from a small town newspaper, but would rarely be available from the English language media in a city of 150,000 people.

Programs

The most difficult aspect of library service to our Hispanic immigrant popula-

tion has been programming. We have tried several different types of programs in the library, most of which have been underattended to the point that they have not seemed to merit the effort.

El Grupo Cañaveral

One of the categories in our start-up grant from the State Library was fees for professional authors, storytellers, and musicians. In collaboration with a Smart Start "Day of the Young Child" and with the public schools we invited Nelson and Hilda Zuleta, the leaders of the Miami based "El Grupo Cañaveral," to come to Forsyth County for some concerts. They spent a day in Hall Woodward Elementary School, one of the largest ESL centers, giving several concerts of Latin songs, singing games, and dance. When the Zuletas present children's programs like this, they use tapes of their full band's recordings, *Cantemos con los Niños Hispanos*, creating a very lively, full sounding performance that was enthusiastically received. At the end of the day, we passed out Spanish language flyers about their concert the next day in our Southside Library and about their performance in the "Day of the Young Child/Día de los Niños" program. We left flyers throughout the city's restaurants and flyers gave them to all the Hispanic churches to be passed out at their services. The only people to come were a group from one area church who attended the library concert and two families to attend the Day of the Young Child. It appeared to me at that time that the Hispanic population simply did not know and trust the library well enough at that point, and that we would be better off to defer any large expenditures on performers until we were better known in the community.

Aprendiendo Juntos

My original concept of Spanish language and bilingual story times was to do them for a certain period of time in outreach locations such as the churches before trying them in the library. However, at one of our Hispanic Service Coalition meetings I was approached by Jim Weiss, the basic skills coordinator of Forsyth Tech, and Mary Jo Winkle, executive director of ABCD, with the idea of doing a story time combined with an English lesson. I would present the story time together with the ESL teacher, a Puerto Rican woman named Maria Selles who was also a social worker for Head Start; then Maria would give a short English lesson while a representative of ABCD would entertain the kids with toys and activities from their collection. On some occasions a special resource person would come during the English lesson time to talk about a subject of interest to the parents, such as immigration, jobs, education, or health. ABCD would provide transportation to families that needed it. We decided to call it *Aprendiendo Juntos (Learning Together)*. One of the books used each week in the story time would be bilingual, and we would provide enough copies so that parents could each take a copy home and read to their children during the week. The enticement of the English classes and ability to provide transportation led us all to feel that it would be a good idea to hold the programs in the public library so that people would get to know it. After polling people in an ABCD program and several churches for time and place preferences, we set up a Monday evening program in our Southside Library and a Thursday morning program in our Kernersville branch.

In Kernersville I enlisted the help of Vicky Utsman, the Hispanic outreach coordinator of Holy Cross Catholic Church in Kernersville, who spoke to the parishioners personally and spent a morning with me going around to the houses and apartments of people she thought might be interested. We ended up with a small, but somewhat stable group of between 2 and 5 families. Being mostly somewhat middle class, the families were fairly motivated to learn English and share books with their children. One parent who was fluent in English came because she wanted her son to be exposed to Spanish, which he rarely got to hear or use. Still, it seemed like a lot of work for three staff people to be tending this small group. When the fall came and we set up a longer series, we ran into problems because some of the children were now in school, others could no longer come for other reasons, and we developed difficulties providing transportation. So we were down to 0-3 families per session, hardly worth the effort.

At the Southside Library we generally had a larger group, about 3 to 8 families, but most of them had to be transported, sometimes requiring two pick-ups with the one van, which could present timing problems. Most of the families were quite poor and unaccustomed to listening to books; this plus an age span from 2 to 12 or so with sometimes a large group could lead to sessions being unruly. In the fall, to cope with transportation and personnel problems from ABCD, we added a new partner, SOS (Support Our Students), a middle school program of the YMCA, which took over transportation and provided a little extra attention for the children. Numbers began to drop off here too, perhaps because of the time and weather change, possibly because some of the women may have felt nervous about riding with the new male driver. At the end of the fall program, all of leaders felt that the results were not worth the expenditure of energy. Also, due to the interests and basic skill level of most participants the English lessons came to focus almost entirely on standard English conversation and vocabulary lessons oriented around everyday survival lessons. The use of the bilingual books as teaching tools, a major reason for this collaborative effort, never quite took off. After the fall semester of the *Aprendiendo Juntos* series, we decided to close it down.

Linternas de la Paz— Lanterns for Hope

Beginning in 1988 every year around Hiroshima Day (The anniversary of the August 6 bombing of Hiroshima), Forsyth County Public Library has sponsored a multicultural program honoring the hope for peace and understanding in the world and in our community. The evening event begins with some kind of supper—a picnic, covered dish, or free meal provided for the guests. Children and interested adults then make a Japanese peace lantern, decorating the paper shade with pictures and phrases that express their thoughts and hopes on the program's theme. the excitement builds as several groups or individuals perform music, dance, drama, or storytelling representing various cultural traditions. Finally, the program concludes with the moving ceremony of lighting and linking together the lanterns, that are gently set into the water and towed in a loop around the lake by a canoe. At the request of the library's Associate Director, the program has moved around to several locations to make it more appealing and accessible to different segments of the community.

In 1997, for the second year, we wanted to create a bilingual ceremony that would involve Hispanic families. Whereas in 1996, before our library program had begun, we tried with no success to attract the Hispanic community, in 1997 we did fairly well in this regard. This was most likely due to our inviting the Hispanic choir of Our Lady of Mercy Church to perform, for they, in turn, invited family members and friends to come see them. It was interesting, however, that no members of the adjoining Lakeside Apartments, which our bookmobile visits and where we publicized heavily, attended. There was also an African American storyteller and bluegrass group. It was very moving to see the group effort of linking together and floating the lanterns, a situation in which many Hispanics, White, and Black residents who had experienced little previous contact, were joining together in this symbolic effort. On the whole we felt the Hispanic involvement in this event was a success.

In the 1998 Lanterns program, conducted at Tanglewood Park, a beautiful but more remote location several miles outside Winston-Salem, we drew about 150 Hispanic participants, forming nearly half of the attendees. Very likely they were attracted by the presence of "Los Viajeros," a well known local Mariachi band, as featured performers, and by a free meal provided by *Mi Pueblo* restaurant. The 1999 program, conducted at Salem Lake in the south central part of town and including a Mexican dance performance group from neighboring Yadkin County, also drew a large Hispanic turnout. At this point it seems that *Lanterns of Hope/ Linternas de la Paz* has established a reputation for being an exciting program which both affirms Hispanic culture for its participants and enables them to feel a connection with other segments of the community. In fact, I think it accomplishes this goal of building multicultural bridges better than any other event I am aware of in Forsyth County.

Aprendamos a Leer

One of our bilingual assistants, Yolanda Pou, who has taught literacy in the past as a missionary, approached me one day about starting a small class in learning to read in Spanish. We knew there were many people who couldn't read or could barely read, and we knew this was key to the parents being able to share books with their children. Since reading Spanish is relatively easy compared to learning to read in English and is not taught at Forsyth Tech, we thought there might be some interest in it. Yolanda brought a few friends to care for young children who might accompany parents. We advertised for several weeks through the churches, radio stations, schools, and other channels. For the first few weeks a couple that was referred to us by ABCD came, then they decided it was too difficult for them to get there. Other than that there were no takers. Hopefully, this important goal of teaching first language literacy can be more effectively accomplished through the larger joint effort being planned by the Hispanic Services Coalition and Forsyth Technical Community College.

Hispanic Film Festival

Observing the popularity of our video collection, the idea occurred to me to present a Hispanic Film Festival that would bring people into the library on Saturdays at the time of our bilingual assistance. At 1 P.M., the time when assistance would generally begin, we scheduled a library tour and short story time and we advertised refreshments and registration for prizes, although people could really take advantage of these at 2 P.M., which is when the film was scheduled. So as not to draw all interested Hispanic patrons into one library on a given Saturday, thus ignoring other branches providing bilingual assistance, I decided to show each of the first four out of five films two times and at two different locations. A variety of film types were selected that would generally reflect Hispanic culture and generally be of interest to children as well as adults, although not being all children's films per se. All the titles were taken from our video collection. I naively thought I had finally found an idea that would draw large numbers of our Hispanic families into the library. There was widescale publicity through 5,000 brochures distributed in churches, ESL classes, restaurants, and libraries. Frequent announcements were made in churches and on the radio, and there was excellent coverage in *Que Pasa* newspaper. In spite of this, attendance ran only between 5 and 15 people per film, about half of the audience arriving at 2 P.M., just in time for the film. Although several bilingual assistants approved the selection of films, some subsequent comments by other Hispanic residents said they thought the selection was too classic, and that attendance would have been much better with new feature films.

The Problem with Programs

Although usage of the libraries is slowly increasing, we have had little luck bringing people into the library during specific times for specified programs. Hispanic people I have spoken with have suggested a number of reasons: the immigrant population simply does not see the library as a place to relax and spend time. They say they are very shy and slow to trust a new place and organization. They also report that they resist committing to a given time. Another reason given is that for those lacking much education this leads to downplaying reading as a valuable and interesting activity. For others, their experience with education in Latin America inclines people to leave the business of reading and education entirely up to the schools. Another reason given is that when Saturday necessities are taken care of, people want to be on their own turf, doing things and going to places they are familiar with. Concerning evening hours, on the other hand, they don't see the library as a necessity like ESL classes, so they are reluctant to give up a weeknight to come there. Outside of their jobs and church attendance, which the Hispanic immigrants attend faithfully, they show little motivation for other commitments. Many other agencies have reported extreme difficulty in bringing out people to programs and have mainly resigned to bringing them in to them. Even Forsyth Tech, which is the most demanded educational service, reported two years after beginning their ESL program that they often had a drop off from 30 registered students to two or three attending by the end of a semester. In order to draw Hispanic immigrants into the library for programs, there would probably have to be a much longer, more extensive lead-up established through personal contact on their own turf—in their churches or homes. For whatever the reason, at this point in the development of library service to Hispanic immigrants, it does not seem to warrant the effort to plan many programs at the library for this population.

Plans for the Future

Plans for the future are to provide more programs at outreach locations and, if possible, to expand outreach service generally. I think the most effective programming at this point will be story time series for parents and children, primarily in churches and apartment complexes. In a series running six to nine weeks, parents would observe their children listening to and enjoying stories; discuss the benefits of this process among themselves; discuss some of the actual stories themselves in terms of their form and meaning; learn how to read aloud and discuss stories in an interesting and effective manner and practice sharing stories with their own children; and visit the library on two or three occasions to check out materials and become familiar with the environment. Several churches have already expressed interest in such a series, as well as ABCD Best Start and the Cooperative Extension Services. Irania Patterson, the Hispanic outreach programmer for Charlotte/Mecklenburg County, North Carolina has done many such workshops on a regular basis and feels they have been successful in drawing many patrons into the library.

Where possible, I will train interested and able members of the churches and other bilingual assistants to do this series, since they already have the confidence of church members and can converse with them more easily than I can. I have an English language training manual that I developed as former head of Children's Outreach, where we train nearly hundreds of day care providers in story sharing skills, and I have a Spanish language training manual a little different in approach, that comes from the Nicaraguan organization, *Libros Para Niños*. A North Carolina organization entitled "MotheRead" has also developed an extensive curriculum of ideas for sharing nearly 100 different picture books with one's own children. Many of these titles are available in translation.

Plans for a radio story time have been in the works for some time. This is something which families can enjoy in the security of their own homes, yet hopefully inspire them to share books and stories themselves. Two of the bilingual library assistants, Maria Selles and Luli Beckles, have spent some time helping select stories and songs for potential programs. They will co-host the program with either myself or a native Spanish speaking man. Other Spanish speakers will assist as readers on certain programs and children will be brought in on occasions to participate as audience members. Two radio stations discussed broadcasting the story time series with me. However, one program, *La Fiesta Mexicana*, which had agreed to do the series for free, later decided it wanted money, and since the program has been in questionable financial status, does not seem worth the investment. The other station stopped doing Spanish language programming. The current plan is raise grant money to pay for the program on *La Movidita*, the most prominent of the commercial Spanish language programs.

There is some question about whether to make the radio story time a bilingual program or present it all in Spanish. Oralia Garza de Cortés has advised me to do it all in Spanish because the students are already exposed to so much in English. Doing the program entirely in Spanish would provide a greater reinforcement of their culture and might make the program more attractive for syndication in other areas of the country. On the other hand, there is a great desire of our immigrant population to learn English, and a bilingual program might promote the idea of

integrating the two cultures and languages. Even if English were incorporated, the bulk of the program would still be done in Spanish.

I think the radio program would help build enough interest in story time programming to begin offering some limited story times at two or three key branches. A bilingual story time, craft, and friendship hour one evening a month seems like a promising program to bring together Hispanic and English-speaking patrons. Using the MotheRead model of focusing on one story could help limit the repetitiousness of doing several stories bilingually, providing more time for mixing of the multicultural participants. Luli Beckles, the Hispanic outreach member of the Sawtooth Center for Visual Design, could lead the craft activity as well as help with the story sharing.

While I hope to considerably expand usage of our traditional public library facilities by the Hispanic immigrants of Forsyth County, I also think that many people who would benefit from our materials will never come into our branches. I think we need to expand our outreach service on a permanent, not just promotional, basis, in order to reach the majority of Hispanic immigrants. Most of this population lives concentrated in apartment complexes, making them fairly easy to access. Our bookmobile stop at the low income Lakeside Apartments is quite popular, and a special Hispanic services bookmobile with a Spanish-speaking driver and assistant should do even better. I plan to apply for a grant within the next six months to fund the bookmobile and a program assistant. The bookmobile could possibly stop at the homework assistance centers as well as residential areas, providing some special programming as well as a varied supply of books.

I anticipate needing two full time assistants to accomplish these new programming needs. Since funding from Forsyth County government does not seem likely in the immediate future, I plan to seek funding for one position from foundation sources, initially the Winston-Salem Foundation, and then others if necessary. There is a lot of awareness, among local businesses as well as foundations, of the needs of the Hispanic population and of the need for enhancing education generally, so I don't think it should be too hard to come up with the money. I hope to obtain another position through Americorp's *Access* program, which is designed to help recent immigrants utilize available services and adapt to their new home. *Casa Guadalupe* has hired at least one staff member through this program, and the Glenwood Branch of the Greensboro

Public Library system has used it to fill four positions! In addition to conducting programming, these new staff members could assist with clerical functions that tie up too much of the department head's time. I also hope to have one of them start a library newsletter featuring articles written by Hispanic library users as well as the editor about our collection and services.

Serving the Hispanic immigrant population of Forsyth County over the past two and a half years has been a new and challenging experience for our public library system. We have met with some successes, which I think will continue to grow. We have also met with some failures, which I hope we can learn from. I hope also that this discussion of our experiences, both positive and negative, will provide some assistance to other libraries seeking to serve Hispanic immigrants.

CHAPTER THIRTEEN

Ethnographic Perspectives on Trans-National Mexican Immigrant Library Users

Susan Luévano-Molina

This article explores selected results of a qualitative case study pertaining to the perceptions of the public library and library use patterns among Spanish-speaking Mexicano/Latino adult immigrants. The data are extrapolated from an expansive ethnographic study conducted in the city of Santa Ana, California, during 1995-1997. [1] This study focused on the impact of post-1994 anti-immigrant legislation on Spanish speaking Latino immigrants. The article provided here intends only to describe an urban transnational Mexican immigrant community's perceptions and usage of the Santa Ana Public Library.

The city under discussion is a low-income, highly immigrant and primarily working class municipality located thirty miles south of Los Angeles. Considered an inner city community, Santa Ana is home to one of the largest concentrations of Mexicans living in the United States and outside of Mexico.

The study transpired during a period of intense local, state and national debate on immigration and immigrants. This socio-cultural context exacerbated an already hostile environment for Latino immigrants or those Latinos perceived to be immigrants. The study locale is home to the highly active "Save Our State" anti-immigrant organization which spearheaded the legislation passed by California voters in 1994, known as Proposition 187.

Research Methodology

An ethnographic approach was selected for the study field work. [2] As practiced in the social sciences, ethnography entails extensive observation, interviews, descriptions of people and contexts. These techniques contributed to the success of the study as the methodology required that all data gathering be done on community turf. This added not only to the rich cultural context in which the study took place but contributed to the reliability of the study evidence. This distinctive research design offered a format in which complex cultural, political and social factors could be equated into an assessment which could give shape and meaning to library attitudes and use factors. Given the highly charged political climate surrounding immigrants use of public services in the United States it was envisioned as an excellent tool for assessing the project goals as formed through the social action of the society. The study was structured to entail a highly focused approach requiring a relatively short period of field work.

This investigative technique was also preferred for it's populist selection of informants. Common ordinary people, not community leaders or "gatekeepers" (Metoyer-Duran 1993), were encouraged to express their viewpoints and experiences. Ethnography allowed for comments to be gathered and analyzed in the native language of the informants. Although language occupies a tremendous part of the human experience it is often taken for granted by library researchers. In conducting this ethnographic study, the Spanish language structured field notes, analyses and insights. It also greatly enhanced rapport and confidence between informants and the research team during encounters. Furthermore, the presence of undocumented immigrants with clandestine identities in the Santa Ana community made ethnography an excellent research method for all the reasons listed above. Names, addresses and phone numbers were not requested and very few sessions were taped. These factors contributed to the willingness of the informants to participate.

Instrument

A six part open-ended instrument was created in English and translated into Spanish. The instrument included, but was not limited to (1) a detailed introduction to the research process, (2) consent of the participant to be interviewed, (3) personal background data, (4) awareness of the public library in the home country and in the United States and (5) use patterns of the public library in the home country and in the United States, and (6) income and immigrations status. A post-evaluation was filled out by the investigator for each completed session. The instrument was administered in Spanish by bilingual/bicultural librarians, and selected community members. The research team used the appropriate anthropological data gathering techniques of observation, engagement and dialogue. Great efforts were made to understand what was happening from the perspectives of the participants. This demanded many hours of field work, gathering and interpreting layers of context in neighborhood settings. Data gathering was incredibly labor intensive and could not have been achieved without the assistance of a highly skilled research team and other organizational support.[3]

The summary qualitative results provided here are the result of the openness and patience of the interviewees who trusted us with their stories, experiences and opinions. While a few residents declined the invitation to participate, most generously gave of their time to participate. The interviews targeted fifty Spanish speaking adult Mexican/Latino immigrants, including 25 men and 25 women. The exchanges were conducted between January 1996 and November 1996, at local elementary schools, neighborhood markets, at a donut shop, on street corners where men wait for work, in public plazas and parks, as well as in private homes. All interviews were conducted within a three mile range of a library facility or bookmobile stop to ensure that access to a public library was not a factor in the informants potential lack of use or exposure to a public library facility. All participants were required to be residents of the City and be at least 18 years old.

The full scope of the project had to be explained to all informants before initiating the interview process. Confidentiality of the respondents remarks were stressed. Potential interviewees were instructed that there were no right or wrong responses. They were also made aware that declining to answer a question(s) was always an option. All respondents were also provided contact information so that they could ask follow-up questions or express concerns of the primary investigator. Participation in the study was contingent only on the verbally consent of the informant.

A taxonomic analysis followed the data gathering stage. That is, a set of categories were organized on the basis of a single semantic relationship. The taxonomy revealed subsets and the way in which these subsets related to the whole. This analyses enabled the primary investigator to determine perception and library usage patterns.

Unlike other social science research, the nature of ethnographic research requires constant feedback from one stage to another. Consequently, preliminary findings were shared with members of REFORMA beginning in August 1996.[4] The study findings have continued to be examined and challenged by other librarians specializing in library services to Latinos. Revisions and further analyses have followed these sessions.

Study Objectives

Selected research objectives included but were not limited to the following areas:

1. Documentation of *Mexicano*/Latino immigrants' **perceptions** of the public library in their home country or the United States.

2. Documentation of *Mexicano*/Latino immigrants' public library **usage** in their home country or the United States;

3. Analyses of how *Mexicano*/Latino immigrants **perceptions** of the public library may be similar or dissimilar to the dominant culture in the United States;

4. Analyses of how *Mexicano*/Latino immigrants library **usage patterns** may be similar or dissimilar to the dominant culture.

5. Refinement of the use of ethnography in library research.

Findings

The demographics of the informants reflected a young population, primarily low-income and working class, with minimal formal education. Although some respondents had arrived as recently as the previous day others had resided in Santa

Ana for over 40 years. The participants averaged 8.8. years of residency in Santa Ana. The majority of participants were of Mexican origin (88 percent) while the remaining 12 percent were from Central and South America. The educational characteristics of the informants were intriguing as they have traditionally served as the pivotal indicator of potential library use (Berelson 1949, Marchant 1991, Scheppke 1994). The participants' educational attainment was low by mainstream standards. Some 20 percent had less than three years of education; 30 percent had completed elementary school (in Mexico this includes 6 years of formal education known as *primaria*); 28 percent had completed *secundaria* or high school; 6 percent were college graduates, and 6 percent had attended professional schools.

Slightly over half of the participants were citizens or legal residents, 12 percent and 42 percent respectively. Almost half the participants (44 percent) were undocumented residents or what is popularly known as *sin papeles*, that is "without valid immigration papers."[5] Another 2 percent of the informants identified themselves as having the unique status known as political asylum. These informants were Salvadorean refugees.

Spanish was the dominant language of the majority of participants and the majority of library users. Most indicated that their grasp of English was limited. However, even among informants who indicated that they spoke English fluently, Spanish was their preferred language. The participants were a young population. The 18-29 age cohort was the largest at 32 percent, followed by the 30-39 group at 30 percent. The over 40 respondents comprised 36 percent of the respondents. Participants with school age children were more likely to be library users than those

who were single. This was the predominant indicator of potential library use among respondents, regardless of gender.

As noted earlier, *Mexicanos* are the predominant immigrant population in Santa Ana. States of Mexico that were widely represented included Michoacan (21 percent), Guerrero (17 percent), and Jalisco (15 percent). Participants from other Latin American countries cited El Salvador, Guatemala and Ecuador as their native home. Income was low for all respondents regardless of education, immigration status, fluency in English or years of residency in Santa Ana. Most respondents could be categorized as working poor. Only 32 percent made more than $10,000 per year. This finding is consistent with other social science studies that indicate that Latinos in urban and suburban areas experience disproportionately high poverty rates and that these rates are evident even in the third generation after settling in the United States (Hayes-Bautista 1989, Hurtado 1992). Informants were more likely not to answer this inquiry than any other question raised during the interview session.

Interestingly, among the informants there was a high awareness of public libraries in their home country. High awareness of the Santa Ana Public Library was also documented. The majority of the participants had very positive impressions of the city library system, even though 50 percent had never entered a public library or bookmobile in Santa Ana. This type of awareness and regard for the public library is similar to research findings in more mainstream populations (Estabrook 1997, D'Elia & Rodgers 1995, 1996).

A fascinating revelation was the high use of public libraries in the home country. Almost half (48 percent) indicated that they had used a public or school library in their native land. [6] Half of the participants had personally visited a library or bookmobile in Santa Ana. Among the group of current Santa Ana Public Library users, 50 percent were library users in their native country. Of those using the library over half felt that neither the passage of Proposition 187, nor more recent nativist legislation or pending legislation had deterred them in any way from using the public library. Library use among those who identified themselves as undocumented immigrants was 33 percent.

An impressive 36 percent of the respondents had Santa Ana Public library cards as compared to an estimated 10 percent–28 percent for the general population (Berelson 1949, Marchant 1991, Scheppke 1994). Among library card holders 16 percent noted that the entire family had valid library cards. Most respondents noted strong sentiments regarding the library as a neutral, tax supported space which should be available to all city residents regardless of immigration status. Many immigrants discussed the various ways in which they utilize the public library. The primary responses were either for life long learning, to expand employment opportunities, or to assist children in completing school assignments. The library was also cited as a needed and valued space for relaxation and study.

Many participants expressed increased anxiety when using the public library during the last couple of years. Given the prevailing anti-immigrant mood in Orange County, this was not surprising. What was striking was the fact that 95 percent of library users stated that they had not noticed any difference in treatment at any permanent library or bookmobile stop since the 1994 passage of Proposition 187.

Significance of the Study

Findings of the Santa Ana case study challenge the existing research on library users as a whole and particularly transnational Mexican populations. First of all, *Mexicano* immigrants are very much aware of the public library and hold it in the same high esteem as the normative population. The library as an institution is a symbol of hope in the Mexican community. It signifies the proverbial "equal playing field" so often discussed in other diversity debates. This is where informants feel they can go, for self or family improvement. As one informant stated *la biblioteca es una fuente de oportunidad* (the library is a center for opportunity).

Immigrants' lack of exposure and access to public library systems in their home countries is a well accepted axiom in the library field (Padilla 1991). However, among the informants who had used the public library in Santa Ana there was a high number who had been library users in Mexico. The Mexican public library system has experienced tremendous growth in the last decade and a half. Between 1982 and 1992 over 4,000 new public libraries have been established (Magaloni 1993). These figures represent a 1,000 percent expansion of public libraries in approximately ten years. These libraries serve over 71 million Mexican readers in urban and rural areas of Mexico. Their rapid development has depended on the help and support of local communities. Libraries have been integrated in the cultural fabric of many communities that twenty years ago had no access to a public library.

Many of the younger respondents in this case study had benefited from Mexico's budding national library system before moving North. This finding indicates the emergence of a trans-national library user not before documented in the literature.[7] Given immigration trends of Mexican nationals to the United States, particularly to California, it should be expected that the number of transnational library users who reside in Mexican/Latino communities will continue to increase in the coming decades.

The ramifications of Mexican immigrants' appreciation and exposure to libraries in their home countries cannot be overstated. Further documentation and analysis of this finding is critical to understanding how trans-national library experiences may assist incorporation of recent immigrants to a new home country. How does library interaction influence immigrants accountability to the city where they reside? One must also question immigrants' expectations of public library service in the United States as opposed to Mexico. Future researchers need to determine how trans-national cooperation between Mexican and United States public libraries in the borderlands of the Southwest have influenced library user trends. Outcomes of Trans-border Library Forums should be carefully examined (Hoffert 1993).

We must also consider how transnational library use might be sustained in the United States. Clearly the inclusion of appropriate materials and bilingual staff were effective in the Santa Ana study. What happens in communities where these services and staff are not provided? Can we really assume that Mexican/Latino immigrants will not use library services or facilities that do not meet their needs or will they force a modification? How might immigrants be persuaded to openly demonstrate social agency for public libraries in this country? These are but a few of the questions that

deserve the attention of library researchers.

This study also documented the racialization of Latino immigrants, both legal and those out-of-status (Miles 1989, Urciuoli 1996). Immigrants sustain a heightened awareness of the bitter social-political context of life in the United States. Informants consistently expressed an overriding sense of societal rejection and erasure. Remarkably, the public library in Santa Ana is perceived as a neutral institution despite the many hardships faced by informants. Findings indicate that the public library is venerated by the *Mexicano*/Latino community. It is viewed as a pivotal community symbol of opportunity and upward mobility. Research on the dominant populations' perceptions of the library is similarly positive (Estabrook 1997, D'Elia & Rodgers 1995, 1996).

Despite this mutual esteem for the public library, the profile of the Mexican immigrant library user is very different from the dominant society. The results of this case study indicate that educational achievement was not a key factor in determining library use. Library users in this study achieved an average of six years of education. This finding runs contrary to most other adult user studies where a direct correlation exists between the level of educational achievement and potential library use (Berelson 1949, Estabrook 1997, D'Elia & Rodgers 1995, 1996). Also, notable is the low-income status of the participants. Income level is another rule of thumb in determining library usage and is closely linked to educational achievement (Scheppke 1994). Again, the informants in the Santa Ana study did not conform to this profile. The majority of library users in this case study would be classified as working poor.

The most salient feature of adult

library users in this study was the presence of school age children in the household. Participants noted a lack of discretionary income to support the buying of books or videos for children. Consequently, respondents with dependent youth increased their library use to supplement educational and recreational material in the household. The Riskind study in New Jersey also found that low-income communities with large numbers of dependent children have higher rates of library use than higher income communities with lower rates of dependent youth (Riskind 1991). Also, a new survey from the National Center for Education Statistics (NCES) indicates similar national results (Lynch). In addition, it is important to reflect on the unique characteristics of individuals who make up the immigrant population as noted by other social scientists (Hayes-Bautista, Schink and Chapa 1989, Chávez 1992, Portes and Rumbault 1996, Hayes-Bautista and Rodríguez 1996, 1997). Immigrant populations are often the best and brightest members of their home countries. They also tend to be highly motivated people. Furthermore, Latino immigrants have the highest labor-force participation rate of any U.S. ethnic group (U.S. Bureau of the Census, 1983).

These characteristics were validated in the Santa Ana study. Informants cited employment opportunities as the primary reason for their migration to Santa Ana. Library users consistently indicated self-improvement as their primary reason for using the public library. Immigrants indicated an apprehensiveness about contact with any public institution, even those that have served them well in the past, such as the public library. The staff survey conducted by Knox verifies Santa Ana Public Library staffs' impression that immigrants in general seem more hesitant to ask for assistance since the passage of Proposition 187 (Knox 1998).

Current library users expressed some anxiety about using the library facility and asking for assistance. This attitude was documented among informants regardless of their immigration status. The reasons cited by informants for this hesitancy centered around recent anti-immigrant legislation that was overwhelmingly supported in Orange County. This legislation along with increased immigrant bashing during the last decade has created a climate of uncertainty among the immigrant community.

Yet, despite the obvious sense of alienation from the mainstream society the participants expressed a vigorous consensus regarding ownership of the public library system and services in their community. Concerns about the possible denial of library services to undocumented residents of the city brought expressions of outrage from both legal and undocumented respondents. The library is regarded as an important neutral institution in the community. Many respondents clearly and forcefully articulated the collective good that comes from an educated and well-informed community.

The opinions of participants in the study indicated that as long as residents pay taxes they have a right to expect public services. Informants clearly desired that the public library be a communal resource available to those who live, work and contribute to the community. These sentiments are in sharp contrast to opinions of the dominant society regarding immigrant populations. The 1990s discourse on local and statewide immigration reform was charged with expressions of anger about recent demographic and cultural changes brought about by the massive immigration of the 1980s. Immigrants, in general, have been deemed less worthy of public services than other community members. To be an immigrant today is to be a burden or cost to society rather than an asset (Gutiérrez 1996, Urciuoli 1996, Perea 1997).

Santa Ana Public Library: Services and Staff

The Santa Ana Public Library collection, staff and services received high grades from respondents who had used them. The quality and quantity of services, collections, and bilingual staff were mentioned constantly as the drawing card for community residents. Appreciation of the excellent facilities were noted. Bookmobile services also received high marks from regular user.

It is very likely that the results of this case study would have been quite different if not for the dynamic nature of the Santa Ana Public Library leadership, services and staff. The public library, has done an outstanding job reaching its majority population which is primarily Mexican, young, highly immigrant, low-income and predominantly Spanish speaking. The library provides appropriate services including Spanish language collections, bilingual staff, after-school study centers, and constant outreach activities (González 1997). Children's services have the highest service priority. In addition, the Santa Ana Public Library staff survey conducted by Knox indicates a strong level of commitment to and understanding of the immigrant community (Knox 1998).

Library leadership is clearly focused on the foremost population it serves and provides direction to staff on these issues. As a result, the men and women who work for the Santa Ana Public Library have

managed to make the highly immigrant community feel accepted and well served during a period of unprecedented Mexican immigrant bashing. The staff's high public service standards have been clearly transmitted to the immigrant community. This is especially noteworthy given that Santa Ana is in the center of Orange County where nativist sentiments abound.

Conclusion

The findings of the Santa Ana study attempt to provide insight into the perceptions and usage patterns of Mexican/ Latino immigrants during an increasingly polarized political, economic and social climate. The major implications of this study concern the success of inclusionary library services and the cultivation of a new type of user. Other public libraries would do well to examine the many successful programs and services offered by the Santa Ana Public Library. Libraries with large immigrant populations may consider implementation of similar programs, resource allocation and personnel management. The emergence of transnational library users must also be recognized as a reflection of the new global order that has become international in its economic, social and demographic structure (Sommerville 1995). Other fields of study in the social sciences, particularly anthropology, cultural studies, economics, sociology, have studied trans-national trends in other environs for many years (Smith and Feagin 1987, Sassen 1988, Scott 1993). The continued maturation of the Mexican library system along with the trans-national features of migrating Mexican populations will make this type of user more common in the decades ahead. This study suggests that Mexican immigrant populations are highly motivated individuals, with increasing exposure to public libraries in their home country. They will use the public library regardless of minimal educational achievement, low-income or immigration status. Immigrants appear to have the same high regard for public libraries as the dominant society. The presence of school age children in the household will greatly increase the probability of library use. Library services are viewed as a positive avenue for self-improvement. Library access to all residents of the community, regardless of immigration status, is strong supported.

The thorny issues surrounding the immigration debate show no signs of disappearing nor does a drop in trans-national migration appear eminent. Consequently, public library administrators must continue to seek innovative methods to legitimate the complex and multifaceted Latino groups in the communities. Library leaders must consider issues of power and domination of the "establishment," while facilitating themes of community engagement, agency, democracy and empowerment. The Colorado statewide model is one example of a comprehensive attempt to proactively address services to diverse populations that can inform other efforts (Alire 1997).

Librarians as a profession must transform their expectations of trans-national Mexican library users as more, not less, likely to become avid library users and supporters. Transition and incorporation of Mexican immigrants into mainstream library users will continue to challenge public libraries to fully and consistently implement their basic service mission.

Kinship and social networks have long influenced the construction of Mexican/Latino communities in the *barrios* of Santa Ana. Neighborhoods tend to mir-ror communities from the native country. For example, residents of a village in Michoacan will relocate to an area where other village residents have settled. Communities such as these found in the City of Santa Ana are often referred to by social scientist as "trans-national communities" (Vélez-Ibañez and Greenberg 1992, Moore 1993, Hurtado 1994). Latinos who fall under this description often maintain homes, families or businesses in Mexico and provide a continual cash flow back to the home country. In fact, it is estimated that approximately 90 percent of Mexican immigrants in California send money home to family members. They practice income sharing, resource pooling and mutual assistance with other more recently arrived relatives or friends. In addition, household members of trans-national families often spend many months a year in their home country. Many social scientist are abandoning the term "immigrants" for the more descriptive "trans-national migrants" (Rouse 1992, Zabin 1993).

An important context note to this study is that it was conducted during a period of intense statewide and national immigrant bashing.

Immigrants, legal and undocumented, had been targeted during the latest economic recession as taking jobs away from "Americans," to overburdening the schools, social and health services. Anti-immigrant sentiments have been expressed at the polls by California voters via the passage of the English-Only Initiative (1986), the "Save Our State" initiative, Proposition 187 (1994) which sought to severely limit educational and health opportunities for undocumented residents of the State of California and the passage of Proposition 209, the so called "Civil Rights Initiative" which bans Affirmative Action programs administered by the State of California (1996). However, the most vexing issue among the white majority electorate appeared to be the resistance of Latino immigrants to assimilate to Euro-American culture. (Perea 1977, Gutiérrez 1996).

Recently, reciprocal borrowing privileges borrowing between the cities of Reynosa,, Tamaulipas Mexico and McAllen, Texas have been established to meet transnational migrants needs. Will international agreements such as these become common place in the next millennium? Hard work and perseverance in the face of adversity were often noted by the informants as key characteristics of Mexican immigrants. Both attributes are highly valued and respected in Mexican communities. These virtues are considered necessary qualities for immigrant survival and eventual economic success (Chávez 1992).

References

Alire, Camila A. 1997. Ethnic Populations: A Model for Statewide Service. *American Libraries* 28 (November): 38–40.

Berelson, Bernard. 1949. *The Library's Public.* Westport, CT: Greenwood.

Boger, John Charles, and Judith Welch Wegner, eds. 1996. *Race, Poverty and American Cities.* Chapel Hill, NC: University of North Carolina Press.

Chavez, Leo R. 1988. Settlers and Sojourners: The Case of Mexicans in the United States. *Human Organization* 47: 95–108.

_____. 1992. *Shadowed Lives: Undocumented Immigrants in American Society.* New York: Holt, Rinehart and Winston.

D'Elia, G., and Rodger, E. J. 1996. Customer Satisfaction with Public Libraries. *Public Libraries* 35: 292–297.

_____. 1995. The Roles of the Public Library in the Community. *Public Libraries* 34: 94–98.

de la Peña McCook, Kathleen, and P. Geist. 1995. Hispanic Library Services in South Florida. *Public Libraries* 34: 34–37.

du Gay, Paul, Stuart Hall, et al. 1990. *Doing Cultural Studies: The Story of the Sony Walkman.* London: Sage Publications.

Durrenberger, E. P. 1996. Ethnography. In *Encyclopedia of Cultural Anthropology.* Vol. 2, New York: Henry Holt.

Estabrook, L. S. 1997. Polarized Perceptions. *Library Journal,* 122 (1 February): 46–48.

Flores, W. V., and R. Benmayor, eds. 1997. *Latino Cultural Citizenship: Claiming Identity, Space and Rights.* Boston: Beacon.

González, Cecilia. Santa Ana Public Library Services to Latinos. 1997. Paper presented at the conference of REFORMA, National Association to Promote Library Services to the Spanish Speaking, Orange County Chapter, Fullerton College, Fullerton, California (April).

Gutiérrez, David G. 1995. *Walls and Mirrors: Mexican Americans, Mexican Immigrants, and the Politics of Ethnicity.* Berkeley: University of California Press.

_____. 1996. *Mexican Immigrants in the United States.* Wilmington, DE: Scholarly Resources.

Hayes-Bautista, David. *Los Angeles Times,* 17 May 1997.

Hayes-Bautista, David, and Gregory Rodríguez. *Los Angeles Times,* 29 December 1996.

Hayes-Bautista, David, Werner O. Schink, and Jorge Chapa. 1988. *The Burden of Support: The Young Latino Population in an Aging American Society.* Palo Alto, CA: Stanford University Press.

Hoffert, Barbara. 1993. Crossing Borders: U.S./Mexican Forum Tackles Common Concerns. *Library Journal* 118(July): 32–35.

Horton, John. 1995. *The Politics of Diversity: Immigration, Resistance and Change in Monterey Park, California.* Philadelphia, PA: Temple University Press.

James, Stephen E. 1985. The Relationship

Between Local Economic Conditions and the Use of the Public Libraries. *Library Quarterly* 55 (July): 255–272.

Jones, Richard C., ed. 1984. *Patterns of Undocumented Migration: Mexico and the United States.* Totowa, NJ: Rowman & Littlefield.

Kanellos, N. 1994. *The Hispanic Almanac: From Columbus to Corporate America.* Detroit, MI: Visible Ink Press.

Knox, Kenneth. 1998. Working Paper. In *Anti-Immigration Legislation and the Public Library.* Westport, CT: Greenwood (forthcoming 2000).

Luévano-Molina, Susan, ed. *Anti-Immigration Legislation and the Public Library.* Westport, CT: Greenwood (forthcoming 2000).

Lynch, Mary Jo. 1997. Using Public Libraries: What Makes a Difference. *American Libraries* 28 (November 1997): 64–66.

Magaloni, Ana Maria. 1993. The Mexican Library Revolution: Taking Books to the People. *Logos,* 4: 81–83.

Marchant, M. P. 1991. What Motivates Adult Use of Public Libraries? *LISR,* 13: 201–235.

Miles, Robert. 1989. *Racism.* New York: Routledge.

Metoyer-Duran, Karen. 1993. The Information and Referral Process in Culturally Diverse Communities. *RQ,* 32: 359–371.

Moore, Joan W., and Raquel Pinderhughes, eds. 1993. *In the Barrios: Latinos and the Underclass Debate.* New York: Russell Sage Foundation.

Padilla, Amado M. 1991. *Public Library Services for Immigrant Populations in California.* Sacramento: California State Library Foundation.

Perea, Juan F., ed. 1997. *Immigrants Out! The New Nativism and the Anti-Immigrant Impulse in the Untied States.* New York: New York University Press.

Portes, Alejandro, and Robert L. Bach. 1985. *Latin Journey: Cuban and Mexican Immi-grants in the United States.* Berkeley, CA: University of California.

Portes, Alejandro, and Rubén G. Rumbaut. 1996. *Immigrant America: A Portrait.* 2nd ed. Berkeley, CA: University of California Press.

Riskind, Mary. 1992. Library Use As an Economic Indicator. *New Jersey Libraries* (Winter): 4–7.

Quezada, Shelley. 1992. Mainstreaming Library Services to Multicultural Populations: The Evolving Tapestry. *Wilson Library Bulletin* 66 (February): 28–44.

Sassen, Saskia. *The Mobility of Labor and Capital: A Study in International Investment and Labor Flow.* New York: Cambridge University Press.

Scheppke, Jim. 1994. Who's Using the Library. *Library Journal,* 194 (15 October): 353–357.

Smith, Michael Peter. 1992. Postmodernism, Urban Ethnography, and the New Social Space of Ethnic Identity. *Theory and Society* 21(1992): 493–531.

Smith, Michael Peter, and Joe R. Feagin, eds. 1987. *The Capitalist City: Global Restructuring and Community Politics.* New York: Basil Blackwell.

Sommerville, Mary R. 1995. Global is Local. *Library Journal* 120 (15 February): 131–133.

Urciuoli, Bonnie. 1988. *Exposing Prejudice: Puerto Rican Experiences of Language, Race, and Class.* Boulder, CO: Westview Press.

U. S. Bureau of the Census. 1983. "Labor Force Participation Rates by Age, Sex, Ethnicity, and Nativity, California, 1980." *Census of Population and Housing, 1908: Public Use Microdata Sample A, California.* Washington, D.C.

Notes

1. A more comprehensive report of this ethnographic study is to be published by Greenwood. The study was funded by a

grant from the Research and Publications Committee of the California Library Association in 1995. Also, an Affirmative Action Development grant awarded by California State University, Long Beach provided additional funding and release time for the primary investigator to conduct the study in 1996.

2. Ethnography is defined as "The empirical study of people which documents how people of a particular culture think and how they see their world. Culture here is defined as the totality of local "public" meaning in terms of which people understand, think about, talk about, and describe behavior, institutions, events, and processes. The objective of an ethnographic study is to draw large conclusions from small well contextualized facts that include the physical, biological, economic and political realities of everyday life. These theories may provide answers to fundamental questions about human existence" (Durrenbeger "Ethnography," in *Encyclopedia of Cultural Anthropology*).

3. The excellent research team on this project included Anita Varela, M.L.S., Frank Castillo, B.A., J.D., and Becky Flores, community member and recent Mexican immigrant.

4. REFORMA, the National Association to Promote Library Services to the Spanish Speaking, represents the interests of Latino communities across the United States within the library community. An affiliate organization of the American Library Association, founded in 1971, REFORMA's membership is made up primarily of librarians and library staff who serve Latino constituencies.

5. Participants were carefully queried at two points during the interview process to be sure that they understood the difference between a library *biblioteca* and *libreria* as these terms are often confused.

6. The terms "undocumented" and *sin papeles* refer to people who are in the United States without the proper immigration papers. These are the preferred terms as they are not judgmental but descriptive and neutral. This is untrue of more commonly used loaded term such as "illegal" or "wetback" which imply criminality, as well as other negative connotations (Kanellos 1994, 180).

7. Trans-national communities are constructed by immigrants that maintain binational ties to a home country and a new host country. Trans-national families often maintain homes, families or business in both countries. They also provide a continual cash flow back to the home country that is integral to the stabilization of the economy. Thus, trans-national immigrants operate simultaneously in local and globalized modes of communication, economics and social interactions. Social, cultural, and economic situations can no longer be analyzed within nation states alone. The globalization of migrant communities is a normal condition that has become a part of everyday existence (Smith and Feagin 1984, Sassen 1988, Smith 1992).

OUTREACH

CHAPTER FOURTEEN

Effective Outreach Strategies to the Latino Community: A Paradigm for Public Libraries

Ben Ocón

Library outreach to the Latino community is needed today more than ever before. A new paradigm for effective library outreach must now be implemented to counter balance the barriers that have been created by the anti–Latino political initiatives which have surfaced in the 1980s through the 1990s. Initiatives such as the English Only/Official Language legislation[1] (nationwide) and state initiatives such as Propositions 187 [2] (in California) exemplify a political environment that is openly antagonistic to the Latino community and which is affecting all sectors of society including libraries. Libraries will need to assume a leadership role and maintain a sense of professional integrity if they are to remain bastions of information, lifelong learning, intellectual freedom and enrichment. This chapter will present a paradigm for effective outreach strategies to the Latino community that public libraries can implement. An effort has been made to share examples of successful outreach programs.

Formulating an Outreach Plan

A recommended first step is in formulating a library outreach plan that will help set a course of direction for the library. A plan is needed to identify goals, to help assess the resources (time, staff, and funding) that will be needed to accomplish those goals and to establish evaluative measures that will gauge the overall success of the library's outreach program.

Effective planning requires sufficient investment in information gathering as well as in solicitation of community input. Such planning will involve the following:

- *Studying the demographic statistics in your library's service area*
- *Getting acquainted with Latino community leaders*
- *Hosting a Latino focus group*
- *Surveying the Latino community*

Know the Community

Library outreach begins with knowing the Latino community and knowing it well. One will likely begin with an intuitive understanding of the Latino community's increased presence. It will be important not to rely on an intuitive judgment; rather, a quantifiable measurement of the Latino population will be needed and research will provide demographic data that will substantiate this presence. A good beginning is in finding out statistical data from the Census tracts that comprise the service area of the library. In addition, local school districts can provide a reliable profile with regard to student enrollment statistics. This is especially useful for statistical information on the Latino student population in the district. Other useful sources are the human services providers [social services agencies] and churches in the area which also maintain informational records that will prove beneficial. As in any effort to substantiate census information, it is important to acknowledge that whatever statistics are obtained, they will likely be lower than what is, in fact, to be true. This can be attributed to various factors such as the distrust by a large segment of the Latino community of government agencies; this understandably results in low numbers at

all levels.[3] Other factors that compound this include ambiguous instructions on forms requesting ethnicity/racial information or simply poor census methods and lack of professional follow-up to verify whether the statistics are accurate.

Equally important is the need to get acquainted with leaders in the Latino community. Knowing community leaders will greatly enhance efforts to become familiar with the issues affecting Latinos in the library's service area. Seek community leaders in the school, church, business, and government sectors. In addition, seek leaders of community organizations who will, in turn, introduce you to members in their respective organizations.

The focus group is an effective option for soliciting information and suggestions in a controlled setting. Whatever standards one uses to form a focus group, it is critical to understand that a focus group is, in essence, an opportunity to obtain information directly from the invited participants as well as the opportunity to share information about one's organization. The participants should include a cross section of the Latino community in order to maximize the opportunity to solicit perspectives from various vantages (e.g. professionals, trade laborers, students, men, women, Seniors, etc.). The size of the focus group should remain manageable and small (6–10 participants). The questions which will be asked should be made available to the participants in advance; this will help the participants better prepare for the focus group meeting. Finally, the focus group meeting should include a few library staff who will transcribe the proceedings of the meeting. The information which is gathered from focus group meetings will be invaluable in the drafting of an outreach plan. The Denver Public Library exemplifies a library that has effectively utilized the focus group option to solicit patron input.[4]

Develop a Spanish Language and Latino Oriented Collection

One of the essential goals of an effective outreach plan is to develop a collection that is pertinent to the Latino community. Input from Latino patrons will invariably point to a need to develop a Spanish language collection of library materials (books, magazines, newspapers, videos, cassettes, and compact discs). In addition, the collection should also expand to include Latino oriented materials. These are titles which document the Latino experience in the U.S. and throughout Latin America and may include materials in the various disciplines such as the humanities (e.g. literature, arts, fine arts, etc.), social sciences (e.g. sociology, education, folklore, etc.) and history and biography. It is important to acknowledge that Latino oriented materials will likely be in English and aimed at Latinos who have been in the U.S. for many generations.

A good first step is to get on the mailing lists of Spanish language and multicultural publishers and distributors. Being aware of what is being published will help in identifying the types of materials that are available. In addition, it is highly advantageous to begin getting familiar with the services and discounts being offered to libraries by such publishers and distributors. Services may include cataloging kits or special binding options; and competitive discounts that may range up to 40-45 percent off the list price.

Visiting the exhibitors booths at library conferences will help in making direct contact with publishers of Spanish

language and multicultural materials. Attending the American Library Association's (ALA) Annual and Mid-Winter Conferences and the Public Library Association's (PLA) biannual conference exemplify worthy conference opportunities. A special opportunity is the REFORMA National Conference which not only provides exposure to the publishing industry but also offers outstanding conference programs on collection development. For Spanish language materials, the Feria Internacional del Libro (FIL) which is hosted annually in Guadalajara, Mexico, represents the premiere conference opportunity to meet publishers and distributors of Spanish language materials.[5] Every year, FIL and ALA sponsor special grants to help make this special buying trip possible for libraries across the U.S. and Puerto Rico.

A second step in developing Spanish language and Latino oriented collections is to become familiar with the review sources in the professional literature. While getting on the mailing lists of publishers will help in knowing what is available, review sources will help distinguish the recommended titles. Professional journals such as *Library Journal* and *Booklist* exemplify two outstanding review sources of Spanish language and Latino oriented materials. In addition, professional organizations such as REFORMA also feature reviews in the quarterly *REFORMA Newsletter* which is available to members.

A critical step is to involve library staff who have Spanish language proficiency or who are bilingual. Involve such staff in the selection process of materials to ensure that the best titles are being added to the collection. Also, involve Latino patrons who can also recommend good titles. For Latino oriented materials in English, involve staff and patrons who have an interest in multicultural materials. Encourage Latino patrons to submit on a regular basis collection development ideas and recommendations.

Notable public library collections that have gained notoriety as exceptional examples of Spanish language and Latino oriented collections include the Chicano Resource Collection at the East Los Angeles Library (County of Los Angeles Public Library), the Rudy Lozano Library (Chicago Public Library), Latin American Library (Oakland Public Library), the Biblioteca Latino Americana (San Jose Public Library)[6], and the Latino Collection at the San Antonio Public Library.[7]

Develop the Library's Services

In addition to developing a good Spanish language and Latino oriented collection, it will be imperative to also develop some of the library's services into services that can be promoted to the Latino community. It is critical that a public library be attentive and responsive to the community it serves.[8] Children's services such as storytimes, children's reading programs, or raising readers programs for parents illustrate the type of services which can be developed and promoted to the Latino community. For example, consider developing a preschool storytime in Spanish or a bilingual version; or consider conducting a raising readers program for parents in Spanish.

Programs that are geared for adults such as book discussion programs can also be developed in Spanish or bilingually. An example of such reading programs for adults that were developed for the Latino community was the *El Lenguaje Que Nos Une/The Language That Unites Us* series of bilingual book discussion programs which

were conducted at the Salt Lake City Public Library. This programming was made possible through a special coordination by the Human Pursuits/Western Humanities Concern (with funding from the National Endowment for the Humanities). These book discussion programs were designed for adults and presented bilingually by Dr. Eduardo Elias (University of Utah) and included the works of authors such as Sandra Cisneros, Rudolfo Anaya, and Laura Esquivel.

Another example involves technology instruction services. As libraries offer patrons training on accessing the Internet and the new electronic resources, it is important to expand such training to the Latino community. Offering such training in Spanish will enhance the service; equally important is to inform patrons on how to utilize Latino pathfinders to facilitate accessing information pertaining to Latinos on the world wide web. Library signage is another aspect of library services which also merits special attention. Translating basic library signage into Spanish will improve access to services for the Latino community. More important, a welcoming environment is created when library signage is provided in Spanish.

Involve All Library Staff

An integral part of an effective outreach plan is the inclusion of all library staff as participants. It is imperative that opportunities are created for library staff and that they be involved and informed of outreach efforts. Staff must understand that outreach efforts will bring in new patrons who will need assistance as they learn about the library and its services. Staff at all levels of the library organization should be ready to assist the new patrons. From the moment of registering for a library card to the instance of asking for help, new Latino patrons will be developing an understanding of library services. It will be critical that their experience be a positive one.

Involving library administrators in outreach efforts is essential to guaranteeing a an enhanced level of success. Administrative support will ensure that the necessary resources are allocated: Staffing, money, and time are the ingredients that will be needed to fulfill the goals of the outreach plan. In addition, involving administrators will also bring a positive effect on important areas such as in human resources [recruitment, retention, and promotion of bilingual staff] and with the projects involving the management team [strategic planning, budget formulation process, collection development]. In the state of Colorado, EthnicPops (Committee on Library Services to Ethnic Minority Populations) has introduced a mentoring program that is worthy of special mention as an outstanding program designed to recruit, hire, and retain minority staff who can relate to, and understand diverse cultures.[9] Finally, outreach endeavors must even involve the library's Board of Directors/ Trustees, the Friends of the Library, and the volunteer workforce. One cannot underestimate the power of the web of inclusion in the area of outreach. Every staff member should be informed and understand that they can play an important role.

To ensure that all staff are receptive to welcoming new Latino patrons, training of staff should include insight to the cultural and socioeconomic factors influencing the Latino community. Involve members in the community with sensitivity training of the library staff; educators, human services providers, and community

activists can each provide a perspective that will help implement this important training of staff. A safeguard measure to ensure that staff are providing quality library service to the new patrons may be in adding this expectation in their job descriptions or performance evaluations. Effective supervisors will recognize and reward their staff for outstanding work in this area. Conversely, supervisors should work closely with staff who are unfamiliar with serving underrepresented minority communities such as the Latino community. Again, it is critical that new Latino patrons encounter a friendly and courteous library staff when they visit the library.

Translate the Library's Basic Forms and Brochures Into Spanish

Efforts to promote library services to the Latino community should include the need for translating the library's basic forms and brochures into Spanish: Registration forms, welcome brochures, loan borrowing privileges, calendar of programs, and hours of service all exemplify the type of basic forms which would greatly enhance the library's services to the Latino community.

While the majority of Latinos in the United States speak English, the new immigrants from Latin America will benefit greatly from such translated forms. In addition, the library will be establishing much goodwill by offering these forms in Spanish and, essentially, in facilitating their transition in a new country—a transition which is likely to be traumatic.[10] Also, these forms could be distributed at select outreach projects and would maximize the library's outreach efforts especially when the targeted audience is comprised of first generation immigrants. An outstanding program which has created community partnerships to help immigrant populations is the One With One program in Boston (MA). One With One provides an important gateway for immigrants to adjust to a new world and using libraries as a vehicle.[11]

Marketing the Library's Collection and Services

An effective library outreach will require an effective marketing of the library's services, collections, and programs. In tandem with the efforts to develop library services for the Latino community are the efforts to incorporate the promotion of such services into the library's marketing operations. Outreach to the Latino community will require various marketing strategies: utilizing the Spanish language media (newspapers, radio, and television); designing special flyers and distributing them in strategic locations in the community; and disseminating the information through strategic alliances (e.g. school districts, churches, parks and recreation, etc.).

Libraries must learn to use the Spanish language media in their communities. Beginning with newspapers, the library should nurture a healthy relationship with the local press. All programming and services should be shared on an ongoing basis. Also, convince the newspaper's publisher into creating a library column or library corner in an section of the newspaper; library staff may wish to volunteer to write that column or in preparing regular press releases. Involve bilingual staff to write the press releases in Spanish. In the event that bilingual staff are not available, explore options whereby the newspaper staff will translate the library's press releases into Spanish.

One of the most effective vehicles of publicity is the single sheet flyer that promotes library activities at the most rudimentary level. Yet, in promoting library services to the Latino community, the effectiveness of the flyer lies not so much in its design but in its placement in the community. The location for posting flyers should include Latino owned businesses or businesses patronized by the Latino community. For example, the best locations will include *tortillerias* [tortilla factories], *panaderias* [bakeries], *tiendas de abarrotes* [neighborhood grocery stores] and restaurants. In addition, other businesses can be identified by simply walking through the community and leaving flyers at select businesses such as restaurants, beauty/hair salons, and hotels. In the cases of some businesses, the outreach efforts are principally aimed at reaching the employees many who are Latinos working in service occupations. The Redwood City Public Library (CA) used this strategy in the early 1990s; under the coordination of Valentín Porras, restaurants were contacted in an effort to reach their employees to inform them of the library's ESL collection and services.[12]

Information about the library should also be displayed at community centers, day care centers, clinics, hospitals and schools. It is important to aim outreach efforts at children and their parents. Through special promotional material, parents can become aware of library services which will benefit their children and themselves. Some libraries have developed outreach to maternity wards at hospitals. The Salt Lake City Public Library created a special program entitled, "Best Beginnings," which introduced parents of newborn infants to libraries and services; included in the brochure was a *Raising Readers* insert which was translated into Spanish, *Como Criar un Lector*. Also, the County of Los Angeles Public Library has been successful in planned outreach efforts involving health clinics; library staff visit with expectant mothers and make them aware of the library's services and resources.[13]

Make Presentations to Organizations and Schools

Effective outreach requires public speaking presentations. It is essential that library staff assertively seek out opportunities to speak to community organizations, service clubs, elected officials, educators, church congregations, etc. After developing Spanish language and Latino oriented collections and after introducing new services, library staff need to connect with the community and inform them of the library's resources. The first step is to identify key agencies and organizations in the community that serve the Latino population. Identify the presiding officer(s) and invite yourself to speak on the resources of the library. Prepare a packet of handouts and brochures for each person who is in attendance. Involve library staff who are fluent in Spanish or who are bilingual. If the first attempt to schedule a presentation is unsuccessful, keep trying. Outreach is not for the easily discouraged; maintain a clear vision of the outreach plan and remain persistent.

Presentations that are the most effective are those that create opportunities for immediate follow-up on the part of those in attendance. A well-prepared presentation will provide ideas and suggestions that are easy to implement. For example,

a presentation to human services providers (e.g. refugee services, senior centers, social services agencies) may suggest that case workers ask their clients whether they have a library card; and, if not, they can furnish the clients with an application form on the spot. A presentation to a school's faculty will offer a convenient opportunity for teachers to schedule class visits to the library.

One of the most successful outreach efforts involves presentations to English as a second language (ESL) classes. Latinos who enroll in ESL classes are eager to seek resources that can help with their language learning endeavors; they also are appreciative of knowing about the library as a place with resources that will help their family especially their children. Presentations to ESL classes are ideal win-win opportunities: the students benefit by knowing about the library's services and resources and the library benefits by increase usage of its collection and services as well as the fulfillment of their mission. A notable characteristic of ESL classes is the strong advocacy that is demonstrated by ESL teachers to facilitate and create opportunities for their students to become fully acquainted with the library's resources.

Establish Strategic Alliances with Community Organizations

One of the most effective outreach strategies is in involving others to speak on behalf of the library. Word of mouth promotion within the community greatly ensures the success of the library's outreach plan. To attain this desirable level of effectiveness, library staff should seek to establish strategic alliances with community organizations. If possible, library staff should also secure a membership for the library in such community organizations and attend the membership meetings. In addition, the library should support community based projects and events. Street festivals, parades, charity activities, information fairs, and activities at schools all exemplify the types of community events in which the library's presence is necessary. Utilize such activities to promote the library's collection and services by distributing the library's brochures and in registering new patrons. Above all, seek to establish community partnerships that will strengthen the library's presence in the community. For example, in developing new services, consider applying for a grant that will involve community organizations as partners and identify them as a site for the project's implementation.

Utilize Technology in Outreach Efforts

Technology has become an important tool to libraries in facilitating access to electronic resources and information; and technology can also serve as an important ally in the area of outreach. The new electronic resources can serve both as a conduit for information about the library to reach the Latino community as well as a vehicle for technology training. The latter will ensure that equal access on the information superhighway will be available to Latinos as they become proficient and aware of the new technology.

The opportunity for libraries to develop home pages on the Internet has greatly enhanced outreach efforts. Libraries now have the ability to electronically transmit information about the library to not only the immediate community but also the entire world. Libraries that have a home

page should design access links to Spanish language and Latino oriented sites. In addition, libraries can post information about their services and resources on their home page. The advent of the Internet has also necessitated an advocacy for technology instruction to the Latino community. This can very well be incorporated in the outreach plan. As library staff have opportunities to conduct outreach to the community, it is important to be mindful of opportunities for technology instruction. One of the most shining examples of technology outreach is the grant project that was coordinated by the Center for Virtual Research at the University of California at Riverside. The Riverside Community Digital Initiative, under the direction of Richard Chabrán, established a computer laboratory and educational center at the Cesar Chavez Community Center in Riverside's Eastside community and targeted youth between the ages of 14 and 23 years.[14]

Closing Comments

The true success of any public library is directly tied to its outreach efforts. A commitment to outreach ensures that a library's services and resources will be utilized and that the library's mission will genuinely fulfilled. More important, libraries that invest in outreach are also ensuring that access to library services are being promoted to their community. Conversely, a library that fails to invest in outreach will fail to attain its goals; there is no other way to soften the dire consequences that result from such inattention and complacency. When weighing the cultural and political obstacles facing the Latino population and other underrepresented ethnic minorities, libraries must view outreach from a different vantage. The library's mission to serve *all* members of the community dictates that a stronger investment in outreach be made. Outreach from this vantage must be aggressive and relentless. It becomes imperative that libraries realize that outreach is an essential, indispensable part of the public service goals. In light of the overt political initiatives aimed at immigrant populations and the subsequent barriers to services that are created, libraries have a moral obligation to invest in outreach. To do otherwise is to fail in fulfilling the mission of the library. Libraries who accept this call for action demonstrate the organizational courage and true leadership that is needed today.

Appendix: 10 Steps for Effective Outreach to the Latino Community

1. Know your community
   - Study the demographic statistics of your service area
   - Obtain a copy of the local school district's statistical profile of student enrollment
   - Get acquainted with community leaders (e.g. church, schools, elected officials)
   - Patronize the local Latino owned businesses (and businesses patronized by Latinos)

2. Develop your Spanish language and Latino oriented collection
   - Get on the mailing lists of Spanish language publishers and distributors
   - Become familiar with review sources of Spanish language materials
   - Involve staff who have Spanish language proficiency or expertise in multicultural materials
   - Seek input from Latino patrons

3. Develop your library's services
   - Identify library services which can be promoted to the Latino community
   - Children's services (e.g. storytimes, raising readers)
   - Book discussion programs
   - Internet instruction
   - Offer these services in Spanish (if possible)
   - Provide basic library signage in Spanish or in bilingual format.

4. Translate your library's basic library forms and brochures into Spanish
   - Registration forms
   - Welcome brochures and loan borrowing privileges
   - Hours of service

5. Involve fellow staff members in outreach efforts
   - Create opportunities for fellow staff members to be involved and informed of outreach efforts.
   - Seek support from Administrators, Trustees & the Friends.
   - Support staff training on service to diverse populations (e.g. being sensitive to new patrons)

6. Market your library's collection/services
   • In local newspapers (especially the Spanish language press, radio, and television)
   • Post flyers in Latino businesses and church bulletin boards
   • Distribute information to faculty and students at local schools; PTA functions.
   • Display the library's brochures at human services providers (hospitals, clinics, day care centers)

7. Participate in local community events/activities
   • Events in neighborhood (e.g. street festivals, parades, charity runs/walks, activities in parks, etc.)
   • School activities held for the community

8. Make presentations to Latino service organizations & ESL classes
   • Form community alliances that will facilitate the Library's outreach efforts
   • Identify ESL programs in your community; provide each class with an overview of Library services

9. Establish strategic alliances with community organizations
   • Seek membership in key community organizations (e.g. Latino chamber of commerce)
   • Support special community projects

10. Utilize technology in outreach efforts
    • Incorporate technology training in special presentations to the Latino community
    • Facilitate access to Latino oriented electronic resources and Spanish language databases/sites
    • Utilize the new technology to improve access by Latinos to the library's resources

Notes

1. Ingrid Betancourt, "The Babel Myth: The English-Only Movement and Its Implications for Libraries." *Wilson Library Bulletin* 66 (February 1992): 38.

2. Edward McGlynn Gaffney, Jr., "Immigrant Bashing: Proposition 187." *The Christian Century* 112 (March 1, 1995): 228.

3. Barbara Hoffert, "¡Se Lea Español Aqui!," *Library Journal* 117 (July 1992): 35.

4. Kathleen W. Craver, "Bridging the Gap: Library Services for Immigrant Populations," *Journal of Youth Services in Libraries* 4 (Winter 1991): 127.

5. Hoffert, "¡Se Lea Español Aqui!," 34.

6. James Fish, "Responding to Cultural Diversity: A Library in Transition," *Wilson Library Bulletin* 66 (February 1992): 36.

7. John Barnett, "Para Servirle: At Your Service," *American Libraries* 28 (November 1997): 42.

8. Fish, "Responding to Cultural Diversity," 34.

9. Camila Alire, "Ethnic Populations: A Model for Statewide Service," *American Libraries* 28 (November 1997), 39.

10. Leonard Wertheimer, "Library Services to Ethnocultural Minorities: Philosophical and Social Bases and Professional Implications," *Public Libraries* 26 (Fall 1987): 59.

11. Margaret Kin Van Duyne and Debra Jacobs, "Embracing Diversity: One With One's Bold New Partnerships," *Wilson Library Bulletin* 66 (February 1992): 43.

12. Hoffert, "¡Se Lea Aqui!" 36.

13. *Ibid.*, 36.

14. Susan Sullivan, *Digital* [News Release], University of California at Riverside 11 (August 8, 1997)

CHAPTER FIFTEEN

Public Libraries and Improved Service to Diverse Communities

Ghada Kanafani Elturk

When I started working for the Boulder Public Library in Boulder, Colorado, as its first Outreach librarian in April 1996, I asked the usual question a new employee asks of an employer: *What do you expect from me?* And the answer was, "You tell us—that's why you were hired." With this directive, my work began.

The Outreach Librarian position had been newly created by our library director, Marcelee Gralapp. Although it is usually demographic changes which trigger institutional and organizational changes in library policies and services to the public, no such changes in our community had occurred. Rather, our director had observed for years that public libraries usually do a good job in serving the middle class, whose members are generally the

traditional users of the library. She realized that although historically, public libraries are very much associated with being a safe haven for newly immigrated populations in the United States, these communities, together with low income communities and non-English-speaking communities, find it very difficult to use the public library. She also had observed that though we always have our hearts in the right place, the fact that we as librarians and library staff people are "outsiders" means we often don't know how to approach these communities, much less what to do to make the library more accessible to them. As a result, she created the position of Outreach Librarian and broadly defined its purpose to be to identify smaller local communities that don't use the library, find out the reasons why, and then try to meet needs. How, specifically, these three tasks were to be successfully performed was left up to me. The communities I would approach were those whose needs were not being expressed for reasons such as cultural preconceptions or language barriers, or for socioeconomic reasons that can leave no time for luxuries—in which category the library is unfortunately sometimes considered to belong.

My First Steps

One of the first things I did was to attend meetings held by community and neighborhood groups, grassroots organizations, the school board, youth organizations, other City departments, and gatherings of families and parents. I asked for input from the people in these community groups so I could begin to understand what their needs were and encouraged them to talk about ways the library could do a better job in serving them. This process is ongoing. Because the outreach program should always belong within the community, I still attend meetings, and in part based on the value I've found in attending them, we've initiated other groups in cooperation with individuals and City and County agencies. One example is an "Immigration and U.S. Citizenship Advocacy Group" that I will discuss about in detail later on in this article.

It became part of my job to evaluate the Library's non–English language, Easy English Reading and English as a Second Language acquisitions, as did collection development in these three areas. Because these areas receive limited funds, I write for grants from the Boulder Public Library Foundation and other organizations in the community. Most of my purchases and programs are funded by grant money. What also helps is that the cost of running my program is kept to a minimum because I work with volunteers from the communities I reach out to. Thus, all the grant monies we receive go to the core of the service, *i.e.,* books, audio and video tapes, and arts and crafts materials.

Requirements for Success

Following are eight reasons I think my job has been successful:

1. Administrative commitment

The library administration was committed from the beginning to what I was doing. I always felt that my volunteers and I were able to be as creative as possible, primarily because the library administration and omission were supportive. This eliminated wasting time in convincing people to provide funding, find room, buy books, approve of time spent, and so on. My energy has been spent listening to what the diverse communities need, and to explore ways to meet their needs. Without the trust of the library administration, and its understanding and conviction, I could never have implemented what I did, nor could I have continued to find new avenues to attract people to the library. Rather than losing time to bureaucracy, hierarchy, and the need to justify every action and instead use the time to find out what is needed to be done and doing it, in my opinion an essential requirement for success, if not the primary one,

2. The Boulder Library Commission includes diverse

*and active representation
of the community.*

3. Raising awareness
among library staff

Another necessity was to work to increase the level of understanding among library staff as to what Outreach is trying to do, particularly in the context of the mechanisms of working with people who traditionally have not used the library. Good relations and understanding among various library departments and employees minimizes friction and decreases the negative way things may look during the implementation of a new department service. What may seem to be "special treatment" or "teacher's pet" is in fact a product of the need for immediate feedback and input regarding programming that is being implemented for the first time in a library's history. Thus, keeping the whole library abreast of what I was and am doing, and why, has been a significant factor in avoiding counterproductive tension or bad feelings.

One example is our library calendar of events. Information for each upcoming month's issue is expected to be turned in by a certain deadline. But for some of my programming, because the communities I'm dealing with are unaccustomed to deadlines, pertinent information is not likely to be ready on time. It helped staff relations to discuss the situation with our publicist so that she understood why I was not always faithful to her deadlines. And when we've failed to make it into the calendar, we've relied on flyers to publicize events.

Another example is the requirement by our library's Volunteer Services that each volunteer turn in his or her schedule of hours. It was and continues to be a major waste of time for me to attempt to convince Outreach Program volunteers to do such a thing that could be "showing off." Their attitude is simply that they are doing what is needed—why make a big fuss over it? To get around this endless impasse we now turn in estimated monthly hours, and only updates on new people coming in to volunteer, or leaving and going back to their home countries; these are submitted to Volunteer Services.

4. The goal is
to have the library be
more accessible to people

Attending community meetings usually results in people calling back for more information or asking for a special service for themselves, their families or their friends. The first thing I do is to schedule a meeting with the individual(s) calling; I always avoid telephone conversations to explain or exchange ideas, especially if the person I am dealing with is a non-native-English-speaker. Meeting in person sets the tone for a personal and warm relationship instead of the feeling of "conducting business." The time and place of meeting is left entirely to the caller, although I suggest we meet in the library if they don't have a transportation problem. I also offer to drive them to the library if they wish to do so.

These meetings are conducted in a very informal manner. I usually ask what they think of the library, and ask about their experiences (if ever) with other libraries in the U.S. or abroad. I leave them free to talk about what they want or expect. Then together we try to figure out how to accomplish what they want. Usually this turns out to be by them becoming involved in volunteering to help accomplish what they think is good for their family, friends and community in general.

Following are examples of what Outreach has been able to offer as the result of people's (volunteers') ideas, combined with the support of the Library administration, Commission and Foundation:

A. BILINGUAL HANDOUTS

Two major communities were identified as needing translated library materials and related handouts that were formerly produced only in English. The Russian-speaking community elected to name eight volunteers to whom I provided detailed information about the library and its services and programs. I also trained them on how to search the library computerized catalog to find books and other library materials. They in turn are working with their own community, and with people whom I refer to them for help.

The other major language group that has been identified were Spanish speakers. As a result of their requests, the library monthly calendar of events is now translated each month into Spanish by volunteers, and distributed through the various community residence areas.

Another need was to explain "what all these numbers are for." It has been a common question, not only from Spanish speakers, but also from other people who wanted to know why and how the Dewey Decimal system works. A Spanish/English one-page, three-fold flyer was created by volunteers to explain the system. It has accompanied the Spanish calendar distribution, and has been sent to elementary schools for students to take home.

B. BILINGUAL TOURS
AND COMPUTER TRAINING

With the help of volunteers who speak languages other than English, we offer pre-scheduled bilingual language tours of the library, and individualized training in how to access the computerized catalog of library materials. Tour groups and individuals include both people who speak and understand limited English and others who speak only their own languages. In our specific community, the groups who request these tours are primarily Russian, Bosnian, and Latino. Our computer training is always conducted in one-on-one sessions (sometimes with a translator). Most people requesting the training lack even the most basic experience with computers or typewriters, and we feel that placing them in a classroom with others, and the resulting potential for intimidation, would unfairly put them in a position of fearing that they might "make a fool of themselves" among "strangers" at the very time when they were brave enough to begin. After the initial one-on-one training, most of these students decide to attend the "Public Access Catalog" training offered by the Training Department, and most show up at the library in the role of translators with friends who want to learn.

C. NON-ENGLISH LANGUAGE ASSISTANCE

The Outreach office matches volunteers with people in the community who seek translators or other foreign-language assistance. We maintain and utilize a list of library staff members who know another language, and the fact that the university is in walking distance from the library also helps attract international student volunteers.

D. IMMEDIATE RESPONSE
TO RECOMMENDATIONS
AND IDEAS EXPRESSED BY PATRONS

An immediate response to phone calls from people who don't speak English as a first language is a must. We might not be aware that it takes a great deal of courage for someone who doesn't speak English, or is not well versed in speaking it, to pick up a phone and speak to a machine through another machine, but I have found that an immediate response to such phone calls have a great positive effect in assuring the caller that we really want to listen to what they say and be of help to them. A long conversation is not recommended, rather an acknowledgment of the receipt of the message and an invitation to set a time to meet.

Encouraging people to speak, and understanding what they are saying, have been a great promotion for our Outreach Program. So many people afterwards admit to me that it was their first phone call in the U.S., or that this was the first phone call "that I did not have my children or my husband do for me." It might sound obvious, but little "successes" add up in the face of all the hard experiences such a person is bound to experience during a day. The people we deal with do not come to us first thing in the morning after a relaxing moment over coffee, but after they've gone with limited success to the store, to the school with their kids, to the mall, to the doctor, to fix their car... As you know, each of these visits is a challenge for a newcomer or a speaker whose first language is not English.

5. Collection development (including on-line)

Non-English language acquisitions should take into account not only foreign language materials but also requests by patrons for materials which tell about and make reference to their culture the way they know it. All of our volunteers are involved in suggesting titles as we make relevant catalogues available for them.

Examples are the ongoing development of our Spanish language collection, a visit last year for the first time by a staff member of our library to the Guadalajara International Book Fair, and good relations established with local Spanish-language book distributors and book stores.

Another unusual example was the Russian collection. A volunteer suggested expanding the collection because most of our Russian-speaking community are older people who will take a while to be able to read and listen to English material, and at the same time they would like to be able to share with their grandchildren the literature, songs, and stories that they grew up with. Russian-language catalogues were given to the volunteer, who distributed them among people in that community and then came back with suggestions. After we learned how much we were authorized to spend, titles were selected and purchased immediately. As soon as they arrived, eight volunteers read the books and summarized them in English to enable our Technical Services Department to catalog them, whereupon they were added to our collection. For people to see their suggestions taken seriously, and see their selections on the shelves, was a major event. They flocked to the library with family and friends, showing others where the Russian collection was shelved and how to check out its materials.

Where non-English language materials should be shelved was an issue for discussion. It was understood that because we want all people to have access to all library materials, the materials should be integrated into the collection. On the other hand, it was felt that because our building is fairly large, integrating the materials could be intimidating to people who were neither accustomed to big buildings nor experienced library users. The decision was made to have these materials shelved in one section of the library, together with the Easy Reading and ESL collections. This proved to be effective. We have found that people are finding what they are looking for in an easily accessed location. How long this arrangement remains will depend on the feedback we receive and the library's long range space availability.

As in all the programs and services we offer, the support we get from the Library's administration and Commission in this aspect of our work is tremendous. An amount of money in the Library's budget is set aside for the purchase of non–English language titles.

6. Library programs and services

In general, libraries should offer diverse programs and different times and locations, so that all communities have a chance to attend, participate, and benefit from them. Beyond that general premise, our Outreach Program has thus far offered the programs and services listed below. Each of them was requested by volunteers, and was implemented to answer a need that had been expressed in community meetings.

A. CONVERSATIONS IN ENGLISH

The Conversations in English program was initiated because volunteers and others in the community sought help in learning to speak better English. It is well known that a person's reading and writing skills in a second language is often at a better level than his or her conversational skills. Thus, people specifically asked for a way to improve their conversational skills.

We recruited American-English native speakers to lead the discussion groups.

Because we did not want any kind of well-intentioned mistake to spoil the program or cause people to turn away, we decided training was a pre-requisite for volunteers. We wanted them to be sensitive to cultural mores and needs that they were not familiar with, or had not served before to be aware of different learning styles, and aware of how each of the cultures communicates and what offends them. Thus, the volunteers attended training on adult learning (conducted by the Library's Learning to Read Program Coordinator); how to deal with and communicate with people whose English is a second language or who are newcomers to the U.S. (Conducted by the Library's Outreach Librarian); we also provided orientation on the Library's book discussion groups in general—how they function and how they are conducted. This was offered by the Library's Book Discussion Groups Coordinator.

We wanted to emphasize for participants that the Conversations in English groups were part of the library's many book discussion groups. Finally, our plan was to begin by using the "Easy Reading" (books written for adults learning English) and English as a Second Language library collections, which include books, magazines, newsletters, audio and video materials. Once we were certain we could offer the program on an ongoing basis, we advertised it targeting the appropriate communities through volunteers, flyers, library calendar as well as ESL classes. Initially, four meetings were scheduled in a month period. Those meetings were offered at different times to allow for as many schedules as possible to be taken into consideration. In the first meetings, we talked about ourselves, where we came from, and why we wanted to attend these discussion groups.

We wanted people to break the first barrier by calling to register, and for them to take control of the content of discussions. Thus we made it clear that people who wanted to attend should make the necessary phone call or visit the library to register. The first meetings consisted of introductions, discussing what times we could meet, and what library location was most convenient. What we hoped to read and converse about was also a major item of discussion.

Difficulties we faced included the fact that some participants asked to belong to groups consisting of their ethnic/language group only, while others came from countries at war with one another and did not want to be in the same group. For both objections we made a rule that the only parameters we had for groups were day, time, and location. When the desired topics were decided upon, the librarian, group leaders and participants researched the library's collection. In this way people who had never used the library learned how to find and request materials.

At present, materials being read and discussed include short stories, simplified versions of novels, U.S. history, and American-English slang. Groups are restricted to six participants and one volunteer group leader. Forty-eight people from sixteen countries participate. They are very enthusiastic, requesting more to read, happy to be able to check out books in English and in their native languages. They bring friends and family members to join them, disregarding the rule of having only six participants, by suggesting that the more people the better because "then we will have more to talk about."

B. Immigration and
U.S. citizenship information

Information about this ever-changing topic was and still is very much in demand. Our library has purchased multiple copies of new and updated material on the subject and currently maintains a vertical file as well. Information in languages other than English is included. Another avenue we took was to offer classes on becoming a U.S. citizen, after having established a good relationship with an attorney specializing in immigration. This individual is committed to the community and its well-being, and to keeping it well-informed about matters that have immediate effects on human and civil rights. The attorney volunteered to lead citizenship classes on a monthly basis, and offered one-on-one counseling for people who had special questions. Thus far the Outreach Program has offered six classes in becoming a U.S. citizen. Each class has dealt with qualifications, requirements, and the new immigration-law updates. The initial class was also designed to get input from people attending as to what stage of the process they had reached, so that we could tailor classes around people's needs.

Principal needs included wanting to know more about the law, how to fill out the forms, and preparing to study for the U.S. history and civics test. In some cases we were able to match volunteers with people at the last stage (studying for the test), and in these cases they worked together on studying and learning more about the subject, using library books, video tapes and other materials. The Outreach Program is one of three City and County entities to start a group called Immigration Advocacy and U.S. Citizenship Efforts in Boulder County. This group now meets on a monthly basis and consists of all City and County agencies that deal with this specific population, including Social Services, schools, adult education and literacy programs, hospitals and others.

C. INTERNATIONAL/DIVERSE FAMILIES STORYTELLING

Volunteers, in many cases parents, have expressed a willingness to tell stories from their cultures and their countries of origin. The Outreach librarian is part of this group. We provide a diverse range of international storytelling in the library, at schools and for community events. As with any library event, we also use these occasions to promote library materials and services, as well as bringing in personal items from our own homes.

D. FACES OF LATIN AMERICAN LIFE

This series was suggested by volunteers from Latin American countries, who are constantly puzzled when people approach them with questions about a certain aspect of their lives, not realizing that the traditions, foods, and celebrations of Venezuela, for one example, are often quite different from those of Mexico or Puerto Rico—or for that matter any other Central or South American country.

Volunteers from various countries, primarily Venezuela and Mexico, led the presentations, concentrating on cultural similarities and differences and comparing what different traditions did and didn't provide for various occasions. Because the volunteer speakers spoke both English and their native languages, the series on occasion was offered in English with Spanish (or, for the Russian community, with Russian) translation and visa-versa, depending on audience needs.

The series has been presented on a monthly basis, and as always promoted library materials and web sites related to the subjects being highlighted. Topics included national foods, heroes, holidays and independence days, social celebrations, music, dance and costumes, religious celebrations and discussions of santos,

milagros, and Dia de los Muertos. The volunteers have worked on the content and the style of the presentations; the librarian's role has been to book a library meeting room for the occasion, purchase materials as needed, advertise the event, and be around if assistance is needed.

E. ARABIC LITERATURE DISCUSSION GROUP

In 1994 and 1995 I offered two classes on Arabic language and culture. The theme was "Learn a Culture Through Literature." Those classes were very well attended and liked, apparently because they combined language, conversations, reading and discussing literature by Arab authors from different Arab countries. Partly as a result of the level of interest in the two classes, in October 1996 the Arabic Literature Discussion Group was launched and has gone on to become one of the library's many standard book discussion groups. This group is also well attended, attracting participants who are of Arabic origin or who have lived in Arab countries, or are learning or know Arabic and are familiar with the culture. The group meets on a monthly basis, choosing each month's selection from a different Arab country. Our belief is that through literature we find common ground and a better understanding of each other.

F. LATIN AMERICAN LITERATURE DISCUSSION GROUP (BOOKS ARE READ AND DISCUSSED IN SPANISH)

Also suggested and run by volunteers from Latin America, this group started primarily because although our library has long had a Latin American Literature discussion group, the books are always read in translation and discussed in English. Our Latin American volunteers suggested, "Wouldn't it be better to read Latin

American literature in the original language it was written in?" The group has its own regular attendees and its books, all of which are read and discussed in Spanish, are chosen to represent authors from countries throughout Latin America (in 1998 we will include books written by Spanish authors as well). Group members are native Spanish speakers and people who know Spanish well enough to love to read "original" works and practice their Spanish.

G. LATINA/CHICANA
ORAL HISTORY PROJECT

In recent years a local museum planning group called Women of the West Museum collaborated with the Boulder Public Library to start discussion groups. The aim was to read from, and discuss, a wide variety of original and published sources that dealt with the history of women of all ethnic backgrounds in the American west. One group, which planned to study Chicana and Latina history, found very little printed material about the subject. As a result, we decided to work with our library's separately housed branch, the Carnegie Branch Library for Local History, and learn how to conduct interviews and document them as part of the long-term Carnegie Oral History Project. We learned that a few interviews with Chicana or Latina women were conducted in the 1970's, but they did not in any way capture the history of women in our area. This project is at its beginning stages. We use information posted on the REFORMA listserv and other web sites as a basis to start up a collection of resources.

H. YOUTH PROGRAMS AND SERVICES

Being an active member of the city's organizations that deal with services and programs for youth, and through relations established with the School District and Headstart programs, Outreach program works closely with youth, offering Multicultural Storytelling workshops, Storytelling, Arts and Crafts programs.

7. Avoid "celebrating" ethnic cultures

One of the goals of our library's Outreach Program has been to avoid "celebrating" a certain culture at a certain month or day and then forget about it for the rest of the year. It is our belief that cultural celebrations should be left to the people in a community to decide whether or not they want to share with the rest of us. Further, some "celebrations" can be, and have been, offensive when performed by people outside the originating culture. Moreover, some aspects of a culture or ritual are properly performed in special settings, and so on. Hence I believe the library's role is to have the right materials (for example, books, video tapes, and posters) available and to make meeting rooms and other spaces available for people to use. All diverse cultural events and celebrations the library has offered through our Outreach Program have been initiated by people from the originating cultures and were not imposed from the library.

8. Beyond the library buildings

Some of the people we wish to serve live in situations that do not allow for frequent use of the library. Some are living in conditions of economic hardship, others in emergency housing. We work with the agencies that take care of these people's needs to deliver books, video tapes, magazines and similar materials. Other communities live in very close neighborhoods where they have a community house that they use for after-school homework and other activities. The library maintains a presence within these communities by providing a mini-library with materials which we change every two months. The mini-collection is selected according to people's requests. We decided not to have bookmobiles, primarily because we want people to feel that as part of the community they can come to the library any time it is open and be a library patron like other people in the community. Though bookmobiles might be successful for migrant populations, and for communities that live at "distant" locations, we felt that it would have a negative effect for people permanently living in a community but secluded and hence excluded from participating like other community members. Library services such as issuing library cards, children's storytimes, and arts and crafts programs are offered on site for people who have no means of transportation. These programs, which are offered to families as a whole, tend to be very well-attended and eagerly anticipated. Through our program, additionally, families without other means of transportation are sometimes driven to library events that interest them. Our calendar of events as well as programs and services announcements, both in English and Spanish, are made available throughout the Boulder area and posted in places where people are sure to see it, such as laundry rooms and club houses.

The Leadership Role of the Library

The above description of the Outreach Program and its responsibilities in the context of library services might give the impression that the sole role of the library is to answer to the needs and requests of various communities. If that were the case, libraries would lack a leadership role—a regrettable state because librarians have access to a wide array of information and resources and hence a responsibility to their less informed patrons. However, in my opinion, a leader is one who is able to balance his or her vision with people's needs and aspirations.

The communities I deal with come from Third World or totalitarian countries whose people have long histories of subjugation, and, as a result, an equally long history of asking themselves what do they represent, or how they must change to measure up to the colonial/white culture. That is precisely why we choose to leave it to them to say what they want— and then do it the way they want. I don't think it is anyone's place to make decisions for them or place a value (or devaluation) on aspects of their cultures.

The leadership role of the library is accomplished through being accessible and responsive to community needs, providing all our communities with information and support to help them know what's available for them, from and through the library. The library is one component of a diverse society. Our role is to serve people. We inherited a history here in the U.S. of exploitation of minorities and people of color, with one result being that many of our ethnic communities don't demand services from us—and don't to the degree that part of what we must do is show them how to demand rights, show them that it is appropriate to do so, and by our immediate responses to their needs, create trust between institutions and people.

ELECTRONIC RESOURCES

CHAPTER SIXTEEN

Latino Resources on the Web

Susan A. Vega García

Introduction

Use of the World Wide Web in academic libraries has grown exponentially since the mid–1990s and the introduction of easy-to-use browser software such as Mosaic and Netscape. In academic settings, librarians, faculty, and enterprising computer science or engineering students were among the first to recognize and to make use of the potential of this new publishing medium. Early pioneers saw the Web as a unique space in which to organize through hypertextual links various Internet resources. Besides organizing existing material, new information sources could easily be created, mounted on a server, and accessed by others. A solid Latino presence was quickly established on the Web in the form of librarian Richard Chabrán's scholarly CLNet, then at UCLA, and in the irrepressible EgoWeb, constructed by Felipe Campos

at the University of Texas, Austin.[1] It is odd to look back at that time—not that long ago—and recall the marvel and excitement of waiting for Mosaic to load the CLNet home page onscreen. Since those early days, numerous other Latino Web resources and hypertext lists have been developed, but in many ways, these two pioneering sites still represent the opposite poles of Web site development—those sites developed by subject and content specialists, and those developed by amateur enthusiasts. For Latino resources, there is value in both approaches.

Librarians have long recognized and utilized the Web as a means of enhancing traditional library services in the areas of collection development, reference, and instruction. In academic libraries, daily Web use has become commonplace as librarians organize and build their own Web pages, develop Web-based reference services, collect sites for instruction and outreach services, catalog Internet resources of all kinds, and build electronic collections for our patrons. For most academic librarians, the first blush of novelty and excitement in using Internet and Web resources is (sadly) long gone. Instead, the focus is now on questions of separating the hype from the reality of how best to make this new tool truly useful in our own work and for our patrons.

Hal R. Varian succinctly states this concern as follows: "The problem most of us now face is not access to information, but rather its overabundance. The challenge is to winnow what is useful out of the vast amount of information available: to select, evaluate, describe, store, retrieve, manipulate and present relevant information."[2]

While access to computers and electronic information is indeed still a serious problem for the majority of Latinos nationwide, this study is an evaluative description of the kinds of Latino resources that are currently available on the Web, and identifies those that appear most useful.

Latino Identity Issues

Finding Latino resources on the Web is not always an easy matter. This is due in large measure to the complexities of Latino identity in the U.S. Mexican Americans/Chicanos comprise the majority of Latinos in the U.S., with Puerto Ricans and Cuban Americans comprising the other largest groups. Of the smaller groups, Salvadorans, Dominicans, Colombians, and Guatemalans are the most populous. Although there may be some broad cultural, historical, or socioeconomic commonalities among these groups, above all else, Latino identity is diverse. A Latino Web site of interest to a *Tejano* patron may

not be relevant at all to a Dominican raised in New York. Librarians assisting patrons will need to be aware of the often substantial cultural differences between various Latino groups, and resist the assumption that all Latino cultures and information needs are alike.

There is no one single monolithic Latino culture or heritage. This is reflected in great part by the sheer quantity of ethnic identifiers that describe individual Latino groups, and by the ongoing lack of consensus on which collective term— Latino or Hispanic—is to be preferred.[3] As Latinos, even what we choose to call ourselves varies from group to group, and at times moment to moment, depending perhaps on the geographical region in which we live, personal politics, the level of cultural awareness of those around us, and many other factors. Oboler[4] and others have researched Latino ethnic labels and their use, suggesting a lack of a common or generic "Latino" or "Hispanic" identity altogether. There are also important gaps: for example, distinct terms to describe Puerto Ricans, Dominicans, Salvadorans, Colombians, and Guatemalans born and raised in the U.S. do not always exist, and hyphenated labels (such as "Colombian-Americans") seem not to be in widespread use by many of these groups in describing themselves.

As librarians, we are aware of the lack of standard terminology from one classification system to another, from Library of Congress subject headings to the vocabulary of various indexes and abstracting services. In varying systems, subject headings such as "Hispanic Americans," "Latinos," and the anachronistic "Spanish Americans" (this latter currently used by Library Literature) are all viable subject terms in use today. But despite this multiplicity of terms, there is in fact order within any given catalog, index, or abstracting service. The Internet and the Web, however, lack this kind of bibliographic structure. Thus, all ethnic identifiers for a particular group must be considered and searched, and all identified resources must be evaluated for relevance.

Librarians, the Internet, and the Web

There is a growing body of professional literature devoted to the topic of how and why librarians can evaluate, collect, and use Web resources. In academic libraries, the collection and organization of various Web resources has been undertaken by many bibliographers and subject-area selectors as a service to the students and faculty in their area, and as a valid means of supplementing physical, in-house collections. The majority of publications address the immediate and practical issues of how to find and use relevant Web resources quickly, particularly for reference desk assistance to patrons. Journal columns, articles, and bibliographies providing or reviewing useful Web sites are now commonplace in the professional literature. To cite one example, in 1997, Díaz edited a special issue of Reference Librarian on the topic of reference resources on the Internet. She states in her introduction that "[s]urfing may be fun, but it's no way to do reference," and that today's reference librarian "...faces a challenge to find the exact piece of information needed without having to wade through irrelevant, unreliable and out of date material."[5] For that reason, twenty-six "core lists" in various subject areas were compiled in that volume to provide immediate practical assistance to reference librarians. Besides this type of published literature, there are also numerous examples of local electronic pathfinders and Web resource guides that bibliographers and other librarians have constructed for their own local libraries and clientele.

Other articles focus more on the theoretical issues of how the Internet has changed libraries,[6] how the Internet and its resources can be categorized by librarians, and on evaluation. Of particular interest is Edmund F. SantaVicca's evaluation of Internet resources as reference tools.[7] SantaVicca applies Bill Katz's well-known typology of reference sources to Internet (but not specifically World Wide Web) materials. The three relevant categories named by SantaVicca are (1) control-access directional tools that "typically do not aim to present needed information but rather indicate where the information exists or can be accessed," (2) source tools "that do, in fact, present the desired information rather than a path to the information," and (3) unconventional reference tools such as "community information centers (information and retrieval agencies), vertical files, clearinghouses, and individual experts."

Clearly, hypertext documents and materials on the Web have the potential to function as all three of these traditional types of reference tools (and indeed often function as hybrids that do all of the above). In particular, hypertext is well-suited to serve as control-access-directional bibliographies, "netographies," or indexes that point the user to relevant information elsewhere, and thus provide some organization to resources scattered across cyberspace. Such sites typically take form as directories or meta-sites.[8] Part of the initial excitement of the Web was that it offered unique and unprecedented publishing opportunities to anyone granted access to Web server space. In other words, anyone could create his or her own content source tools, meta-site, or information clearinghouse. In time, however, this same capability for self-publishing became an often cited drawback to the Web as "vanity publications," as Smith calls them, began to flourish.[9]

Consequently, there has been ongoing debate among librarians as to whether the Internet and World Wide Web can and should be used as a research and reference tool. In their 1998 study, Zumalt and Pasicznyuk state that while "[t]he answers the Internet provides might be flawed, since self-publishing is more of an option,"[10] any other print reference tool may be similarly incorrect, incomplete, or not current, and that all reference materials, regardless of type, must be evaluated by the librarians using them. Overall, they conclude that the Internet is stable and has much to offer libraries, and that using the Internet for reference is highly worthwhile.

On the other hand, Devlin and Burke suggest that at the most, only some ready reference questions can be answered using the Internet. They state that the overall lack of bibliographic structure and quality control on the Web make it very difficult, realistically speaking, for a reference librarian to quickly choose an appropriate search tool, find a relevant Internet or Web information resource, thoroughly evaluate the site from which the information came to ensure its authority, and then answer the patron's question all in a matter of minutes. The authors write:

"A number of criteria including purpose, authority, scope, and audience have traditionally been used to evaluate information quality. These criteria should always be used intelligently; for example, using the reputation of an author or publisher as the sole test of accuracy and impartiality leaves much to chance. Despite their flaws these criteria do provide cues for identifying quality information. The problem is that they are not easily applied to Internet resources. These resources often lack minimum levels of descriptive information, have ill-defined boundaries, and are subject to rapid revision."[11]

Continuing on the topic of evaluation, Alastair G. Smith presented evaluation criteria for Internet and Web resources, much of which were based on traditional criteria for examining print resources, CD-ROMs, and other electronic services.[12] Smith cautioned that librarians and patrons alike must understand the difference between content evaluation, which examines factors such as accuracy, authority, currency, usefulness, purpose, breadth, and ease of use, and evaluation that centers on more superficial matters such as trendiness, attractive presentation, or what Smith's article calls "coolness." Smith developed criteria specific to Internet and Web materials such as links made to other resources, graphic and multimedia design, and a category called "workability," which addresses issues such as user-friendliness of the resource, its organization and "browsability," connectivity, whether a search engine has been provided, and an assessment of the resource's "required computing environment." This latter refers to whether any specialized hardware or software is necessary to view, "experience," or make use of the site in question.

Smith also stressed that librarians have a role to play in teaching patrons how to evaluate Web resources as well, and cited, among other guides, one developed by Esther Grassian at UCLA as providing a good model from which to work.[13] Grassian has appropriately posted her guide on the Web, and offers numerous questions for patrons and students to consider, focusing on the categories of content evaluation, source and date of the resource, and its structure.

Despite this proliferation of publications and research attention on the topic of the Internet and Web resource evaluation, collection, and use in libraries, research specifically on Latino Internet and Web resources is just beginning to be published, with much of it at the level of theses and dissertations.[14] In the professional library literature, publications in this area often have been little more than unannotated lists of Web sites and their URLs, while others have included few if any Latino Web sites.[15] On the whole, U.S. Latino Web resources have remained marginalized, left un-addressed, un-reviewed, and uncollected, or are often misunderstood in the professional literature and librarian Web guides. For example, it is not unusual for bibliographies and local pathfinders that supposedly focus on U.S. Latino resources to include more Latin American than U.S. Latino materials. Diversity among Latino Web resources has also not been well represented in the library literature. Thus, the overall lack of attention on finding, evaluating, using, or categorizing Latino resources on the Web may be due in part to a general lack of understanding of the complexities of Latino identities and cultures in the U.S. and reflected on the Web.

Identifying Latino Resources on the Web

This research project was intended not only to identify and evaluate the most useful Latino materials on the Web, but also to analyze which Latino groups were making use of (or being addressed by) the Web, and for what reasons. In compiling data for this study and its accompanying bibliography, an objective approach was taken in order to identify and review as many Latino resources as possible, not simply reiterate or promote personal favorites. For that reason, two Web search engines, HotBot and AltaVista, were used to search and retrieve Latino Web sites. Separate searches were done for each of the seven Latino groups under consideration, those being Mexican Americans, Puerto Ricans, Cuban Americans, Salvadorans, Dominicans, Colombians, and Guatemalans. Search terms used were simple ethnic identifiers (e.g., "mexican american," "chicano," "chicana," "puerto rican," "boricua," and so on), and consistent for both search engines. Separate searches were also done on the collective terms "Latino" and "Hispanic."

The first two hundred results of any one search were reviewed and screened for relevance. Sites that were Latin American in content were not collected, nor were classified ads, on-line news threads, advertisements, recipes, real estate or tourist information, ephemeral one-page material or other sites judged to have little added value. Duplicates were also thrown out. After this initial screening, collected materials were then analyzed and organized by Latino subgroup and by type of Web resource. Sites were then evaluated for content, breadth, perceived authority, currency (or signs of ongoing maintenance), stability, usefulness, accuracy, ease of use, and what Smith terms "required computing environment." Sites that were evaluated as particularly noteworthy and of potential use by librarians were compiled into an annotated list of recommended Web sites.

Types of Latino Web Resources

It was discovered that collected sites could be organized into two main categories, according to type of resource. Broadly speaking, these categories were (a) those sites judged to be of most potential use to librarians and patrons for research or reference services, and (b) those sites that, however well-designed, had a much more limited or specialized purpose, and were not as likely to lead the user to authoritative, related sites or other quality content-rich information on the Web. Sites that fell into this latter category were further analyzed and organized into the following categories, with individual representative sites included for illustration. Latino group information on each type of resource is also summarized here.

a. Commercial services. These are sites that sell services or products aimed specifically at Latino groups. Some commercial services are on-line shopping catalogs or sites with added value, such as links to various cultural resources. A good examples of this kind of site is Isla (*http://www.IslaOnline.com*), a mail order site for Puerto Rican and Caribbean folkart, textiles, food, and music. After screening and evaluation, the majority (57 percent) of all commercial sites collected pertained to or addressed Mexican Americans (21 percent) or were "generic" Latino/Hispanic (36 percent) in nature (meaning, they used the rather monolithic ethnic labels "Hispanic" or "Latino," and did not refer specifically to any one Latino group).

b. Cultural sites. Broadly defined, these are sites that promote distinctly Latino arts, dance, music, history, literature, and so on, whether traditional or contemporary, as well as serve as directories, promotions, or services for Latino artists and writers. Also included in this category are pages that explore issues of individual or group ethnic identity. CreArte (*http://www.crearte.org/mainmenu.html*) is one example of an excellent Chicano-focused ambitious art site with numerous multimedia effects, such as sound files (that not everyone will be able to access). Heavy use of graphics also increases the time it takes to load each page. Just under half (48 percent) of all cultural sites collected were Mexican American (30 percent) or Puerto Rican (18 percent).

c. Health. Pages and Web sites related to various Latino health issues were numerous. The Hispanic Health Council (*http://www.hispanichealth.com/*) from Connecticut provides a good example of a typical health-related page. More than three quarters (81 percent) of all health sites collected were "generic" Latino/Hispanic (50 percent) or Mexican American (31 percent).

d. Latino Studies programs, or descriptions of various academic Latino Studies programs and Latino course descriptions. For example, the Chicano Studies Program at the University of Madison-Wisconsin page (*http://polyglot.lss.wisc.edu/chicano/*) is a good model of how colleges and universities are using the Web to promote their Latino Studies programs and curricula. Forty-six percent of all such Web sites collected were Mexican American.

e. Libraries, research institutions, and museums. Web sites or pages that describe these institutions and their collections, services, or programs; these may or may not include noteworthy links elsewhere. UC Berkeley's Chicano Studies Library (*http://eslibrary.berkeley.edu/cslhome.html*) is a good example of a well-designed library site. Over half (58 percent) of all such Web sites collected were Mexican

American (42 percent) or "generic" Latino/Hispanic (16 percent).

f. Research projects. For the most part, these were materials for academic or individual research; also, descriptions of specific Latino-related research projects. An interesting example of a research project presented on the Web is the Cuba Project (*http://www.soc.qc.edu/procuba/*) from Queen's College, CUNY. Again, more than half (68 percent) of all such Web sites were Mexican American (37 percent) or "generic" Latino/Hispanic (31 percent).

g. Organizations. Individual pages or directories of community and professional organizations and associations are becoming quite numerous on the Web. Organizations as varied as the Association for Hispanic Theological Education (*http://www.aeth.org/index.html*) and the Colombian American Bar Association (*http://www.latinet.com/colbar/*) are examples. Over half (59 percent) of all these Web sites collected were either "generic" Latino/Hispanic (40 percent) or Puerto Rican (19 percent).

h. Personal pages. Personal pages merit a note of explanation. These are Web sites or pages produced by individuals that typically focus on that person's occupation, studies, likes and dislikes, friends, and so on. Although typically considered to be ephemeral material, this study found many examples of value-added Latino personal pages. One of Grassian's questions to consider asks "What other resources (print & non-print) are available in this area?"[16] Particularly for the smaller Latino groups, such as Dominicans, Colombians, Guatemalans, and Salvadorans, this question is indeed relevant. Where are the other resources that tell us first hand what it is like to be Colombian American, or describe Dominican, Sal-

vadoran, or Guatemalan realities in the U.S.? Many of these histories have yet to be published in traditional print formats. Web personal pages constructed by members of these groups can be enlightening. One example is New York State Committeeman Carlos Manzano's Colombian page (*http://www.midtownmedia.com/manzano/Colombia.html*). The majority (60 percent) of all such Web sites was either Dominican (24 percent), Guatemalan (19 percent), or Colombian (17 percent).

Latino Web Resources as Reference and Research Tools

Those sites judged to be of most potential use to librarians and patrons for research or reference services fell into two categories. These were control-access-directional tools (mostly meta-sites and directories) or clearinghouses, and source tools, such as e-journals and newspapers. These were further analyzed, with the most noteworthy and useful examples being listed on the accompanying select bibliography. Meta-sites, clearinghouses, directories, and electronic publications not included on the original bibliography were either not found by the two search engines, or duplicated the efforts of other, better organized or more comprehensive sites. More than half (54 percent) of all meta-sites and clearinghouses collected were either "generic" Latino/Hispanic (37 percent) or Mexican American (17 percent). Of source tools, the majority (60 percent) was either Puerto Rican (23 percent), "generic" Latino/Hispanic (23 percent), or Mexican American (14 percent).

The growth and changeability of the Web is one powerful reason for focusing only on control-access-directional tools and source tools. It is no longer feasible to list every interesting or unique Web site, but rather to highlight those that seem dedicated to provide a reasonable attempt at bibliographic control or original, authoritative content.

Since the compilation of the original "Recommended Latino Web Sites" list in May 1997,[17] changes have inevitably occurred. One recent change is the development and promotion of portals, some of which are being marketed for a Latino audience. In a 1999 article appearing in *Hispanic Magazine*, Vidueira defined Latino portals as "one-stop Web sites that serve as gateways to the Internet."[18] More specifically, portals are competitive commercial services that offer (often for a price or registration) numerous services such as Web search engines, electronic communities and interactive chat forums, e-mail, daily news or daily stock exchange quotes, banner advertisements and direct links to popular merchant Web sites, and so on. User lists may be released or sold to other companies and used as mailing lists. On the Web, familiar search engines such as Lycos, AltaVista, Excite, Yahoo, and many others have transformed quickly from simple search systems or subject directories into these multi-purpose electronic communities.[19] A number of Latino-focused portals have recently emerged offering similar on-line services as well as a means to search for Latino-relevant Web sites. Currently, these Latino portals seem to promise more than they actually deliver as few actually provide adequate searching and retrieval of U.S. Latino Web sites, but they are included and evaluated on the list in the event that they improve in the near future.

Other changes include the unfortunate demise of such Web sites as Daily Roots Stand, an alternative and innovative electronic newspaper from Brooklyn that featured Dominican and Afro-Latin perspectives, *El Colombiano*, an excellent Colombian American newspaper from Miami, and SQARIK, a Guatemalan collection of scholarly articles on politics, economics, finance, the U.S., contributed short stories, poems, and essays. A handful of Latino Web sites have revised their focus significantly, while changes on other selected Web sites primarily have been cosmetic, such as the addition of JavaScript. A few sites have added necessary search engines; a few sites have changed URLs, and a few of the source tools now show signs of a lack of maintenance. Like many minority periodicals, these sites may be operating on shoestring budgets, with new releases issued only sporadically and irregularly. Time will tell whether this is the case, or whether they are simply interesting but apparently abandoned cultural relics in cyberspace.

Recommendations

The fact that a particular Web site is on the recommended list does not indicate that some changes are not in order. Resources were evaluated comparatively, but no ranking system was used. Had this been the case, a number of recommended sites might not have scored high. Inherent with providing links and information on the Web is the need for ongoing maintenance of Web sites and their data. Depending on their subject matter, resources that are not routinely updated become stale and can decline in usefulness. Web site administrators should be encouraged to routinely check the viability of links and content, particularly if it is information about the Internet or other topic that changes rapidly. Correcting HTML code errors, spelling mistakes (in English and in Spanish), and clearly indicating when pages were last updated is also necessary.

Conversely, as Web sites are maintained and new information is added, administrators need to keep in mind the "browseability" of their site and the needs of their users. The larger a Web site grows, the more pressing is the need for a search engine or, at the very least, a clearly understood organization scheme must be used, such as organizing resources by broad and intuitive subjects, and then listing materials by finer topics or in alphabetic order. These suggestions seem quite basic, and are among the most fundamental guidelines in most evaluative schemes, yet they are not routinely followed by many Latino Web resource developers. The overall quality of Latino Web resources can be improved if these fundamentals are observed.

The push towards commercialization of the Web has also had an impact on many Latino Web sites, and not always for the better. A number of major Latino Web sites have rushed to transform their sites into commercial-centered portals that often have user traffic and marketing in mind much more than the actual quality of the content they offer. An editorial from PCWeek Online stated the following:

> The drive to consolidate operations, expand on-line services and gobble user lists has one goal: to create a way to funnel the most sets of eyes to the most targeted banner ads. Yet, as portals trip over one another in those efforts, they are producing sites that look and feel like one another. The winner in this race may not be the site with the most toys. The site that knows what to do with them will separate itself from the pack.[20]

To date, the majority of Latino portals appears to have concentrated most on gathering together a cluttered collection of advertisements, e-mail and chatroom services, on-line "member" surveys and quizzes that do not benefit the user but are designed instead to compile user e-mail addresses for market surveys and commercial use, and faulty search engines to pull up unevaluated Web pages submitted or self-nominated by individual Web page authors. Use of such portals results in a distorted and incomplete picture of quality Latino information on the Web. Currently, noncommercial Latino meta-sites and source tools are more successful at pointing the user to relevant information by and about Latinos in the U.S.

There is also a need for more research, and better access to relevant information. For example, *Library Literature*, the primary index to the professional periodical literature, regularly indexes book reviews but does not yet include indexing for Internet or Web resource reviews. Although a number of mainstream professional journals regularly include Internet review columns and features profiling various Web sites, the usefulness of this information is decreased if we in the profession do not have easy and regular access to it through indexing.

As a final note, the concept of a static bibliography of World Wide Web resources is akin to taking a photograph of a dancer in movement, whose expression and interpretation will never be exactly duplicated again. The bibliography will best be used as an historical document of a piece of Web history, and as a starting point for librarians and their patrons to make their own discoveries and augment local library services.

Recommended
U.S. Latino Web Sites

This list includes Chicano (Mexican American), Puerto Rican, and Cuban American Web resources, as well as sites that pertain to Salvadorans, Dominicans, Colombians, and Guatemalans residing in the U.S. Only Web sites that are reflective of U.S. Latino realities were considered; sites that are exclusively Latin American in focus are not included. Recommended Web sites listed below were evaluated for breadth, perceived authority, stability, usefulness, and accuracy. Meta-sites, clearinghouses, directories, e-journals and electronic newspapers are the focus.

Meta-Sites, Clearinghouses, and Directories

Andanzas al Web Latino
http://lib.nmsu.edu/subject/bord/latino.html

Annotated and well-organized long list of predominantly Mexican American Internet and Web resources, by librarian Molly Molloy. Includes some evaluative comments, and a useful list of newsgroups and discussion lists. Increasingly includes Latin American items, making it a bit more difficult for non-subject specialists to locate specifically U.S. Latino materials. In English (bilingual main menu only); no search engine.

The Azteca Web Page
http://www.azteca.net/aztec/

A clearinghouse of Chicano and indigenous Mexican historic and cultural facts, opinions, debates, definitions, and information; includes a mailing list, listserv, and numerous advertisements. In English; includes search engine.

Boricua.com
http://www.boricua.com/

A clearinghouse that serves mainly as a directory for Puerto Ricans on the Internet and links to their Web creations. Includes a bulletin board, calendar, electronic communities, and Puerto Rican facts. Increasingly, this site has been transforming into a portal, offering instant daily news, numerous surveys, commercial advertisements, services such as sending e-cards with Puerto Rican images, and links to Puerto Rican-relevant bookstores and a mall. In English and Spanish; includes local search engine and GoTo.com search for the rest of the Web.

CANFNet (Cuban American National Foundation Net)
http://www.canfnet.org/

CANF is the largest Cuban American organization in the United States; this Web site functions as a clearinghouse for CANF publications, editorials, articles, news and opinions, some of which are available in PDF format. In English; no search engine.

Chapines Online
http://www.nortropic.com/chapines/

Major directory of Guatemalans online; includes many in the U.S. Includes a Guatemalan Web ring, listserv, e-mail services to contact members, and links elsewhere. In Spanish; includes search engine.

CLNet (Chicano/Latino Net)
http://clnet.ucr.edu/

Major meta-site that points to academic research, creative arts, and community outreach materials. A unique service offered is the opportunity for users to create their own personal Web page to add to CLNet. Focus on Chicano and general Latino materials, but increasingly includes links to Puerto Rican and some Latin

American materials. In English (bilingual main menu); includes search engine.

Coquí Net
http://www.coqui.net/

Major Puerto Rican Internet service provider, with many links to Puerto Rican sites. Strong island and Latin American focus. This is another site that has been transforming into a portal, with numerous advertisements, webmail services, links to daily news, many help pages with networking information, and links elsewhere. In Spanish (main menu in English); no local search engine but Yahoo (in English and in Spanish) search for the rest of the Web, plus a listing of other specialized search engines.

Cuban Committee for Democracy
http://www.us.net/cuban/

Bilingual clearinghouse of moderate viewpoints on Cuban and Cuban American issues; includes Cuban Affairs newsletter, news on relevant legislation and events, and demographic information that challenges the belief that the Cuban American population is homogeneous and monolithic. Includes interesting Cuban and Cuban American links elsewhere; still being maintained? In English with parallel site in Spanish; no search engine.

CubaWeb
http://cubaweb.com

Major site features viewpoints, articles, on-line bookstores, chat forums, classified ads, calendar of events, a business library, and other Cuban American and Cuban resources. In English (bilingual main menu); no search engine.

Dominican Studies Institute
http://www.ccny.cuny.edu/dominican/home.html

Brand new to the Web, a description of this institute at CUNY, its programs, publications, activities, and contact information. A fledgling meta-site, included because scholarly information on the Web and on Dominicans in the U.S. is otherwise scarce. May it develop into a more content-rich resource, specific to Dominican materials and information on the Web. In English and Spanish; no search engine.

EgoWeb: Felipe's Things Latino
http://edb518ea.edb.utexas.edu/html/latinos.html

Massive collection of unalphabetized and unannotated links from Felipe Campos, one of the Latino Web pioneers. Focus on Chicano and Mexican sites; includes Latin American materials. One of the few sites that includes Latino gay and lesbian resources and Web ring. In English (bilingual menus); index jump feature, includes search engine.

¡Guanacos Online!
http://www.nortropic.com/guanacos/

Massive directory of Salvadorans on-line, in U.S., El Salvador, and abroad. This site has begun calling itself a portal ("un directorio tipo Yahoo"), but currently offers just a subject directory and numerous links to news stories of interest. In Spanish; includes local search engine (for user directory information only, not subject content of Web site).

Guatemala, la tierra del Quetzal
http://www.serve.com/MarioVillalta/guatemal.htm

Long list of unalphabetized links with brief annotations, organized by broad subject area. Includes some resources that look at Guatemalan identity and issues in the U.S. Fully bilingual with parallel sites in Spanish or English; no search engine.

Guatemalan Cyberspace: Internet Services
for Guatemala
*http://mars.cropsoil.uga.edu/trop-
ag/quienes.htm*

Annotated list of numerous discussion and chat groups, directories, a Web ring, and news links, some of which include issues related to Guatemalans in the U.S. In English.

HispanicBiz
http://www.hispanicbiz.com/

Large meta-site with a business focus. Includes helpful links to U.S. and Latin American financial news, demographic and business-related facts about U.S. Latinos, resources and publications on technology, networking, education, and community resources. Focus is general U.S. Latino and Latin American. In English (some links in Spanish, Portuguese); no local search engine but a long list of search engines for the rest of the Web.

Hispanic/Latino News Service
http://www.latinowww.com/

Well-organized abstracting service of current news articles and editorials on Latino and some Latin American topics from Web news sources. Includes partial archives dating back to late 1998, though links may no longer be active. Includes additional features such as a discussion list and selected links elsewhere. In English; smaller, parallel Spanish site features abstracts of Spanish-language news articles from the Web; includes search engine.

The Hispanic/Latino Telaraña
http://www.latela.com/

An extensive site that has included links to creative arts, careers, cultural centers, E-publications, newsgroups and mailing lists, and organizations. Focus is on Latin American, peninsular Spanish, and some Chicano, general Latino, Cuban American, Puerto Rican sites. The site has been off-line for renovations for an extended period of time, and may not return. In English (bilingual main menu); no search engine.

Hispanic Pages in the USA
http://coloquio.com/index.html

Includes a few useful U.S. Latino resources, particularly a "Who's Who of the Hispanic Web" directory and the e-journal Coloquio. Includes Chicano, Puerto Rican, Cuban American information; Latin American, peninsular Spanish, and Basque sites. Extensive use of graphics detracts from the site. In English and Spanish (some sections in Spanish only).

Hispanic Vista.com
http://216.55.26.177/

News service that links to news articles, information and services of interest from elsewhere on the Web, many of which are on Latino topics and issues. This is another site that has begun transforming into a portal, offering e-mail, voice mail services, a growing subject directory, magazine subscription services, and an on-line mercado. From San Diego. In English; includes search engine.

HOLA: Hispanic On-Line Association
http://www.hola.com/

Organizes noteworthy Latino Web sites by language (bilingual, in English, etc.), and provides links, annotations, and grades to HOLA's selection of the best of the best (many of which are Latin American). Includes Hola! Magazine, a chatroom, shareware archives, a Web guide for children, and various networking tools, as well as portal-like commercial advertisements and user surveys for members. Many features are not Latino or Latin American in focus. In English; no search engine.

IPRNet (Institute for Puerto Rican Policy Network)

http://www.iprnet.org/IPR/

Previously a major research and policy site that included articles, publications, news, statistical releases, events, the on-line newsletter *Crítica,* and other resources, including a discussion list. The Web site currently is undergoing redesign due to IPR's merger with the Puerto Rican Legal Defense and Education Fund. Previous Web site was in English; no search engine.

LatinoWeb

http://latinoweb.com/

Previously one of the largest and most inclusive sites, collecting and annotating links ranging from arts, business, jobs & bilingual classifieds, education, history, government agencies, non-profit organizations, newspapers & magazines, and personal pages. The site has now become a full-fledged portal, whose main page features Latino-relevant news stories, as well as e-mail services, and numerous advertisements. Much of the previous authoritative news focus has been replaced by a growing subject directory of user-contributed (self-nominated) resources. In English and Spanish (some sections bilingual); includes search engine.

LULAC

http://www.lulac.org/

The Web site of this well-known organization functions as a clearinghouse to their own weekly policy briefs, and includes much useful information such as a Congressional scorecard (detailing Senate and House votes by state and name), sections on immigration, Puerto Rico and the statehood question, voter rights, "English Plus," briefs on upcoming legislation relevant to Latino populations, a discussion list, and much more. Very well designed and timely. In English; no search engine.

Mexico's Index Channel

http://www.trace-sc.com/index1.htm

Previously, a numbered list of unalphabetized, unannotated links about immigration, Proposition 187, NAFTA, and news. Focus on Chicano, Mexican, and general Latino sites. The site has been enlarged and revamped with graphics and new sections on topics such as "Mexico for Kids," "Hurricane Season," and "Fighting Drugs" added. Much of the previous coverage on specifically Chicano and U.S. Latino issues seems to have disappeared. Fully bilingual with parallel sites in Spanish and in English; includes search engine.

Las mujeres

http://www.lasmujeres.com/

Biographical profiles on selected U.S. Latinas and Latin American women, ranging from Julia Alvarez, Cristina García, Mary Helen Ponce, and Gloria Estéfan to the ubiquitous Frida Kahlo and Sor Juana Inés de la Cruz. Although the site quotes liberally from copyrighted print sources (often reprinting entire articles from periodicals and reference books not on-line), at least the sources have been cited. Includes many Web links for each profile, as well as banner ads and links to on-line commercial bookstores. In English; no search engine.

National Council of La Raza

http://www.nclr.org/

Well-organized Web site from this policy focused organization provides extensive annotated lists of NCLR publications for sale, news briefs on issues such as health, education, immigration, and policy, and an unannotated list of other Web sites of interest. An excellent resource for staying current on Latino issues. In English; includes search engine.

New York Semanal
http://www.cdiusa.com/NYSemanal/
Most of the major portions of this weekly news service link unexpectedly to well-known sites such as CNN en español and PBS Online, but it also includes major sections from En español.com (see listing below) and other resources. Worth exploring. Mostly in Spanish, some English; no search engine.

Nueva Vista: Latino Perspective
http://www2.epix.net/~escobar/Vista.html
    Presents news, viewpoints, and partially annotated links on many topics. Puerto Rican, Chicano, and general Latino sites; also includes some Latin American information. This Web site has been redesigned significantly since this list was first compiled, and was off-line for redesign again in October 1999. In English; no search engine.

¡Qué hubo!
http://www.quehubo.com/
    Massive directory of Colombian and Colombian American businesses and individuals on the Internet. Recently, this site has been growing into a subject directory as well. In Spanish, with parallel English language site currently under construction; includes search engine.

El Salvador a Wonderful Country
http://www.ecst.csuchico.edu/~william/
    Lots of links to general information about El Salvador, but also discussion groups, dictionaries, e-journals and other resources by and about Salvadorans in the U.S. In English; no search engine.

Latino-Focused Portals

Oyeme.com
http://www.oyeme.com/

    Obviously patterned after Yahoo and other mainstream portals, this one bills itself as "100 percent Latino" and offers standard portal features such as selected news (much of it world news or Latin American in content), chat rooms, personal ads, membership registration (without detailing what services members might receive, if any), and so on. The search engine was fast but retrieved little U.S. Latino content. (For example, a search on the word "chicano" pulled up sixteen matches; October 20, 1999.) Worth a visit, particularly if Latino content and retrieval is improved. Bilingual with parallel sites in Spanish and English; includes search engine.

Picosito.com
http://www.picosito.com/
    Bilingual site from San Francisco with full-text news articles, plus business news, health, immigration, culture, and sports. Also offers e-mail services; home pages, a discussion forum, horoscopes, and a generic e-mall. Currently, the site seems low on overall content and retrieval, both Latino-centered and otherwise. (No matches were found with a search on the word "chicano," October 20, 1999.) Worth a browse, but not recommended until Latino content and retrieval is improved. In Spanish and English; includes search engine.

QuéPasa.com
http://www.quepasa.com/
    Yahoo-like portal with typical services (e-mail, chat, etc.) and a search engine dedicated mostly to Latin American and some U.S. Latino Web site retrieval, from Phoenix, Arizona. The organization of the site is crisp, but search and retrieval is very slow, and the content retrieved is often quite uneven and not comprehensive. (A search on the word "chicano" pulled up 186 matches, many of which came from per-

sonal pages and a single PBS Web site.) Nonetheless, a site to watch particularly if search speed, content, and retrieval are improved. Bilingual with parallel sites in Spanish and in English; includes search engine.

StarMedia.com
http://www.starmedia.com/

Collection of selected world news stories and an extensive array of services such as shopping, interactive chat sites, Internet guides, games, and related ephemera. On the surface, this New York site focuses on world news and Web resources from Spain, Portugal, and selected Latin American countries. Searching is slow, but retrieval of U.S. Latino Web sites is more impressive than other portals. (A search on the word "chicano" pulled up over 8,000 matches, many of which were academic or authoritative in nature; October 20, 1999.) Worth visiting, particularly as searching speed is improved. In Spanish, Portuguese, and (some sections) English; includes search engine.

TodoLatino.com
http://www.todolatino.com/

Billing itself as the "premiere Hispanic/Latino portal," this site may be the closest to living up to that claim, at least in terms of Latino diversity in the Web sites organized in its subject directory. The site also provides standard portal features such as news, career information, several surveys, on-line shopping, and a search engine. Searching was fast, but relevant retrieval was low. (A search on the word "chicano" pulled up forty-nine matches; October 20, 1999.) A promising site, particularly if content and retrieval is improved. In English; includes search engine.

Yahoo en español
http://espanol.yahoo.com/

Spanish-language version of Yahoo that focuses on classification and retrieval of Web sites written in Spanish, with a special focus on Argentina, Colombia, Chile, Spain, Mexico, Peru, and Venezuela. Note that U.S. Latino Web sites (and all Latino-relevant Web sites) written in English are not included, which means that numerous major U.S. Latino sites are explicitly excluded. (A search on the word "chicano" pulled up one match; October 20, 1999.) Possibly an important site for Latin American and peninsular Spanish materials, but currently not recommended for U.S. Latino Web sites. In Spanish; includes search engine.

Yupi.com
http://www.yupi.com/

From Miami Beach, another Yahoo-like portal, this one obviously named after Yahoo as well. Although the emphasis is on Latin American Web sites and information, a search feature allows searches for U.S. Web sites only. Organization of Yupi.com is clean, it offers a vast array of standard services (e-mail, on-line merchandise, translations, and so on) and retrieval was fast. Its weakness, like that of other Latino portals, is the lack of authoritative and representative content retrieved by the search engine. (A search on the word "chicano" pulled up three matches; October 20, 1999.) Just the same, it is another site to watch, particularly if content and retrieval is improved. In Spanish; includes search engine.

E-Journals, E-News

El Andar Worldwide
http://www.mercado.com/andar/

Stylish literary and cultural e-journal hosted by the Electric Mercado. Focus on Chicano and Mexican issues. In English.

Arena cultural
http://www.laraza.com/arena4/index.html
New e-journal hosted by Chicago's La Raza newspaper includes signed literary essays and profiles of Latino and Latin American authors, musicians, and artists. A comprehensive index or menuing system has yet to be built to access all previous issues of this publication. In Spanish.

Borderlines
http://www.zianet.com/irc1/bordline/spanish/espindex.html
Scholarly articles on environmental health, climate changes, immigration law, politics, and related topics concerning the Mexico – U.S. border region. From New Mexico. Fully bilingual with parallel sites in English and in Spanish.

La Campana
http://www.netside.net/lacampana/
Miami newspaper dedicated to "la libertad de Cuba" covers Cuban and Cuban American politics, and many other topics including sports, health, arts & entertainment, and more. In Spanish.

Colombian Post
http://www.colombianpost.com/
Colombian, Colombian American, and Latino current news with portal services, hosted by the Colombian-focused portal Holanet (*http://www.holanet.com/*) and focusing on the Miami area. Still being maintained? In English.

Contacto
http://www.contactomagazine.com/
Sophisticated lifestyle and news magazine from Burbank that calls itself "una revista para el latino de hoy," targeting topics of interest to many specific Latino groups as well as world news and selected Latin American news stories. There are sections on society and culture, immigration, the arts, editorials, current news, music, humor, and food. Fully bilingual in Spanish and English.

Crítica: A Journal of Puerto Rican Policy and Politics
http://www.iprnet.org/IPR/critica.html
Formerly available at the IPRNet Web site (see above), this on-line newsletter focused on policy and identity issues, with no holds barred. The IPRNet Web site is temporarily off-line for redesign, due to IPR's merger with the Puerto Rican Legal Defense & Education Fund. In English.

El cuarto del quenepón
http://cuarto.quenepon.org/
Innovative Puerto Rican on-line creative arts and literary journal, with critical essays. In Spanish (some essays in English only).

Del corazón
http://nmaa-ryder.si.edu/webzine/index.html
Latino arts Webzine written for educators and young students; produced by the National Museum of American Art and hosted by the Smithsonian's Web site. In English.

Diario las Américas
http://www.diariolasamericas.com/
Cuban- and Cuban American-focused newspaper from Miami, that includes a great deal of Latin American news as well. Includes typical features such as sports and editorials, but also includes "Notas evangélicas" and "Cuestiones gramaticales." Also includes links elsewhere, with some general U.S. Latino information. In Spanish.

En español.com
http://www.enespanol.com/home.html

Pan-Latino and Latin American e-zine covers news, sports, food, culture, travel, and other topics, with all articles and information in Spanish. Also includes their lifestyle e-zine, EnteraTe (*http://www.enespanol.com/enterate/*) which covers many of the same topics. Apparently from Atlanta, Georgia. In Spanish.

Frontera Literary Magazine
http://www.fronteramag.com/
Essential literary e-journal with numerous critical articles and interviews in every issue; focus on Chicano/Mexican American literature and authors; only back issues available on-line, with current issues available by paid subscription only. Includes comments and discussion section, plus links elsewhere. Plans are to expand into a CD music store as well. In English.

Generation ñ
http://www.gen-n.com/
Slick and humorous e-zine focuses on first generation Cuban American culture, including definitions of selected Cuban American slang terminology. Still being maintained? In English and Spanish.

Habaguanex Ciboney: Web Magazine of Cuba in Exile
http://www.netside.net/~ciboney/index.html
Includes articles, "factelitos" or little facts about Cuba, movie reviews, poetry, recipes and entertainment for Cuban Americans and exiles; includes extensive links. Another artifact of the Web that seems no longer to be maintained; archived articles and some of the links may still be useful. In English, includes separate Spanish section.

Hispanic Business
http://www.hispanstar.com/hb/
Electronic version of this business mag-azine includes links to some of the feature articles and news stories included in the print version. Many stories also include relevant links elsewhere. In English.

Hispanic Online
http://www.hisp.com
Electronic version of the well-known magazine, with some portal-like features available, such as a chatroom and a career forum. Their "Tesoros del Web" section features a selection of U.S. Latino and many Latin American Web sites. In English.

Hopscotch
http://www.hopscotch.org/
Literary journal edited by critic Ilán Stavans presents selected on-line essays on Latin American, Jewish, and U.S. Latino identities and cultures. Full-text (or in some cases, partial text) of only selected articles available on-line; all others are citations only. Includes annotated list of Latin American and U.S. Latino (mainly Mexican American) Web sites of interest. In English.

Guanaquiemos
*http://www.queondas.com/aqui_estamos/
welcome.htm*
From Miami, literary and cultural e-journal for Salvadorans whose focus is to remember El Salvador "with a smile and with nostalgia"; aimed at all Salvadorans "no importa donde estemos." In Spanish.

'LA' Ritmo.com
http://www.laritmo.com/
Biweekly music e-journal, focusing on Puerto Rican salsa and music of all kinds. Includes interviews, reviews, music charts, and many advertisements. In English.

Latin Music 1OnLine!
http://www.lamusica.com/
One of the best and most extensive

Latin music sites with a focus on salsa, tropical, and contemporary Latin pop and rock music. Features interviews, reviews, New York live music club guide, and suggested resources. In English.

Latina On-line
http://www.latina.com/

Electronic version of the popular fashion and lifestyle magazine aimed at young Latinas. Full text articles provided for some back issues only; current and more recent issues provide selected table of contents and interactive features, but not the stories or feature articles themselves. In English, with some bilingual features.

Latino USA: The Radio Journal of News and Culture
http://www.latinousa.org/

Excellent site provides access to sound files and some text transcripts of Latino USA's recent radio programs on diverse topics such as Latinos in unions, Colombians in Miami, the political situation in Puerto Rico, and Latino baseball players in the Negro Major Leagues. Requires RealAudio Player, and Adobe Acrobat for some text files. In English.

LatinoLink
http://www.latino.com/index.html

Major e-zine provides news, articles, entertainment with focus on many U.S. Latino groups and various Latin American issues; includes bulletin boards and chat forums. In English and some Spanish.

LATNN.com: Latino On-Line News Network
http://www.latnn.com/

News articles of interest to Latinos, in English and in Spanish. Sources of the news include LATNN's wire news service and their superb electronic journal, Gráfico (*http://www.latnn.com/grafico/*),

which includes author interviews, indepth essays, and opinion pieces. Focus is on many Latino groups, and includes relevant articles regarding Latin American events. In English and Spanish.

National Association of Hispanic Journalists
http://www.nahj.org/

Features news articles on various U.S. Latino groups and topics in its "Latino Reporter" section; includes professional information for organization members regarding conferences. In English.

El Nuevo Día interactivo
http://www.endi.com/

On-line version of this excellent daily newspaper from San Juan, Puerto Rico. Features news from Puerto Rico and the world, business, arts, sports, sciences, and other regular sections. Archived issues available for searching, for a fee. In Spanish.

El Nuevo Herald Digital
http://www.elherald.com/

One of the best on-line daily newspapers, from Miami. Includes Cuban section, news of interest to many Latino groups in the Miami area, as well as international, national, and regional news, cultural information, and services. In Spanish.

El Pueblo Magazine
http://www.elpueblomagazine.com/

From Houston, this on-line magazine describes itself as "...dedicated to all issues in the Houston metro-area Chicano, Latino, and Mexican community. Issues from entertainment to politics and an array of issues in between are covered." Bilingual in English and Spanish.

Puerto Rico: Reflections on the Oldest Colony

*http://www.pacifica.org/programs/puerto/
boricua.html*

Digital radio news program from Pacifica Radio Network News focuses on the political status of Puerto Rico and its small island of Vieques. Recorded news features detail protests of the Puerto Rican people seeking to have the U.S. military base removed from that island. Requires RealAudio Player; also includes facts and statistics concerning Puerto Rico and its people. In English.

Pocho Productions' Virtual Varrio
http://www.pocho.com/index.2.html

Chicano humor, comic art, and satire. Offers two versions of the Web site—one laden with JavaScript, audio features, and Shockwave plug-ins, and a stripped down version for the rest of us. In English.

La Prensa de San Antonio
http://www.laprensa.com

On-line weekly edition of this newspaper from Texas. Fully bilingual in English and Spanish.

La Raza On Line
http://www.laraza.com/

Electronic version of this newspaper from Chicago features articles on regional and national U.S. Latin issues and events, and Latin American news coverage, with an emphasis on Mexico, Puerto Rico, and Colombia. One of the most inclusive newspapers in terms of Latino groups covered. In Spanish, with parallel site in English.

El Sol de Texas
http://www.elsoldetexas.com/

Editorials, features, and cultural articles and graphics from the electronic version of this newspaper, the paper version of which has been in existence since 1966. In Spanish (menu items are in English); no search engine.

Urban Latino Magazine
http://www.urbanlatino.com/

Intelligent and flashy youth-oriented e-journal with long critical articles on music, culture, fashion, politics, and various manifestations of hip-hop ethnic pride, with a special focus on Puerto Ricans, Dominicans, Colombians, Cuban Americans, and other Latinos. Includes on-line bodega that sells t-shirts and other items. In English.

Vista Magazine
http://www.vistamagazine.com/

Electronic version of the newspaper insert familiar to many Latino communities nationwide. Includes articles on prominent Latinos, music reviews, Latino success stories, parenting features, and many other topics. In English and Spanish.

Notes

1. A note on terminology: The terms "Latino" and "US Latino" are used interchangeably in this study to indicate persons of Latin American descent born and/or now living in the United States. The author recognizes that these terms and definitions may not be accepted or utilized by everyone.

2. Hal R. Varian, "The Next-Generation Information Manager," *Educom Review* 32, no. 1 (January/February 1997). Available: *http://www.educause.edu/pub/er/review/revie wartic les/32112.html* [Accessed October 22, 1999]

3. "Ethnic identifiers" is a term used by Doris Hargrett Clack, a librarian who devoted her career to advocating for better and fuller subject heading description of African American library materials. In this context, ethnic identifiers are names such as "Latino," "Hispanic," "Chicano," "Mexican American," and so on.

4. Suzanne Oboler, *Ethnic Labels, Latino Lives: Identity and the Politics of (Re)presentation in the United States.* Minneapolis: University of Minnesota Press, 1995.

5. Karen R. Díaz, "Doing Reference 'Off the Shelf'." *Reference Librarian* 57 (1997): 1–3. Simultaneously published as *Reference Sources on the Internet: Off the Shelf and Onto the Web.* Karen R. Díaz, ed. Binghamton, NY: Haworth Press, 1997.

6. See for example Anne Grodzins Lipow, "'In Your Face'" Reference Service," *Library Journal* 124, no. 13 (August 1999): 50–52, and Mary E. Ross & John R. M. Lawrence. "Internet Reference: Boon or Bane?" *American Libraries* 30, no. 5 (May 1999): 74+ .

7. Edmund F. SantaVicca. "The Internet as a Reference and Research Tool: A Model for Educators." *Reference Librarian*, no. 41/42 (1994): 225–236.

8. A note on terminology: Web sites that provide such electronic lists of links are called by many names, including indexes, gateways, directories, netographies, webliographies, meta-pages, and meta-sites (meaning, Web sites about Web sites). In this paper, the term "directory" is used to indicate a Web site that provides straightforward listings of information, such as e-mail addresses, and the term "meta-site" is used to indicate a Web site that functions at least in part as a bibliography, linking to relevant content sometimes on the same site but most especially listing numerous content-rich Web sites elsewhere.

9. Alastair G. Smith, "Testing the Surf: Criteria for Evaluating Internet Information Resources," *Public-Access Computer Systems Review* [Online] 8, no. 3 (1997). Available: *http://info.lib.uh.edu/pr/v8/n3/smit8n3.html.* [Accessed October 22, 1999]

10. Joseph R. Zumalt and Robert W. Pasicznyuk, "The Internet and Reference Services: A Real-World Test of Internet Utility," *Reference & User Services Quarterly* 38, no. 2 (1998): 165–172.

11. Brendan Devlin and Mary Burke. "Internet: The Ultimate Reference Tool?" *Internet Research* 7, no. 2 (1997): 101–108.

12. Smith.

13. Esther Grassian, "Thinking Critically about World Wide Web Resources," [Online WWW evaluation guide, UCLA College Library Instruction] (October 10, 1997). Available: *http://www.library.ucla.edu/libraries/college/instruct/web/critical.htm* [Accessed October 22, 1999]

14. See for example Jonathan James McCreadie Lillie, "Cultural Uses of New, Networked Internet Information and Communication Technologies: Implications for US Latino Identities," (Master's thesis, University of North Carolina, Chapel Hill, 1998), Claudia M. Siervo, "The Internet and the Latino Community in the United States: A Tool for Empowerment or Disenfranchisement?," (Master's thesis, Georgetown University, 1998), and Yolanda M. Rivas, "Emergence of Latino Panethnic Communities on the Internet: Expressions within a New Medium," (Master's thesis, University of Texas, Austin, 1996).

15. See for example "A Guide to Hispanic Materials," *Unabashed Librarian,* no. 99 (1996): 32, and Lisa Pillow. "Selected Ethnic and Gender Studies Internet Sources for Reference Use," *Reference Librarian* 57 (1997): 97–109. Because this latter article addresses so many different ethnic and gender groups, the author limits each category to a very few sites. The "Latino/Chicano" section consists of three primarily Chicano sites and one Latin American site.

16. Grassian.

17. A portion of this study was presented as a poster session entitled "Latino Resources on the WWW" at the ALA Summer 97 meeting. Data and percentages reported in this paper were collected in 1997, and have not been updated or modified. The original version of the bibliography, "Recommended US Latino Web Sites," was distributed at the ALA Summer 1997 meeting to attendees, and via e-mail to those who requested the list after the meet-

ing. An authorized electronic version of the bibliography is maintained and updated on-line by the author, and is currently available at the following URL: *http://www.public. iastate.edu/~savega/reclst.html* [Accessed October 22, 1999]

18. Joe Vidueira, "Rocketing to Cyber-space: Latinos Mine for Internet Gold," *Hispanic* (July 1999): 18+.

19. What distinguishes portals from meta-sites is this commercial focus on user services, selling advertising space, and typically the provision of search engines that have the capability of searching data distributed throughout the Web, as opposed to searching just the contents of one particular Web site or one server. However, a number of meta-sites and even electronic journals have been transforming slowly into portal-like sites, with the addition of numerous banner ads, selected on-line services, and occasionally search engines capable of searching distributed data on the Web, reaching beyond the contents of the local Web site.

20. "Editorial: Rushing to Portals," *PCWeek Online*, August 24, 1998. Available: *http://www.zdnet.com/pcweek/opinion/0824/ 24edit2.html* [Accessed October 22, 1999]

CHAPTER SEVENTEEN

CLNet:
Redefining Latino
Library Services in the Digital Era

Romelia Salinas

The demographic growth of Latinos in the United States combined with the explosion of Chicano/Latino literature has dramatically increased the need for library services targeting this population. Observing this phenomena through the lens of technological advances conjures a myriad of possibilities for how Latino librarianship and technology can intersect. CLNet (Chicano/Latino Network) is a product of that intersection; an attempt to address these information needs in an arena called cyberspace, a "place" where computer networking, hardware, software and people using them converge. This article will discuss the development of CLNet, as an electronic information resource on Latino issues. Included in this article are: (1) an overview of the state of

technology use among Latinos/as prior to the development of CLNet; (2) a presentation of the initial aspirations and ideas for the CLNet project; (3) a discussion of its implementation in infrastructure development, content development, electronic communication and virtual partnership development, training including policy awareness education and; (4) a reflection on how CLNet has impacted Latino electronic information services. I will conclude with some insight on future directions and uses of CLNet.

The convergence of digitized information with emerging technological advances has brought us to a point where libraries and library services need to be re-envisioned and redefined. Libraries traditionally have functioned as sites where printed resources have been stored and open to the public for meeting informational needs. Library services have traditionally facilitated the access and use of informational sources by such methods as the implementation of organizational structures and reference systems. Computerized technology now provides libraries and library services with tools that allow for the function and definition of libraries to evolve in a manner that further benefits library users and library professionals. For instance, the concept of a library collection can be expanded with technology. A library's collection may now be comprised of items beyond its immediate location. It can also include items in many formats such as photographs, maps or digital music without having to deal with the issues involved in physical storage and preservation of such items. In addition to the changes in the concept of collections, library services can also be substantially affected and improved by the implementation of new technologies. For example, computer technology provides more sophisticated searching and indexing capabilities, more efficient modes of dissemination, increased access to geographically distant or rare information sources, and of most value, a mechanism to create new informational systems.

The technology industry has brought libraries new tools but it is up to librarians to visualize how they may be applied to existing library services and to refine them. It is essential for librarians to integrate and make use of computer technology and digital tools to continue providing the best possible service to their users. CLNet is a response to the need for creating an alternative and innovative definition to Latino library services developed by librarians. CLNet has proposed to build a virtual Chicano/Latino library taking advantage of the powerful networking capabilities that the Internet offers. It is a virtual library that would use new technologies to facilitate access to Latino-related information and also foster new research in a creative fashion.

Technology Use and Latinos Before CLNet

In researching the history of Latino library services one finds that computers have had a role in its development. Latinos have been concerned and actively involved in automation efforts affecting information collections, storage and dissemination since the mid 1970's.[1] The first searchable Hispanic database was established in 1975 by UCLA's Spanish Speaking Mental Health Research Center pertaining to Hispanic Mental Health in the United States. In 1976 the Hispanic American Periodical Index (HAPI) was introduced as a database in the area of Latin American Studies. That same year the Chicano Database began at the Chicano Studies Library at UC Berkeley as a pilot project to index ten Chicano Studies periodicals. The Chicano Database has been on-line since 1986. Later it was converted into CD-ROM format to provide greater dissemination. In 1996 it was made available on Melvyl, the University of California on-line library system, and in 1997 was accessible via the World Wide Web. In 1977 the California Spanish Language Database was developed to cater to a Spanish-speaking audience. That database was to provide subject access to Spanish language books in various public libraries in California.[2] These are few examples of how digital technologies have been utilized in building information resources on Latinos. These databases also exemplify the willingness of information professionals to integrate emerging technologies into Latino Library Services.

The Internet

The Internet has revolutionized computer use, communications, and information services. The Internet is a global matrix of electronic networks, a mechanism for information dissemination, and a medium for collaboration and interaction without regards for geographic limitations. It has been heralded as a force for the creation of a true democratic society. It is a place where ideas can be freely expressed and all participating voices are considered equal. However, a "technology gap" has been identified in ownership and use of advance communication technologies between Latinos and Non-Latinos.[3] Furthermore, use of communication technologies, such as the Internet, by Latinos has been uneven. In 1992, the state of electronic networking amongst Latinos was mainly limited to those in academia who were provided access to this technology by their respective institutions. Use of the technology among the few Latino scholars, librarians and students who took advantage of it were mainly for the purpose of communicating electronically, better known as e-mailing. During this time representation of Latino or Latino-related issues in the explosion of information accessible via the Internet was minuscule. There was minimal understanding and awareness of this new technology among the Latino community resulting in a lack of skills for navigating the developing tools to access Internet-base information. Out of this state came CLNet. At that time the Internet was creating an uncharted space that offered

endless potential for redefining library services for the 21st century.

CLEN, the Umbrella Project of CLNet

CLNet was born in 1993 at the Chicano Studies Research Library (CSRL), at the University of California Los Angeles (UCLA). The umbrella project of CLNet was CLEN (Chicano/Latino Electronic Network) a joint project of the UCLA Chicano Studies Research Library and University of California (UC) Linguistic Minority Research Institute (LMRI) headquartered at the University of California Santa Barbara (UCSB). The UCLA campus created and maintained CLNet while the UCSB campus developed LMRINet, an Internet project where focus is on education and language minority issues. While each campus maintains separate servers, with particular foci, close collaboration exists in areas such as training and electronic communication development. CLEN is a UC-wide project funded by the University of California Committee on Latino Research out of the UC Office of the President.

As is the case with many projects venturing into unknown areas CLEN's initial proposal was soon rearticulated in a manner that expanded its target user population and that increased its content scope. In 1993 CLEN was proposed as an electronic utility to bring together researchers and research in Chicano/Latino Studies as well as linguistic minority and educational research programs being carried out at the University of California.[4] By 1997 the major goals of CLEN had changed to develop Internet access, services and training which facilitated and promoted research within and beyond the University of California for those interested in ethnic studies, particularly Chicano and Latino scholarship, language minority education and related areas. The project now provides three principal Internet services: (1) electronic discussion lists for UC work groups, for selected Latino and language education organizations and for the public on various topics of interests; (2) a Gopher server which is a menu-driven program providing access to text data bases and documents; and (3) a World Wide Web server which provides a graphical interface to accessing resources in various formats such as graphics, text, video and sound files.[5]

CLNet Development

The development of CLNet parallels the establishment of Chicano/Latino libraries and library collections during the 1960s and 1970s but with less intense challenges. CLNet encountered both similar and unique challenges than those faced by the founders of Chicano/Latino research collections and libraries. First of all, the struggles that led to the establishment of valuable research collections such as the Chicano Studies Research Library at UCLA, the Chicano Studies Library at UC Berkeley, the Colección Tloque Nahuaque at UC Santa Barbara, the Chicano Studies Collection at Arizona State University, and the Mexican American Library Project at the University of Texas, Austin provided the precedence and the foundation from which CLNet was able to evolve.[6] The ideologies that manifested themselves in those past struggles were similar to the ones that drove CLNet. The drive to create, preserve and generate cultural and historical representation served as the force for the implementation of

CLNet. This drive mirrors the efforts of those Chicano university students who demanded the establishment of library collections that were relevant to their lives and information needs. The significant difference between the two however is that the student struggle focused mainly on a printed and tangible space while CLNet sought to create what is referred to as a virtual representation in an emerging digital space. This is a conceptual representation that is not confined or captured in a physical location but is distributed throughout a space accessible only through the use of computer technology.

On the other hand CLNet faced unique challenges that were not encountered by the student struggle. In the digital world the definition of ownership is still very fluid especially at the onset of the Internet. This fluidity created some disappointment for us over the years. For example, on occasion, pages from our web site were copied by another site without permission or giving CLNet any type of credit. In another incident we had scanned over fifty color images of artwork for a web page after receiving permission from the artists that held copyright. Many hours of work went into scanning, re-sizing and converting these images as well as into the organization of the images. Months after the project had been completed we discovered that someone else had created a web page using all the images we had scanned including the way we had organized the images, without recognizing CLNet's work.

Although we encounter such challenges we believe that creating web sites for free was important in the development of the infrastructure of Latino Internet resources. However, these growing pains have caused us to establish more formal agreements with our partners.

Infrastructure

When CLNet began, gopher was the most innovative tool available to access Internet base information. Gopher is a menu-driven text base tool that allows a user to browse for information on the Internet. Thus when CLNet was born as a gopher site in March of 1993, it was the first Internet site with a focus on Chicano/Latino information.[7] By 1994 the World Wide Web was becoming a major platform for delivering information globally using a graphical interface. At that time CLNet decided to transition over to creating a web site that would incorporate the gopher-based resources.

CLNet's infrastructure development meant more than acquiring the hardware and software needed to establish a server on the Internet. It called for the development of a strategic human network as well. CLNet along with CLEN formed working relationships with key individuals in academic computing units, University Librarians, Librarians and faculty across the University of California campuses and the UC Office of the President. Its networking included professional organizations, research consortia, community-based organizations, institutes, other Latino libraries and academic departments outside the University of California. Through the support and strength of these partnerships CLNet was able to become a vibrant research tool based on collaboration and connections among many different perspectives. This new tool complemented rather than duplicated existing information sources. It became part of the emerging information infrastructures on the UC campuses. In this spirit, by 1994 it was made accessible via MELVYL, the UC-wide Online Library System.

Although CLNet was born at UCLA's Chicano Studies Research Library, its main office and server were moved to the Center for Virtual Research at the University of California Riverside in November of 1996. The expansion of CLEN to the Riverside campus provided an opportunity to further develop the organizational structure of CLEN as well as allot CLNet a greater level of developmental support.

Content Development

As we embarked on the building of CLNet we were well aware that information on Chicano/Latino issues was minimal and not easily found on the Internet.[8] So creating this new information resource was extremely challenging in terms of content development. There were no existing sites at that time to which we could link our services to, as there are today. We needed to actually create the digital content to which CLNet would provide access. Drawing on our experience and expertise as Chicano Studies Librarians, as well as our willingness to learn the new technology, we were able to make CLNet a reality. The importance of familiarity with the field can not be overstated in developing a well organized and quality information system. My academic background in Chicano Studies and my awareness of the historical and contemporary issues that affect the Latino community were indispensable to me as I worked on constructing this information system.

The dynamic nature of the digital world kept the content and structure of CLNet in a constant state of change. In general we applied library practices and principles in our approach in the organization of information. We tried to organize information very much as one would in a library, keeping user-seeking behavior in mind. In the beginning of our gopher development we focused on what was available and how that can be integrated into CLNet in a logic manner to facilitate access. This included the identification of library catalogs with strong Latino studies collections and the provision of access to them via CLNet. Links to related gopher sites such as the Latin American Information Service at UT Austin was also established.[9] In addition to providing links to related sites, content development included monitoring the two existing electronic discussion lists on Chicano/Latino issues. The Midwest Consortium of Latino Research (MCLR) at Michigan State University sponsored an electronic discussion list on Latino research and the University of New Mexico sponsored Chicle, a discussion list focusing on Chicano literature. From these two lists we selected posted messages that we determined were of research or informational value; this included postings such as book reviews, conference announcements, job postings, short reports/abstracts, etc. to reformat and be integrated into CLNet content.

In addition to taking full advantage of these resources we also worked to electronically publish information on Latinos that only existed in print format. Our initial objectives were to bring information about Chicano/Latino research centers, libraries/collections and programs onto the Internet. However in order to accomplish this we needed the collaboration of those who held rights and access to this information. At that time the reality was that people, including academics, had not yet come to understand the functionality or the value of the Internet, thus, our

invitation for collaboration was at times met with perplexity and little ambition. This changed with the introduction of the World Wide Web and the commercialization of the Internet. We also worked to change this attitude by hosting an Internet Summit for leaders in Chicano/Latino Studies research including directors of research centers, librarians and faculty in April of 1994 on the UCLA campus. This two-day workshop was co-sponsored by the Inter-University Program on Latino Research. During those two days hands-on workshops were offered covering tools such as Telnet, email, listservs, newsgroups, gopher, Veronica and Mosaic. Although the majority of the content of the summit focused on the technology the wider objective was to get the participants to recognize how these tools could be applied in their daily lives, including their jobs and research.

Nevertheless, working through already present librarian and academic networks, CLNet was able to bring some valuable information on to the Internet early in its development. Descriptions of Chicano and Latino collections and inventories to their special collections were made available, including an Inter-University Program for Latino Research (IUP) Inventory of Latino-related archival collections. Information and a report on UC Davis' Chicana/Latina Research Center was also brought to the Internet. At this time we also began discussions with Librarian Lillian Castillo-Speed at UC Berkeley's Chicano Studies Library regarding putting the Chicano Database, then published only on CD-ROM and print, onto the Internet. Figure 1 illustrates the gopher structure of CLNet at the time we ceased development of it and incorporated its resources into our web site.

By 1995 there was an explosion of web

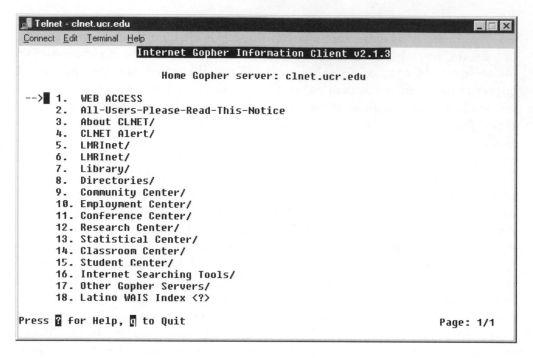

Figure 1

sites development throughout the world including all UC campuses. Recognizing the capacity of web servers CLNet decided to go beyond its initial goal of developing a gopher server. In November of 1994 CLNet brought up its World Wide Web site. The navigational flexibility, interactivity and multimedia capabilities that the web provided allowed for CLNet to take on innovative approaches to information access and creation. By then the Internet and its strength had become well known at least within the academic world, thus providing us with an abundance of opportunities to bring new information onto the Internet. Similar to our gopher site we organized our web site in a manner which facilitated access along functional and subject use of the information. By then CLNet functioned as a general Latino Internet site, organized into areas such as an electronic job center; a virtual museum of Latino art, music,

theater and pictorial essays; a calendar of events; profiles of library archival and bibliographic collections; access to Latino publications on the Internet; profiles of student organizations; profiles of local and national community organizations; statistical information; and an extensive research section covering a variety of fields including the most comprehensive women's studies site dedicated to Chicana Studies.

A great deal of the creation of information CLNet contributed to the Internet were results from our partnerships. Since 1994 CLNet has had the privilege of hosting web pages for a number of Chicano/Latino academic organizations such as the Inter-University Program for Latino Research, the UC Committee on Latino Research and the National Association of Chicana and Chicano Studies. As part of these web sites CLNet has digitized and published electronically many original documents and reports produced by these organizations but never published in any format. The web has proven to be a good medium of disseminating information and CLNet has used this feature to its fullest to increase access to rare information and publications. For instance CLNet worked with publishers such as PathFinder Press to publish electronically small publications that had come out during the Chicano Movement. Publications such as *Chicanas Speak Out* are hard to access in most parts of the country, however, by making them available on the Internet access to its content was increased. Along this same goal of increased access to rare information CLNet created a web page on Latinos and AIDS by publishing electronically documents and conference proceedings from a monumental bi-national conference on Latino and AIDS between Mexico and the United States held at UCLA. In this manner CLNet has used this new technology to make rare Latino literature more accessible.

CLNet has also been involved with the development of other types of information. For example in 1996 CLNet received an award by the National Latino Communication Center to assist in the development of the web site for the *Chicano! History of the Mexican American Civil Rights Movement* series that premiered on PBS in April of that year. This partnership provided a rare opportunity to work with a national board of Chicano scholars and activists in the development of a television series, a CD-ROM product and a web site. CLNet provided technical assistance and advice for the new web site and managed the viewer feedback section for the series on the CLNet server. This provided an electronic forum for people who had viewed the series to share their comments as well as personal experiences relating to those issues or events presented in the series. In this manner CLNet provided an avenue that allowed for the creation of new information such as, personal stories, testimonies, memories and interpretations of historical events and individuals of the Chicano civil rights movement, that could be accessed and read worldwide.

CLNet has also made a great effort to work with community-based organizations. It hosts web pages for close to thirty community organizations, mostly in the Los Angeles area. Finally, CLNet developed a web page on Latinos and Health in California that contains the results of a survey on work and health conducted by the Field Institute and sponsored by the California Wellness Foundation.[10] These are a few examples of how CLNet has contributed to the development of Internet-based information on Latinos.

The last few years has seen a growth in the content development of CLNet and in the development of Internet resources on Latinos in general. Today there are a number of Internet sites, many of them focused on specific subjects such as music, art, or history while others are web pages for programs, library collections or organizations. Many of these new web sites are making great contributions to the Latino library services on the Internet. Sites such as CEMA[11] (California Ethnic and Multicultural Archives) at the University of California Santa Barbara have made great use of the web in providing information and visual access to some of its special collections.

CLNet has always encouraged others to become what are referred to as information providers—those who provide the information to publish on the Internet. REFORMA (The National Association to Promote Library Services to the Spanish

Speaking) has been a key partner of CLNet and a strong information provider.[12] REFORMA was an organization that had its web page developed and hosted on CLNet. Eventually REFORMA took on full responsibility of the development of the web site by organizing a National Virtual Web Team to work on its development and maintenance.

There are still many areas that are underdeveloped. We encourage their development and we are willing to provide guidance to those who are willing to take on the development of innovative areas, such as those targeting Latino youth or the elderly community. With the growth in the number of Latino related Internet sites CLNet has attempted to keep current with the newly available resources and to organize them in a manner to increase access.

Electronic Communication and Virtual Communities

While gopher and web sites are great tools for disseminating and accessing information they fall short in terms of facilitating ongoing communication between people. In order to enhance the communication and the development of virtual communities a series of electronic discussion lists more popularly called listservs are sponsored by CLEN. The electronic discussion lists pull together individuals in areas such as bilingual education, immigration, Chicana Studies, etc. They also connect work groups such as the UC Latino Eligibility Task Force and various organizations such as REFORMA. The success of these electronic discussions cannot be overstated. For instance, in one of our discussion groups researchers on various campuses communicated with government officials in Washington D.C., on issues related to immigration and bilingual education. In another discussion group Chicana graduate students and faculty have share their experiences and resources with each other.

In addition to providing a means for dialog, electronic discussion groups contribute to the development of the foundation that facilitates and invites the Latino community to engage this new technology. E-mail is the tool that is most commonly used by newcomers to the Internet. To join lists all one needs to know is how to use email. However, it is easier for one to interact with something that is pertinent and embraces one's issues, language, and culture. Thus, having discussion groups such as those hosted by CLNet provided Chicanos/Latinos a possible stepping-stone into the digital world and into the creation of a virtual community. It is a community that can come together unlimited by geographical borders, to exchange information, provide mutual support, and create awareness on issues affecting Latinos. This is done similar to how Chicano Studies libraries have provided a comfort zone for culture-shocked students and a place to exchange information. CLNet has used such lists to create such spaces on the Internet.

Training

From the beginning of the project and the development of our electronic resources, we were concerned that access to Internet services be made widely available. One of the methods we employed to facilitate access was training. While many faculty and students were familiar with electronic mail few had ventured beyond those borders into other areas of cyberspace. In

1993, there were few training resources available for Internet resources especially for people outside of academia.

The initial phase of our training activities focused on the identification of relevant training materials; this led to the development of an in-house training manual. We developed major components for various levels of training workshops. Keeping in mind that using the Internet in 1993 was much more complicated than it is today we developed components that focused on Telnet; Email; Electronic Discussion Lists; Newsgroups; Gopher; Archie and Veronica; and later the World Wide Web. With the increase in Internet training resources and a greater number of people familiar with the Internet, CLNet training has become more focused, tailoring content to particular audiences and specific access tools. As a means of electronically sharing this information we created a web page for Internet training. It consists of an electronic workshop with a series of courses, to teach new Internet travelers how to navigate the rapidly expanding information superhighway. The various activities allow the users to experience the fundamental tools of the Internet in action, to grasp their function and use, and to understand their role in Internet navigation. Furthermore, these workshops introduce users to Latino and/or linguistic minority Internet resources.

We have made presentations to a wide range of audiences including researchers, research organizations, high school students, community organizations, librarians, librarian organizations and administrators, as far away as Harvard University, and as close as our own campus. These presentations cover the basic principles for Internet use as well as a general orientation to our Internet sites. We found the most successful training to be intensive and hands on.[13] Each workshop is tailored to its participants in order to ensure that the relevancy in their lives or jobs is demonstrated. Incorporation of different technologies such as computer-based slide presentations also functions as a tactic for maintaining attention and explaining concepts visually.

Presentations give us an opportunity to educate on two levels, educate about the technology, basic Internet literacy as discussed above, and introduce relevant policy issues. We present some of the policy issues revolving around the technological revolution and why it is of importance to the Latino community to begin taking an active role in this process. Policy issues are introduced such as those brought out in "Latinos and Information Technology: Perspectives for the 21st Century" a study by the Tomás Rivera Center (TRC).[14] According to the TRC computer literacy is becoming mandatory in an economy that is displacing labor-intensive, industrial-age work. Latino children might not be able to compete for success in a technology-dependent society. Information and services are quickly becoming electronic based; by the year 2000 about 75 percent of all federal and state services will be processed electronically. Information technology is transforming political communication and the delivery of services, and without private and public points of access, many Latinos could be further marginalized from public life.[15] Latinos left out will become an information-poor community as well as lacking the skills to compete in a global economy.

In 1992 studies revealed that nationwide the average Latino student's school has 19 percent fewer computers per capita than the average student's school. Moreover, when schools are evaluated in terms of the involvement of students in manipulating computer networks for communication, including electronic mail, the average Latino student's elementary school uses advance tools 40 percent less frequently than the average students' elementary school.[16] The ramifications of such facts underscores the importance for Latinos to beginning addressing barriers such as cost, access, and computer literacy and to develop structures that motivate the telecommunications industry to make infrastructure investments in Latino-dominated neighborhoods. The Latino community cannot afford to see technology as something foreign or separate from their lives because such attitudes can be detrimental in terms of future economic and educational success and survival. Thus, as librarians we should strive to ensure that Latinos have the access and the skills to make use of computerized information technology. Access is only part of the solution to the problem of closing the gap between the information poor and the information rich. There are other important factors such as computer literacy that also need to be addressed. For these reasons CLNet has made it a training priority to educate the Latino community about such policy issues and future implications.

CLNet Impact on Latino Library Services

CLNet has been a leading agent in the virtual explosion of Internet-accessible information for the Latino community and in many different ways made an impact on information and library services. Today many information professionals refer to it as the premier Internet information resource on Latinos. A pioneer in an uncharted space, CLNet has

accomplished, its objective of becoming a virtual library and a modeled project for Internet-based information services. CLNet has served as a virtual place where researchers, educational practitioners, community organizers, librarians and policy leaders and analysts can easily locate relevant information on the Latino community. CLNet has made a great impact on the Latino representation in cyberspace. CLNet's incipience was at a time when Latino-related information on the Internet was minimal. Since then we have become a site that represents a Latino voice. CLNet has received both regional and national attention as reflected in the news media articles that have reviewed our services. This recognition included mention in such major newspapers as the *Los Angeles Times*, professional journals such as *Library Journal*, and trade publications like *Internet World*. We have also received many unsolicited comments as to the quality and utility of the electronic services.

Our efforts in building a relevant information system provided a tool that could be used by information professionals to introduce library users to a new spectrum of information and to a new method of information access. By working with librarians through organizations like REFORMA, who work with large Latino populations and through our training efforts, we have been able to develop a group of technologically savvy users within the Latino community. In the process we have brought people awareness of the implications this technology will have in our future.

CLNet has also become a technological and informational resource within and beyond the Latino community. We have become an informational resource for people conducting research on Latino issues.

We receive numerous reference questions regarding Internet-based resources and general print resources by those doing research on Chicano/Latino issues from throughout the world. CLNet has become a virtual place to turn to for direction by those geographically far from Chicano/Latino literature and library services. CLNet has also become a resource for technological advice and guidance. This is especially true for the community-based organizations that we have worked with over the years. They turn to us for help on how to get onto the Internet, what type of computer to buy, how to choose an Internet Service Provider (ISP), and a number of other questions and concerns.

CLNet has also impacted the general definition of Latino Library services. Latino Library services are no longer limited by walls. As librarians there is now yet another resource to turn to for answering reference questions on Latino issues. This is especially helpful for librarians who have limited access to Latino related literature. Latino library services now exist in a redefined space. Latino library services exist wherever there is an information need met by the use of CLNet or any other Internet-based resource.

Future Directions

CLNet looks towards developing more collaborative projects with other libraries, organizations and researchers. It looks forward to projects that go beyond reproducing an electronic version of a printed project but that are themselves digitally based, projects that use computers to create new information or re-articulate information in another dimension. We want to be part of creating information systems that further and support research on Latino issues. Some possible areas we are considering is the use of GIS (geographic information systems) to present information visually about Latinos through the use of maps or the use of the Internet to provide computer and library literacy through distant learning. This would be of value especially to people in rural areas of the country.

CLNet recently began to explore the idea of venturing into a new level of training and providing access to electronic information systems. In partnership with other educational centers at the University of California and community-based organizations CLNet has become involved in creating CDI, the Community Digital Initiative. This is a project that has established a community computing center in the eastside of Riverside, an area predominately comprised of low-income Latinos and African-Americans. The Center is equipped with multimedia computers with full Internet access through a T1 line. The lab offers structured services such as a series of computer classes and public forums on issues such as policy as well as unstructured services like drop-in hours. It is into projects like these that CLNet plans to expand.

Since 1993, with the help and support of our partners CLNet has made great strides in addressing the need for Latino-related information in cyberspace. By employing methods such as establishing a valuable Internet-based information resource, increasing access to Latino literature and information by electronic publication, creating virtual communities, Internet literacy training and by developing strong partnerships, CLNet has become a model project. In the process we have offered a new definition to Latino library services, definitions that can better address the information needs of the growing Latino population of the United States. CLNet approaches the future with a continued commitment furthering Latino library services through the use of technology.

Notes

1. Ron Rodríguez, "Library automation, bibliographic databases and Chicano research: a survey," in *Biblio-Politica: Chicano Perspectives on Library Service in the United States*, ed. Francisco Garcia-Ayvens and Richard F. Chabrán (Berkeley, CA: Chicano Studies Library Publications, UCB, 1984), p. 153.

2. *Ibid.*, pp. 158–164.

3. Anthony G. Wilhelm, *Buying into the Computer Age: A Look at the Hispanic Middle Class* (Claremont, CA: The Tomas Rivera Policy Institute, 1997) p. 3.

4. CLEN Progress Report, August 1, 1993.

5. CLEN Annual Report 1996–1997, May 1997.

6. Richard Chabrán, "Notes on the history and future of major academic Chicano libraries," in *Biblio-Politica: Chicano Perspectives on Library Service in the United States*, ed. Francisco García-Ayvens and Richard F. Chabrán (Berkeley, CA: Chicano Studies Library Publications, UCB, 1984) p. 89.

7. Also at about this time LatinoNet was also launched. LatinoNet is a non-profit organization committed to increasing the use of telecommunications technology throughout the Latino community. They provided information about Latinos through a contract with America On-Line (AOL) for those who were subscribers to this service. (http://members.aol.com/lnet03/latinonet/ln.welcome.html)

8. I began working with CLNet as a first-year library school student at UCLA's Graduate School of Library and Information Science in 1993. I was involved with content development from the day the gopher server was installed.

9. Progress Report August 1, 1993

10. CLEN Annual Report 1996–1997, May 1997.

11. http://www.library.ucsb.edu/spec coll/cema.html

12. http://clnet.ucr.edu/library/reforma/

13. CLEN Annual Report 1995–1996, April 1996.

14. Tony Wilhelm, *Latinos and Information Technology: Perspectives for the 21st Century* (Claremont, CA: The Tomás Rivera Center, 1996).

15. *Ibid.*, executive summary.

16. *Ibid.*, pp. 8–9.

About the Contributors

John Ayala has been in library service since 1963. His only time away from libraries was during his military service during the Vietnam War. He drove the bookmobile for Long Beach Public Library for 5 years, worked as a bilingual reference librarian for Los Angeles County Library and directed an outreach bookmobile for one year in 1971-72. From 1972 through 1989 he was the Director of the Pacific Coast Campus Library of Long Beach City College. In 1971-72 he was involved in founding the professional library association REFORMA. During the time he was at LBCC he was president of the Faculty Senate from 1984 to 1986. He was instrumental in redeveloping the Pacific Coast Campus and building a new Learning Resource/Library facility in 1989. He has been dean of the library at Fullerton College since February of 1990. He is currently involved in a major remodeling project of the existing library and expects to build a new

library within the next three years. He is married with two children with one grandchild on the way.

Graciela Berlanga-Cortéz brings fifteen years of experience as a high school teacher and multicultural instructional specialist to the library profession. She has been directly involved in promoting libraries to the Spanish-speaking and Latino communities in Dallas since 1994. While working as manager of the Dallas Migrant Education Program, she organized field trips to introduce Latino families to public libraries in Dallas. Also, she conducted early childhood enrichment workshops for Spanish-speaking parents while their preschool children participated in storytelling and other library-related activities. As a multicultural instructional specialist, Berlanga-Cortéz monitored the infusion of multicultural materials and instruction into the content areas at magnet schools and academies in the Dallas

Public Schools. In 1998 she founded her own firm, Cortéz Education Consultants, and has produced educational supplements for *The Dallas Morning News Newspaper in Education* edition. Currently, she is involved in writing a book, *Jugando Loteria: A Collection of Short Stories*, and is nearing completion of MLS and M.Ed. degrees at Texas Woman's University. Her enthusiasm for helping Latino families to discover the library led her to help establish in 1995 a REFORMA chapter in Dallas. She served as president and vice president of the REFORMA–Río Trinidad chapter from 1995 to 1998. Berlanga-Cortéz is one of the 1998 Spectrum Scholars. She received the American Library Association Spectrum Scholarship, awarded to fifty minority group members during the first year of the Spectrum Initiative Program. Also, she was awarded a national REFORMA scholarship in 1998 and a Texas Library Association scholarship. She completed an internship in the Special Collections and Archives at the University of Texas at Arlington during the summer of 1999. She plans to work in special collections with Latino-related holdings at an academic or public library.

Mônica Scheliga Carnesí received her M.L.S. from Kent State University in 1993. She worked at the Queens Borough Public Library as a reference librarian and as a senior librarian, in charge of organizing Coping Skills Workshops for the library's New Americans Program. More recently, Ms. Carnesí was assistant reference librarian at Kalamazoo College in Michigan.

Luis Chaparro is the director of library technical services at El Paso Community College in El Paso, Texas. He

began his career in librarianship in Mexico where he worked first at the Benjamin Franklin Library and later at the University of the Americas. He played a key role in moving the library to its present location in Cholula, Puebla, and worked there as a reference librarian and Spanish instructor. After receiving a scholarship to continue his studies abroad, Luis moved to Canada where he received a M.L.S. and M.A. from the University of British Columbia. Upon his return to the United States, he entered the Texas community college library field where he has worked since. He was first hired as public services librarian at El Paso Community College and in 1989 became the director of learning resources.

Ana María Cobos graduated from UCLA in 1983 with an M.L.S. and M.A. in Latin American Studies. She worked at the UCLA Latin American Center 1980–86 as associate editor of the *Hispanic American Periodicals Index*. From 1989 to 1992 she had a position at Stanford University Libraries where she worked closely with the Latin American Collections curator on a variety of projects; since 1992 she has been at Saddleback College Library. She has been an active member of SALALM since 1980 and REFORMA since 1982. Her current project is on *Latin American Studies: An Annotated Bibliography of Core Works*.

Danelle Crowley was born in Gulfport, Mississippi, in 1945. She first became interested in the Spanish language at the age of three while living with her grandparents on the Pacheco Ranch in eastern New Mexico. Her bachelor's degree is from Texas Tech University, in secondary education with a teaching field in the Spanish language. Her master's degree in library science from the University of Texas at Austin focuses on Latin American libraries and Afro–Latin American bibliography. She has studied in Mexico; lived in Argentina, Bolivia, and Brazil; and traveled through much of the rest of Latin America. She has utilized her Spanish as Peace Corps Volunteer in Panama, Head Start Home Base teacher, interviewer for the San Antonio Heart Study, assistant at the Benson Latin American Collection, and cataloger for the National Migrant Resource Program and the Spanish language collection of the San Antonio Public Library. She has recently been involved in librarian exchanges to Chiapas and Cuba. Her home is in the Texas Hill Country near Canyon Lake.

Tami Echavarria is coordinator of instruction at Whitworth College. She is the former head of research services at Louisiana State University, Shreveport. She was coordinator for the Undergraduate Student Internship Program (1989–1997) at the University of California, San Diego, which recruited minority students to librarianship. She has been a conference speaker and has published articles on minority librarians, mentoring and recruitment in *Library Trends*, *College and Research Libraries*, *Library Personnel News*, *College and Research Library News*, and *California Libraries*. She has been active in the American Library Association and the California Library Association for over a decade.

Ghada Kanafani Elturk was born and raised in Beirut, Lebanon. She lived three years in Saudi Arabia, and lived and worked in many countries including Syria, Iraq, Jordan, West Bank, Kuwait, United Arab Emirates, the former Yugoslavia, and France. She received her B.A. in 1972 and her M.A. in philosophy in 1982. Elturk has extensive experience as a cross-cultural trainer for academic, community, education, and business environments, and has been a trainer for the Rape Crisis Team, Boulder County, Colorado. As outreach librarian since 1996 for the Boulder Public Library in Colorado, Elturk designed and implemented the outreach program, receiving the Boulder County Multicultural Award for Community Service (1997). Several of her projects received national recognition by the American Library Association, including "Conversations in English" and "Reading to End Racism." Her "Conversations in English" project won the "Innovations in American Government Award 1999 Semifinalist" from the J. F. Kennedy School of Government, Harvard University. Earlier in her career Elturk was International Business Librarian for World Trade Center of Orange County, California (1990–1992). She has been active in many civic and professional organizations, and has represented national REFORMA with the ALA Office of Literacy & Outreach Services (1997–99).

Edward Erazo has been head of reference at Florida Atlantic University's S. E. Wimberly Library since June of 1998. Prior to that, he was outreach/education librarian and assistant professor at New Mexico State University (NMSU) in Las Cruces, New Mexico, 1993–1998. He has also worked at both the El Paso Public Library as head, Mexican American services, and the University of Texas at El Paso as reference librarian as well as acting head, access services. Additionally, in 1992, Erazo worked at Saint

Thomas University in Miami, Florida, as reference and technical services librarian. He earned a Master's in Library Science from the University of Arizona (1990) as well as both a Master's (1988) and a Bachelor's (1985) in Spanish from the University of Texas at El Paso. An active member of the American Library Association (ALA), Erazo has chaired or served on numerous ALA committees, on the Library Administration and Management Association (LAMA) and the Reference User Services Association (RUSA). Erazo has been active in several state library associations. Erazo is a past president of REFORMA, the national association to promote library services to the Spanish speaking. He is a past president of the Border Regional Library Association, and was named the 1995 BRLA Librarian of the Year. Now in Florida, he has given library profession workshops in Mexico and also teaches for the University of South Florida School of Library and Information Science, East Coast Program.

María A. Fiol is the Spanish language collections manager in the New Americans Program at Queens Borough Public Library. Born and raised in Santiago de Cuba, attended the University of Havana and received a degree in optometry. She moved to the States in 1961 and received a B.A. in 1976 from New York State University at Stony Brook, N.Y. In 1979 she obtained her M.L.S. from Long Island University–C.W. Post Center. She worked as a reference librarian in Suffolk Cooperative Library System and as an adjunct librarian at Suffolk County Community College, Long Island. Since 1983 she has been at the Queens Library as a reference librarian and since 1984 as the Spanish

language collections manager and ESOL coordinator in the New Americans Program.

Oralia Garza de Cortés is a leading advocate of library services for Latino children. She is President–elect (1999-2000) of REFORMA, the national association to promote library and information services to Latinos and the Spanish speaking, an ALA affiliate. A library services consultant, she resides in Austin, Texas.

Susana Hinojosa is Latin American & Iberian Documents selector for the Government/Social Sciences Information Service at the University of California, Berkeley, Doe Library. She has been Ethnic Studies liaison for the Library and Chicano Studies 98 instructor for many years. She is the 1998–2000 chair of the Planning Committee for the REFORMA 2nd National Conference scheduled August 3–6, 2000.

Susan Luévano-Molina is the ethnic, women's and multicultural studies librarian at California State University, Long Beach, where she is a tenured full librarian. She has 25 years of experience working in academic libraries in California and Texas. She has conducted numerous community analysis studies for public libraries in Orange County, California. Her current research on the impact of anti-immigrant legislation on the Latino community was funded by a grant from the California Library Association and a California State University, Affirmative Action Development Award. She is currently editing a book on this topic that will published by Greenwood Publishing.

Hector Marino is currently CEO of Bilingual Library Services, Inc. Most recently he was library automation manager for the U.S. Government Bureau of the Census International Library in Washington, D.C. Previously, he was a consultant to public libraries in Colorado and Texas, served as collection development specialist for the Denver Public Schools, outreach librarian for Denver Public Library and information officer at the World Bank. He holds a Master's degree in Library and Information Science from Catholic University in Washington, D.C. He is active member of REFORMA (National Association to Promote Library Services of the Spanish-Speaking) and ALA (American Library Association).

Ben Ocón has served as a librarian for over twenty years and is currently the branch manager of the Day-Riverside Library with the Salt Lake City Public Library. He has previously held positions with the County of Los Angeles Public Library and Stanford University Libraries. Ocón holds degrees from Stanford University (A.B.), California State University at Fullerton (M.A.) and the University of California at Berkeley (M.L.S.). Ocón has been a member of REFORMA since the late 1970s and is one of the founding members of REFORMA de Utah.

Rhonda Rios Kravitz is the head of access services at the Library at California State University, Sacramento (CSUS). At CSUS she plays an active role in promoting educational equality; the recruitment, retention, and promotion of faculty of color; and the mentoring of students of color. She is a past president of REFORMA and currently co-chairs the Association of Mexican American Educators at CSUS. She was a NGO delegate to the United Nations 41st Commission of the Status of Women and to the Fourth World Conference on Women held in Beijing, China. She also was awarded the 1997 YWCA Outstanding Women of the Year Award (Sacramento, California) for her commitment and work in the area of diversity and equity.

Romelia Salinas is a graduate of UCLA's Graduate School of Education and Information Studies. She was co-founder of Chicano/LatinoNet and managed the project from 1993 to summer of 1999. She is currently the Social Science Liaison for the JFK Memorial Library at the California State University, Los Angeles. She continues to be involved with Chicano/LatinoNet by working on special web-based projects.

Jon Sundell is descended from Russian Jewish grandparents. He was born in 1947 and reared in Freeport, New York. He graduated in 1969 from the University of Michigan, majoring in English, with minors in Asian Studies and French. After living for a year in Japan, he moved to east Tennessee in 1971, where he worked as a community arts director and high school teacher in rural Appalachia. After working several years in Atlanta, Georgia, as a professional storyteller and folksinger, Sundell received a Master of Library Science degree at Emory University. He moved to Winston-Salem, North Carolina, in 1984 to work for the Forsyth County Public Library, initially as a children's librarian, then as head of the Children's Outreach Department, and, since March 1997, as head of Library Service to

Spanish Speaking People. Sundell has visited Central and South America on various occasions and, since the late 1980s, has been personally involved in solidarity activities through the Carolina Interfaith Task Force on Central America. Sundell has played and sung on five commercial recordings and has edited a book entitled, *Stay with Us: Visiting with Old Time Singers and Storytellers in the Southern Mountains.*

Susan A. Vega García is a reference librarian and racial & ethnic studies bibliographer and assistant professor at Iowa State University. She received the Master of Arts in Library Science from the University of Iowa in 1992. She has published on bibliographic access of racial and ethnic studies periodical literature, and regularly reviews websites and

reference works for publications such as *Choice* and *C&RL News.* Her current research focuses on access and ownership of African American and Latino serials in research libraries. She also serves as an indexer for the *Hispanic American Periodicals Index.*

Sonia Ramírez Wohlmuth is an instructor at the University of South Florida with assignments in both the School of Library and Information Science and the Division of Language and Linguistics. Her interest in the role of language in providing optimal library services to the non–English speaking is a natural outcome of her professional preparation and work experience. She is currently pursuing a doctorate in Spanish linguistics at the University of Florida.

Index